D0154459

Young people, health and family life

Young people, health and family life

Julia Brannen
Kathryn Dodd
Ann Oakley
Pamela Storey

Open University Press
Buckingham · Philadelphia

Open University Press
Celtic Court
22 Ballmoor
Buckingham
MK18 1XW

and

1900 Frost Road, Suite 101
Bristol, PA 19007, USA

First Published 1994

A catalogue record of this book is available from the British Library

ISBN 0 335 19097 9 (pb)

Library of Congress Cataloging-in-Publication Data
Young people, health, and family life / Julia Brannen ... [*et al.*].
        p.   cm.
    Includes bibliographical references and index.
    ISBN 0–335–19097–9
    1. Parent and teenager—Great Britain.   2. Teenagers—Health and
hygiene—Great Britain.   I. Brannen, Julia.
HQ799.15.Y685   1994
306.874—dc20
                                                              93–22709
                                                                   CIP

Typeset by Graphicraft Typesetters Ltd, Hong Kong
Printed in Great Britain by St Edmundsbury Press, Bury St Edmunds,
Suffolk

Contents

Preface

Three concerns above all others have dominated our work in transforming the research material into this book. The first is the desire to locate issues related to the health of young people in the context of the households and families in which they live. Most previous academic and policy work on young people's health treats young people as though they are free-floating, autonomous individuals. But most young people do live with families of one kind or another, and it is these contexts that help to shape and explain their health behaviour. Similarly, parents – often contended by politicians and policy-makers today to be insufficiently responsible for their young people – do not treat questions of health in isolation from other aspects of their young people's lives. Issues to do with health may be compartmentalized by health professionals, but are part of the complex fabric of everyday life as it is routinely and concretely lived. This is particularly true for young people, whose concerns in accomplishing the transition to adulthood often lead them to focus on the present, rather than on the ways in which their behaviour is likely to impact on their health in the longer term.

In research terms, locating young people's health within the family and household context means the generation of a good deal of rich 'qualitative' material about what goes on between parents and young people. A relatively unexplored research area, it has certainly been a challenge to analyse and write up. This brings us to the second central concern in our writing of the book: the importance we have attached to not treating households and families themselves as discrete, individualized units. Rather, we have tried to explore the ways in which axes of social and cultural difference, notably gender, ethnicity and social class, tie families and family relationships into the wider material and social structure, and help to explain why certain parents and young people behave as, and believe what, they do. There is always a certain tension between attempting to represent research participants as unique, on the one hand, and, on the other, trying to see the patterns in research data – that is, the ways in which individuals and families resemble one another.

Our third concern has been to integrate, as far as is possible, qualitative and quantitative approaches to data analysis. This has been difficult with two large data sets, one based on a questionnaire survey and the other derived from an interview study of households of young people and their parents. Some chapters are more 'quantitative' or 'qualitative' than others depending on the different issues we have chosen to identify, analyse and discuss. It has been difficult to condense a large project with an enormous amount of both qualitative and quantitative data into a relatively compact book. The result may be a certain unevenness in both the data and the text; we have tried to iron most of this out, but some differences remain none the less. Some areas of interest have been jettisoned or treated summarily in order to allow (fuller) discussion of others. To some extent, the decisions taken are arbitrary, and not all readers will agree with them. We hope in due course to make more of the project material available in other publications.

This book is the outcome of a research project which was funded by the Department of Health. It was undertaken from 1989 to 1992 at the University of London Institute of Education. When the project began, three of us were located at the Thomas Coram Research Unit, Institute of Education. Midway through the study, one of us (Ann Oakley) left to head the Social Science Research Unit (SSRU) at the Institute and another of us (Pamela Storey) joined the Thomas Coram Research Unit (TCRU) for the analysis and writing-up stages of the work.

We have had the support of a great many people during the course of the research. Most of all, we are grateful to the young people and the parents who took part in the study. They made us welcome in their homes and gave up valuable time to talk about sensitive issues. (Their names, where they are used in the text, have of course been changed.)

Thanks are especially due to other members of the research team: Gillian Colville, who made a valuable contribution to the interviewing; Mary Douglas, for transcribing the taped interviews, help with the analysis and secretarial work; and Sandra Stone, for secretarial and administrative work. Others provided support in many different ways. We wish to thank: Elizabeth Wilson, our research liaison officer in the Department of Health, and Carolyn Davies in the Research Division of the Department of Health; the head teachers and teachers who co-operated in the study and gave us access to the young people and their families; the members of the project's Advisory Group – Pat Allatt, Christine Griffin, Robyn Young and Martin Richards – for their enthusiasm and interest in the work; Basil Bernstein, for his creative comments especially on Chapter 10; Charlie Owen in TCRU and Tony Crowle in SSRU, for help with computing; Michelle Duff, Theresa Duggan, and Pat Hedges' team, for help with transcribing interviews; John Balding and his team at the Health Education Authority Schools Health Education Unit, Exeter University; Valerie Hey in SSRU, for help with interview analysis; and Gill Poland, for help with the manuscript.

1 Themes and methods

The title of this book embraces three themes – young people, health and family life – which are intimately related. However, for a variety of reasons they are rarely considered together. The need to make these connections was one important motive for undertaking the research which is described in this book. A major focus of our interest was an issue which is singularly under-discussed in both the academic and policy literatures, namely the extent to which parents and young people take responsibility for young people's health. The stage of life we explored in our research is that between ages 15 and 17. It is commonly assumed that many young people during these years are moving towards greater economic and social independence. The particular question we wanted to explore was how the general dimensions of the transition from childhood to adulthood were, or were not, related to autonomy in the area of health and health care behaviour.

In this chapter, we discuss the background to our research: the significant debates, issues, theories and arguments in the area of young people, health and family life. In the latter part of the chapter we describe the methods used in our research, and some of the illuminating problems of trying to carry out a study which is both qualitative and quantitative, and which attempts to tap and include the perspectives of different household members in relation to questions, many of which concern 'sensitive' and usually 'private' matters.

Young people's situation today

We use the term 'young people' in preference to that of 'adolescents' in this book because the terms 'adolescent' and 'adolescence' tend to have a somewhat derogatory meaning – that the essence of being a young person is not in *being* but in *becoming*. That is, adult society values young people primarily because they are adults in the making (Frankenberg, 1993). Historically speaking, the identification of the teenage years as a special period is, like childhood, a cultural invention. Young people did not attract social attention as a distinctive age group until enough of them survived, and until the demands of a specialized labour force, combined with the establishment of universal education, lengthened the period of transition from childhood to adulthood. These conditions only apply in developed societies; in much of the world today, the conditions of young people remain very different.

In Britain and other European countries since the 1950s, public discourses have tended to treat young people as a social barometer of society's ills – from teenage pregnancy to increased delinquency, drug-taking and violence (Jones and Wallace, 1992). A recurrent theme is the threat which youth is said to pose to the social order and the consequent implied moral decline of the nation. The breakdown of familial values is frequently blamed, rather than underlying material or structural factors. As others have observed (Jones and Wallace, 1992), given the diagnosis made especially by the New Right in blaming parents for the growth of deviance among young people, there is surprisingly little research which locates youth in a family context.

Normative definitions concerning what it means to be a teenager are constructed in public discourses, which in turn influence lay definitions of the teenage years. But such definitions are also informed by the ways in which young people are depicted in the academic literatures of social psychology and sociology, and by the ways in which practitioners from different professional groups have defined, and claimed expertise in relation to, the situation of young people.

In contrast to sociology, which has tended to focus on the broader structural context of youth rather than adolescence, psychologists have generally stressed adolescence as a scheduled passage to adulthood which is rooted in its biological events and characterized by tasks of individual development (Coleman, 1990; see Rutter *et al.*, 1976, for a discussion). Conceptualized as a period of emotional turmoil and a time of identity formation (Erikson, 1968), 'adolescence' is supposedly marked by conflict with parents and other adults (although empirical investigation of this thesis has provided limited evidence) (Offer and Sabshin, 1984). Believed by psychoanalysts to be a universal feature of adolescence, young people's ambivalent feelings are said to be linked to nonconformist and rebellious behaviour (Coleman, 1990). Such behaviour is said to be functional for the requisite process of disengagement from parents in the transition to adult independence. This literature largely ignores the social and economic aspects of young people's transitions to adulthood.

In setting out the normative process of adolescence, traditional psychological accounts have paid little attention to gender. As Gilligan (1982) argues, the notion of individuation in adolescence, and adolescents' progress towards autonomy and the exercise of individual rights, is largely based upon a male model of development. By contrast, and as Gilligan shows, a female model of development and relationships lies in the continuing importance of attachment in the human life cycle. 'Women's place in man's life cycle is to protect this recognition while the developmental litany intones the celebration of separation, autonomy, individuation and natural rights' (Gilligan, 1982: 23).

The psychological notion of adolescence is also a particularly Western creation, involving cultural bias; the 'normal' process of development is seen to operate without regard to the cultural diversity of families and family norms. In relation to a study of young people's health in the context of family life, it is important to note that if parents adhere to different cultural norms concerning rights and responsibilities within families and households, they may not consider that parental responsibility and filial duty are automatically modified by biological changes or age stages in their children.

Just as psychologists' perspectives on adolescence are culturally specific, so sociologists' perspectives are historically distinctive (Jones and Wallace, 1992). By contrast with psychology and its preoccupation with notions of adolescence, sociology has largely focused on the broader structural context of youth. The 1960s' ideas concerning socialization and role theory (Parsons, 1956) did not hold up well in the 1970s, when the focus, informed by the sociology of deviance, shifted to peer groups and youth subcultures and the increased demand from young people for self-expression. In the 1980s and thus far in the 1990s – periods marked by widespread unemployment – attention has switched to the nature of young people's transitions to adulthood, as it has become increasingly obvious that there is no necessary connection between the age of theoretical independence and becoming a fully paid-up member of the labour force. As young people's economic dependence upon their parents has been extended, working-class transitions have come to be redefined as premature rather than middle-class transitions as delayed (Jones and Wallace, 1992). These considerations do, of course, reveal the irrelevance of biologically based models of adolescent development to an understanding of the factors shaping the situation of young people. The state of the economy and policy directives and changes relating to this are crucial influences on the timing of educational and labour-market transitions.

As we have already observed, the sociological literature on young people has largely ignored the household context (Jones and Wallace, 1992). Its focus has predominantly been on youth as a social category and the social control problems youth presents for the wider society. Sociological studies have, until recently, investigated youth in relation to schools, peer groups, subcultures and lifestyles, rather than examining the situation of young people in relation to the families from which they come and in which the majority of them live. Much of the British sociological study of youth has also been marked by an implicit concern with male youth and an explicit interest in social class (see notably Willis, 1977). More recently, race (for example, Hewitt, 1988) and gender perspectives (Griffin, 1985; McRobbie, 1991) have been integrated in the structuralist approach to the study of youth. However, the German individualization thesis is now gaining some ground from structural explanations; followers of this school of thought argue that the trajectories of young people need to be understood in terms of the individualized acquisition of cultural 'credentials', both formal and informal, by 'reflexively mobilized' individual processes which, it is argued, produce a growing differentiation within social classes (Chisholm *et al.*, 1990; Jones and Wallace, 1992; Oechsle and Zoll, 1992). Another way of making sense of this process in a British context is seen in the work of Bernstein (1971; 1975) and, more recently, in the work of Cohen (1984) and Walkerdine and Lucey (1989). These authors emphasize how external modes of control and negative sanctions are giving way to invisible forms of regulation and internal controls, and are producing new forms of 'standardization' of youth culture (Chisholm, 1990).

Aside from being the focus of the gaze of social scientists, young people have also been defined as the subject-matter of different professional groups: most notably doctors, health educators and other health professionals, teachers, and social workers. The processes whereby these different groups come to lay claim to young people as a legitimate part of their expert territory are complex and related to the development of the different professional specialisms themselves (see Mayall, 1989). The themes of control, protection, surveillance and promotion in relation to young people can all be identified in professional viewpoints, much as they can, as we see later in this book, in those of parents. Young people pose problems of moral and social order which invite a controlling response (the heavy hand of the police or social workers); their childlike vulnerability may provoke a protective stance, in which young people are seen to be in need of defending not only from the harms of adult society, but also from their own potential internal moral chaos; the surveillance of young people – watching, monitoring, measuring, assessing – is fundamental to the work of some professionals. Promoting the abilities of young people may be seen as the positive side of this work, one which stresses the possibility of capitalizing on the characteristics of this life stage rather than regarding these inevitably as problems to be contained.

Health and young people

It has become commonplace to observe that both the study of health and health care have been dominated by a concern with illness and death, rather than with health in a positive sense. As a consequence, we know rather little about what health 'is', or about how people in general see health and its relation to other aspects of their lives. Some of the data discussed later in this book suggest that health is not seen as distinct from living; that is, practices, behaviours and beliefs relating to health are experienced as an integral part of everyday life.

The roots of the traditional narrow conceptualization of health lie in medicine's concern with the treatment of suffering (see Stacey, 1991) and in the conceptual and administrative organization of health services, which has been more concerned with treating illness than in preventing it. These traditions served to stress illness as an individual, rather than as a socially structured, phenomenon, and led to the development of health education initiatives prioritizing the need to persuade individuals to behave in healthy ways. An enormous amount of energy in many countries has been devoted to health education campaigns of various kinds, and most of these have been unevaluated (for a discussion see, for example, Windsor *et al.*, 1984). As evidence has mounted in recent years of social and environmental influences on health, the rhetoric of health education has been translated into that of health promotion, with a corresponding emphasis on the need for a healthy public policy (Research Unit in Health and Behavioural Change, 1989). In the language of health promotion, individuals are seen to have a limited power to choose healthy lives; their choices and behaviours are understood to be constrained by the social and material conditions in which they live.

Although teenagers are one of the healthiest groups in the population, judged by any standards, they have been a prominent target for health educators. In part, this is because some of the health behaviours in which some teenagers engage – for example, drinking, smoking and drug-taking – have been identified as health risks. Many attempts have been made to educate young people to reform these behaviours. Once again, the lack of evaluation of the effectiveness of these health education interventions is striking, and the extent to which such initiatives and studies have ignored the social context of teenagers' health is impressive. An important part of the wider context is family life. Within families, what parents do for children and young people is traditionally defined as 'childrearing' or 'socialization', instead of being described as health maintenance work (Graham, 1984). The impact of the familial context on the health of adolescents has received little attention. Rather, the health education model conceptualizes young people as free individuals who take autonomous decisions about health and lifestyles quite independently of their families. In so far as it takes account of social relations, its focus tends to be on the ways in which the inculcation of life skills and the consequent enhancement of teenagers' self-esteem can help them to resist peer-group pressures, and conform to the messages delivered by schools and other health educators.

Family life and young people

Sociological conceptualizations of British family life have revolved around classical modernization theory and Parsonian functionalism (Jamieson, 1987). The modern family is said to develop a sense of itself as a bonded, discrete unit, while the wider social world is constructed as 'outside' – a process supposedly brought about by the geographical–physical separation of family members' worlds of employment work from their living space. Within this public–private division, there is a sharpening differentiation between men's and women's roles. Moreover, the focus shifts to the individuals in the family and away from the collectivity. Family members become their own persons, while the child is 'no longer the servant of the family, but an individual who is serviced by the family' (Jamieson, 1987: 595). Children are encouraged by their parents to rise in the world for their own sake and not for the sake of the collectivity. They are trained for independence, and to think of themselves as autonomous individuals. In this perspective, privacy and self-expression are encouraged (Ariès, 1973).

Feminism has transformed some aspects of this classical account, notably bringing into view women's contribution to the material reproduction of the household, and the ways in which both private and public spheres are gender-differentiated. Problems remain, however, in reconciling the fact of women's inequitable share of resources, labour and responsibility, which makes them dependents of men, with their role in bringing about the individuation and autonomy of children and young people. This double positioning of mothers has been articulated and confronted by Walkerdine and Lucey (1989). According to Walkerdine, mothers, as regulators of their children, create the illusion in their children that they are free, self-determining individuals, although mothers themselves have not achieved such a status. This paradox is most acute for working-class women, whose lesser resources in class as well as gender hierarchies render their performance of the illusion particularly problematic and unconvincing.

Postmodernist ideas about family life emphasize the growth of ideas of choice and voluntarism in the creation and maintenance of family ties. According to Giddens (1991), the renegotiation of relationships between parents and young people is also increasingly governed by their achieved status in terms of liking and closeness, rather than by norms of obligation and the ascribed nature of relationships. These ideas resonate with bourgeois individualism and equalitarian ideals.

Though ideas of individualization, voluntarism and equality constitute important ideologies governing relationships between parents and young people, other contradictory discourses are equally apparent. During the 1980s, the British government has tried to redraw the boundaries of adulthood, laying increasing emphasis upon parental responsibility. Many state benefits formerly available to young people as adult citizens of the society have been withdrawn. These changes have had most impact upon unemployed and working-class young people (Jones and Wallace, 1992). Some aspects of this approach which re-emphasizes parental rights over, and responsibilities towards, young people can be discerned in other European countries.[1]

The study's approach

The perspective and findings of our study take issue with a number of the perspectives outlined above. Particular points of divergence are with: normative ideas which portray teenagers as autonomous individuals in respect of their health practices; a monocultural view of young people which sees the movement from dependence to autonomy as 'naturally' scheduled; the idea that health is something different from work and other aspects of everyday life; the notion that youth and the parenting of youth are non-gendered phenomena.

Our aim in this book is to examine the extent to which, and the ways in which, parents and young people negotiate distributional changes in responsibilities concerning health which are earlier and typically shouldered by parents. In so far as responsibilities are subject to change as young people move towards adulthood, our concern is to see whether young people and parents set new parameters in relation to their respective roles and practices. In so far as responsibilities are not transferred to young people at this point, we are interested in the ways in which young people subvert continued control by parents, and the ways in which parents respond to what they may perceive as young people's infringement of household norms.

Central to understanding what goes on in households between parents and young people concerning health are the concepts of rule, negotiation and control. Rules refer to the explicit or implicit norms which govern what parents expect of young people. The term negotiation refers to the ways in which parents and young people 'handle' these rules and expectations in practice. Different patterns of negotiation with respect to responsibility for health matters are identified: (a) consensual, negotiated delegation of responsibility from parents to young people; (b) overt bargaining or resistance involving conflict between parents and young people; (c) covert subversion by young people, when parents refuse to delegate responsibility; (d) parental avoidance or compliance strategies to deal with the latter situation. In addition, we identify the (many) unproblematic instances in which there is no change in the status quo: where responsibility for health is not subject to renegotiation either by parents or young people.

Changes in the balance of responsibility between parents and young people have consequences for the relative balance of power between them. The principal mechanisms for renegotiation take place in the arena of communication. Through communicative strategies of various kinds some parents create new types of relationships with young people as the latter begin to act more autonomously. Within the normative individual rights model of adolescence, the overt exercise of parental power is required to give way to a more democratic model of relationships. However, we also argue that in practice power goes underground and is exercised covertly. Within this model, communication becomes the vehicle of control and is not only the symbol of the new relationship being forged by parents and young people.

Our attempts to understand household negotiations are set against a backcloth of the normative rules and expectations to which parents subscribe and to which young people respond, in particular the meanings which they attach to adolescence, parenthood and health responsibility. Our aim is to examine the ways in which normative rules and their negotiation are structured by gender, ethnicity and social class,[2] though we also pay attention to other factors, particularly household composition and type of school (state versus private).

The three aspects of our analysis – normative rules, processes of negotiation and structural patterns – are examined within households, as well as across the respective samples of young people and parents. This endeavour is particularly challenging in those families in which the generations are differentiated by their experiences of migration. The problem of distinguishing between the norms and values of the first and second generations raises the issue of the differential effects of the migration experience, the cultural values of the old society and the dominant values of the current society within and across the generations. In our sample, the ethnic origins of non-indigenous parents are highly diverse, and this has made us more aware of the taken-for-granted assumptions and sociological perspectives we ourselves brought to the study. Our multi-faceted approach has also made visible the ways in which individualism and an individual rights morality are embedded in the very concepts of parenting and adolescence themselves. This, in turn, has made us more reflective of competing undercurrents – notably ideas of connectedness, interdependence, obligation, and responsibility. Notwithstanding the classical notions of independence which typify adolescence, when relationships between parents and young people are renegotiated, these concepts are also influential and may be reworked. The recent resurgence of ideas of citizenship constitute an example of such a transformation (Jones and Wallace, 1992).

The study design and methods

We decided to focus our study on young people who were aged 15 at the start of the study and 16 or 17 by the end of it, and who were making important decisions concerning their future education, training and employment.

The study involves two stages, with two related samples: a questionnaire survey of young people aged 15–16 in their last compulsory year of schooling, and an intensive interview study of a subsample of households randomly selected from the survey participants. In the interview study both parents (if resident) and the young people were to be interviewed. Our overall approach was to use the two methods – the questionnaires and the interviews – to address different issues.

The schools survey was used to provide quantitative data concerning young people's health-related behaviour and backgrounds. We employed a self-completion social and health questionnaire which fifth-formers filled out in school time. The questionnaire was based on one which had already been extensively used throughout the UK, 'Balding's Health Related

Behaviour Questionnaire' devised by the Health Education Authority (HEA) Schools Health Education Unit at Exeter University (Balding, 1989). This work provides a nationally comparative data set in which to contextualize our survey data. Our own survey thus provided us with the basis for selecting the interview sample, and also a data set for contextualizing the interview material.

In the household study we sought to explore the negotiation of social relationships and transactions concerning health. We employed an in-depth interview approach with separate interviews conducted by three different interviewers with mothers, fathers and young people. The interviews were semi-structured so that interviewees were free to articulate their own concerns and to describe their experiences in their own way. We tape-recorded the interviews, which lasted on average two and a half hours with parents, and about half an hour less with young people. We aimed to produce comparable material from young people and their parents, by using similar questions in some sections of the interviews. In other parts of the interviews, we concentrated on issues only of concern to the parents or the young people. The interviews were transcribed verbatim and the material subsequently organized under sets of conceptual headings and codes. Related comments were cross-referenced. These procedures have enabled the interview material to be treated quantitatively, to be content-analysed by individual interview and to be subjected to a case analysis at the household level.

The questionnaire survey

In order to conduct the survey, we gained access to a number of secondary schools. We chose a West London borough for the following reasons: one of the research team had formal and informal links with some of the schools and the local education authority (LEA); the proximity of the area to the home of the same researcher, who was to conduct most of the interviews with parents; the multi-ethnic composition of the borough; and the LEA had not been over-researched, unlike many inner-city boroughs.

Through direct approaches to schools and indirect approaches through the LEA, we successfully gained the co-operation of four mixed-sex state schools. At the suggestion of our Project Advisory Group, we added two single-sex, private day schools, a girls' school in the borough, and a boys' school just outside, since a significant proportion of middle-class parents in the area use the private sector.

We discussed the survey's content and our research strategy with the schools' head teachers, who in turn sought parental permission for all the schools' fifth-formers to take part. In recompense for their help, we later provided detailed analyses of the questionnaire data pertaining to each school, a service which was warmly welcomed and used in some schools in the design of their Personal and Social Education curricula.

Over a three-week period in November 1989, all the fifth-form pupils from the state schools and the private girls' school filled in the question-naires. They did so under examination-like conditions which did not permit any pupils to opt out of completing the questionnaire, with two research-ers overseeing the exercise in the schools. Teachers who supervised the hour-long period allocated to the completion of the questionnaires in the classrooms were fully briefed by the researchers beforehand. Schools were given a week to gain the co-operation of absentees, though some schools were better than others in following these up. Because we were unable to secure the agreement of a boys' private school in the borough at that time, the survey in the boys' private school was carried out under similar conditions exactly one year later in a school just outside the borough (in November 1990).

The quality of the questionnaire survey data is very good overall, with few spoiled questionnaires and the great majority of students completing all the questions in the allotted time. In a space provided at the end of the questionnaire, pupils' comments suggest that they found the exercise interesting. Certainly most of those who were later interviewed could clearly remember completing the questionnaire.

The overall response rate for the whole survey is 85 per cent (843 out of 989). The average rate for the state schools is 83 per cent (640 out of 769 pupils), with 89 per cent for the girls' private school (72 out of 81) and 94 per cent for the boys' private school (131 out of 139). Variation in response rates occurs between the four state schools, with one school in particular, which was used to pilot the questionnaire, achieving a sig-nificantly lower response rate (78 per cent). The follow-up of absentee students improved the response rates marginally – from 81 per cent to 83 per cent in the state schools; the exercise was considered unnecessary in the private schools. Since teachers said that many of the 16 per cent absentees from state schools had virtually ceased to attend school, we felt nothing more could be done within the resources of the project to improve the response rates. The study, therefore, under-represents this group.

Our survey is not representative of the national population of young people, nor did we intend it to be. Surveys conducted by Balding in over 200 schools in the UK provide a national comparison, but our catchment area is more ethnically mixed. Only 5 per cent of the schools in which Balding (1989) carried out his surveys have more than 20 per cent ethnic minority pupils, compared with all the schools in our study.[3] While a significant proportion of Balding's schools are in rural areas, our study can only claim to represent metropolitan areas. Also, 55 per cent of Balding's surveys were conducted between January and March, with only 14 per cent conducted during October to December, the time of year when our survey was conducted. Therefore the fifth-year young people in Balding's samples are on average older than ours, a factor which might be expected to produce higher rates of smoking, alcohol and drug use, though in practice this did not always turn out to be the case.

Characteristics of the survey participants

Our sample contains a slight gender imbalance; it consists of 57 per cent boys and 43 per cent girls. The four mixed state schools contribute 76 per cent of the total sample, with 80 per cent of the girls, but only 73 per cent of the boys. Compared with the national distribution, therefore, the private school population is over-represented in our study.[4] The private boys' school fifth form was larger than the private girls' fifth year and provided 27 per cent of the total sample of boys compared with only 20 per cent for the sample of girls. Moreover, around 24–26 per cent of Asian, white and 'other' groups are in private education, compared with only 13 per cent of the black group.

The ethnic composition of the survey, based on a number of categories which we later collapsed, is as follows: 64 per cent of white UK origin, including 'other European origin' (referred to as white); 18 per cent who class themselves as Asian (referred to as Asian); 11 per cent who claim to be of Caribbean origin or identify themselves as black British (both subsequently referred to as black); and 8 per cent who are placed in a miscellaneous group, consisting of those of African, Arab, Chinese or different origin including 'mixed ethnicity' (referred to as 'other').

Overall, 71 per cent of our sample report living with their biological mothers and fathers, 17 per cent with their mothers only, 7 per cent with their mothers and stepfathers, and the rest (5 per cent) with their lone fathers, fathers and stepmothers, or in some other arrangement. When we consider ethnic origin and household composition together, differences emerge. Asian-origin young people are more likely than other groups to live with both (biological) parents (86 per cent), compared with 48 per cent of blacks, 70 per cent of whites and 80 per cent in the 'other' groups. Private school girls are more likely to live with both biological parents than state school girls, whereas the reverse is true for boys.

The average household size reported by the sample is just over four persons. However, the Asian and 'other' groups are significantly above the average in this respect, with 4.7 and 4.6 persons, respectively. These differences are accounted for by the facts that Asian households contain more children, are more likely to have two parents and to have other relatives living with them. 'Only children' are least likely to come from an Asian background, and are most likely to be in private schools. Indeed those in private schools are significantly more likely to be only, or eldest, children than are state school pupils (54 per cent compared to 38 per cent).

In terms of fathers' employment status, 92 per cent of resident fathers are in employment and 8 per cent are not at work for a variety of reasons including unemployment, retirement and sickness. The unemployment rate for fathers corresponds with the male unemployment rate for the borough. There are, however, significant differences by ethnic background: 89 per cent of the resident fathers of Asian young people are in (full-time) employment compared with 77 per cent of black resident fathers, 90 per cent of white resident fathers and 91 per cent of those in the 'other' group.

The occupational breakdown of fathers' employment is less easy to assess because of incomplete information. Not all young people live in the same household as their fathers, and, of those who do, 7 per cent did not answer the question on the questionnaire, either because they did not know or because they said they found the question intrusive. Of those who replied, and also have resident fathers, there is a roughly equal split between 49 per cent in high-status jobs and 51 per cent in low-status jobs.[5] Predictable differences are found with respect to school type and housing. Thus state school pupils, those living in rented housing and those living with their fathers only are more likely to have fathers in low status as opposed to high status jobs.[6]

Over three-quarters of young people's mothers (79 per cent) are said by young people to be in the labour market, with 13 per cent housewives, 3 per cent unemployed, and 2 per cent students (3 per cent were unsure). Our study reflects the relevant national figure – 73 per cent of mothers with dependent children aged 10 or over are in paid work (Office of Population Censuses and Surveys (OPCS), 1990). The division between part- and full-time employment status in our study is 33 per cent and 46 per cent respectively, which is again similar to the national distribution (OPCS, 1990). Ethnic background has little effect on the rate of employment among mothers, except with respect to the 'other' group, in which significantly fewer mothers are in the labour market (61 per cent). However, concerning working hours, white mothers are most likely to be in part-time employment – 39 per cent compared with 18 per cent of Asians, 20 per cent of blacks and 27 per cent of the 'other' group. When household composition is taken into account, fewer women work full-time in two-parent households: 43 per cent, compared with those who are single parents (53 per cent) and those cohabiting or remarried (58 per cent). Also, women working full-time are more likely to be in high-status jobs than women working part-time (37 per cent against 24 per cent).

There are no significant differences in mothers' occupational status by ethnic origin, but young people in state schools are predictably more likely to have mothers in low-status occupations (62 per cent against 34 per cent), and those living in privately owned housing much more likely to have mothers in high-status jobs (29 per cent against 8 per cent).[7]

The questionnaire data provide some indication of young people's likely education and employment status at the end of the fifth year: 59 per cent say they intend to stay on in the school sixth form, with a further 10 per cent intending to go to sixth-form college and 15 per cent into a further education college. Eleven per cent expect to go into employment and only 3 per cent into a youth training scheme. Less than 0.5 per cent are contemplating a career on the dole. These figures correspond fairly closely with estimates provided by the LEA concerning the destinations of all those aged 15–16 in the borough for the relevant year. Differences are marked with respect to school type, with no young people in the private schools expecting to join the labour market or enter youth training schemes, compared with 17 per cent of young people in state schools. For those in state schools, there are differences in intentions by household composition: those living with both parents are most likely to be intending to stay on in education (82 per cent), followed by those living with lone mothers (78 per cent), those living with mothers and stepfathers (72 per cent) and, lastly, those living in other arrangements (56 per cent). There are also significant differences between the ethnic groups, with the white group containing the highest percentage not intending to stay on (25 per cent) compared with only 8 per cent of Asians, 13 per cent of blacks and 11 per cent of the 'other' group. Mothers' occupational class has no effect on students' future intentions. However, 91 per cent of those with fathers in high-status occupations are intending to stay on in education, compared with 77 per cent of those whose fathers are in low-status jobs, and 66 per cent of those whose fathers are not employed. Most young people in private schools expect to remain in the same school in the sixth form (81 per cent) in contrast to 52 per cent in the state schools. Moreover, some association is found between intention to enter employment and having a Saturday or after-school job, with 68 per cent of those planning to leave full-time education already working while at school, compared with 53 per cent of those intending to stay on in education.

Overall, 50 per cent of young people in the fifth form have a paid job. This includes 40 per cent with one job and 10 per cent with more than one. Girls are slightly more likely to have jobs than boys (52 per cent against 48 per cent). While both sexes are typically employed in shops, girls also frequently do babysitting and boys paper rounds. Asian girls are least likely to have a paid job of any kind (27 per cent, compared with 52 per cent of all girls). Similarly, only 38 per cent of both Asian and 'other' boys work, compared with over 50 per cent of both white and black boys. The mean number of hours worked per week is, however, significantly higher for boys (7.8) than girls (7.1). Of all ethnic groups, Asian boys work the highest number of hours and Asian girls the least. Private school girls report even fewer hours, but not private school boys. Household composition makes no difference here, while there is some association with parents' occupational class: 45 per cent of those with one or both parents in a high-status job had a Saturday job, compared with 55 per cent of those with parents in low-status jobs.

The household study

We explored the possibility of selecting the household sample from the questionnaire survey with respect to responses concerning patterns of health responsibility. However, since the questions covering these issues were necessarily limited we decided instead to take a sample which was representative of the survey population and stratified by school and sex of the young person. Using a Statistical Package for the Social Sciences (SPSS) sampling procedure, 138 students were selected from the populations completing the questionnaires. This was a larger number than our intended final interview sample size, both because we had originally planned to have a larger household interview sample, and in order to allow for people deciding they did not want to be interviewed. In practice, we only approached the first 97 households. Household responses vary by school, with two of the state schools having somewhat lower response rates than the others.[8] Rates among both young people and parents were particularly high in the boys' private school.

Having chosen our sampling frame, we went back to the schools and sought further co-operation from the head teachers, who agreed to write to the relevant parents asking their permission to pass on to us their names and addresses. In practice only a handful of parents, mainly from the girls' private school, withheld permission. Next we wrote separate letters to the parents and the young people, describing in each the purposes of the study and its links with the school survey. We were especially concerned to reassure the young people that the survey information already provided would remain confidential. We emphasized that, in order to protect them further, we would be using three different interviewers for parents and young people and would make separate approaches to each party. We then approached our sample a few households at a time in line with our interviewing resources.

Less than a handful of households refused at this point by letter or telephone call to the Research Unit. The rest were subsequently contacted, usually by telephone. When respondents made initial excuses, in order to minimize the refusal rate, we frequently left open the matter of participation, sometimes returning weeks and, in a few cases, months later. It therefore took us some considerable time to achieve our final household sample.

A total of 142 interviews were completed with members of 64 households. The household response rate where at least one household member was interviewed is 66 per cent. The rates for the different household members vary considerably, however, with 58 per cent of young people (26 girls and 30 boys) taking part, 58 per cent (55) of mothers, but only 39 per cent (31) of resident fathers. Interviews with all available members were completed in over half the households (52 per cent) – that is, young people and both parents in 27 two-parent households, and young people and one parent in six single-parent households.

The household interview response rates may be considered highly satisfactory when compared with similar studies. For example, Pahl's (1989) study of household finances achieved a 52 per cent response rate with husbands and wives. A study of parents and young people in North-East England (Allatt and Yeandle, 1992) reported a higher rate of refusals, though the method of recruitment was different from our own.

The households' characteristics

Twenty-six girls were interviewed – five from private schools and 21 from state schools. Thirty boys were interviewed – 26 from state and four from private schools. The gender imbalance in the survey is thus reflected in the household study. Nineteen per cent of girls interviewed are from private schools, compared with 20 per cent completing the questionnaire. In the case of boys, 13 per cent of those interviewed are from the private sector, compared with 27 per cent in the questionnaire sample.

It was easiest to gain the participation of all household members in households of UK-born parents and hardest in Asian-origin households, with Asian parents being particularly likely to refuse an interview. The ethnic backgrounds of the parents in the household study are diverse. Under two-thirds (39) of all the young people in the 64 households have two (biological) parents born in the UK. The rest include 11 young people with two Asian-origin parents born either in the Asian sub-continent or in East Africa; four have parents from Middle East countries; the parents of the other four households are from Africa, China, North America and southern Europe. In addition, there are six mixed-parentage young people; each has one UK-born parent, with the other parent coming from various parts of the world – the Middle East, Africa, South-East Asia, southern Europe and the Caribbean (one young person living with a Caribbean origin mother and a UK-born step-parent is included here).

Comparing the questionnaire and household samples

The interviewed group reflects the ethnic composition of the questionnaire sample reasonably well, with 61 per cent of interviewees having UK-born parents, compared with 64 per cent of white young people completing the questionnaire, and 17 per cent being of Asian origin in both cases. If only those of African or Afro-Caribbean parentage are included as 'black', then blacks are under-represented in the interview study, with only four young people, two of whom are of mixed race; they constitute only 6 per cent of the total, compared with 11 per cent of the survey sample. The 'other' group is over-represented – 16 per cent of the interviewees compared with 8 per cent of those completing the questionnaire – though this is partly accounted for by the use of a more detailed classification of ethnic origins in the household study.

Similarly, the wide variation in household composition almost exactly reflects the distribution in the questionnaire survey: 71 per cent of the questionnaire sample and 72 per cent of the interview sample reside with two biological parents (46 households), and 19 per cent of young people in both the survey and the interview study live in single-parent households (12 households). The remaining households in the interview study include five step-parent households (two stepmothers and three stepfathers) and one case in which the young person lives with his sister, who is his legal guardian, and her husband.

The proportion of households with no parent in employment is similar in both samples (7 per cent in the survey and 8 per cent in the household study). We have classified lone-mother households by mothers' occupations where they are in work and two-parent households and lone-father households by fathers' occupations.[9] In practice, there are few cases where classifying household occupational class on the basis of the mother's job would mean reclassifying the household on the other side of the high–low status divide – 6 per cent of cases in the questionnaire survey and one case in the household study. Like the questionnaire survey, there is a fairly even occupational distribution of those in work: parents (mostly fathers) in just over half the households have a higher-status occupation (this category here includes shopkeepers and those with their own businesses); two-fifths are in lower-status jobs – mostly manual jobs, with a few in sales or clerical occupations.[10]

Characteristics of 'refusers' *vis-à-vis* participants

The two samples do not differ significantly with respect to demographic characteristics, despite the lower response rate of the household study. But we can explore the matter further, since we can compare, on the basis of their survey responses, those young people who refused to take part in the household study or had moved away (41 cases in total) with the 52 interview participants who completed the questionnaire.

Few differences emerge in terms of gender, ethnicity or occupational background, though proportionately fewer refusers are in two-parent households compared with the interview sample – 33 out of 40 (83 per cent) against 44 out of 52 (85 per cent). On other issues, more 'refuser' boys have Saturday and after-school jobs (67 per cent) than interviewed boys (63 per cent), but both groups work considerably more than the rest of the questionnaire sample (46 per cent). Concerning relationships between parents and young people, there appear to be differences in quality, with 'refusers' slightly less likely to report good relationships. More significant in terms of the study's focus are health differences. The comparison between the interviewees and the 'refusers' suggests that the household study may under-represent the least healthy young people (because of small numbers the differences do not reach statistical significance). On ill health and diet, the 'refuser' group, especially boys, are less likely to assess their health as good, and to go to the doctor more frequently than the interviewed group. Similarly, on diet, more 'refusers' are missing meals and girls, in particular, are more likely to fall into the least healthy diet group. In addition, compared with the interviewed group, 'refuser' girls are more likely to be smokers, including heavy smokers, and to have tried drugs.

Using different research instruments

Our use of two different research instruments affords the opportunity to compare, in a few instances, responses to similar questions. However, the time lapse of between six and 15 months between the conduct of the questionnaire and the interview needs to be borne in mind here. We found few discrepancies with respect to 'factual' data, such as illness, hospital visits and fathers' employment. Only in the responses to questions relating to drugs is there any evidence of interviewees changing their stories. Four young people, happy to use the questionnaire as a confessional, may have felt too insecure in the company of an adult interviewer to admit to illegal behaviour or, since they were interviewed at home, they may not have dared to risk being overheard by household members. Attitudinal responses, by contrast with most 'factual' data, are less robust, with young people's evaluations of their health emerging as rosier in the interview than in the questionnaire. Since there was no evidence that their health had changed in the intervening period, it is possible that they felt under pressure to be positive in a face-to-face encounter. In this sense, and as we argue later, concepts of health involve strong moral evaluations. Similar differences between responses to self-administered questionnaires and in-depth interviews were found in a study of women's experiences of motherhood and child health (Oakley et al., 1992).

Negotiating access to the interviewees

The process of gaining the agreement of the interviewees to take part in the study generated important theoretical insights, not only concerning power relations between the researcher and the researched, but also as regards the focus of the study – namely the negotiation of relationships between parents and young people.

We were fortunate in obtaining from the schools the telephone numbers of most of the households. After writing separately to the parents and the young people, each researcher telephoned her own pool of interviewees. In general, it proved easiest to secure the agreement of mothers. Despite the fact that most are in employment and have busy lives, mothers were the most ready to accommodate us. When we telephoned, the fathers who answered often referred us to the mothers. Access to fathers often had to be pursued via the mothers, who were not always facilitative. In some cases, they sought to protect fathers, claiming that they lacked the time or interest to take part. Some mothers were protective of our interests, suggesting that fathers have little knowledge of the issues that interested us. There are some striking exceptions to these patterns, however. Asian-origin fathers were particularly disposed to offer themselves for interview as spokespersons for their households. They had a tendency to rule out their wives, claiming they were 'too busy', or had poor English. It was therefore often necessary to negotiate access to them during the fathers' interviews. Somewhat unaccountably, professional fathers of the private school boys were particularly accommodating, despite their long working hours.

Gaining access to the young people, while at the same time protecting their confidentiality, threw into relief power relations in the household. Young people, especially boys, were out a great deal when we tried to contact them. Alternatively, parents answered the phone when the young people were at home. It was often necessary therefore to negotiate access via parents. In these situations, parents often acted as gatekeepers, a process which proved to be instructive and illuminating of the central research issues. It forced the researchers to reflect on the variation in parental norms concerning young people's status in the household.

Where the first approach was made to the young person via the parent, those parents not born in the UK usually demanded that the interviewer give an account of herself and the research before they would allow her access to the young people. The interviewer was unprepared for the inquisition that followed, assuming that the young people were free to take part in the study if they wished. Her overriding concern, based on her role as researcher, was to protect the young people's right to confidentiality, especially in view of their earlier revelations in the questionnaires, and given that their parents were also to be approached. She also assumed at the start of the study that most 16-year-olds would be relatively independent of their parents, at least as far as decisions of this order were concerned. But the interviewer was forced to reconsider her research strategy. Typically she then approached the young person when the issue had already been negotiated with parents.

Except in a few cases, the interviews were conducted in the home. Finding a suitable room in the house was unproblematic for parents with relatively large houses, or for those young people who were available in the day when their parents were at work. Other young people with fewer rights over public space were concerned about keeping out of earshot of parents. The interviewer sometimes took a proactive role here, suggesting that they repair to the young people's own rooms. However, most young people were interviewed in the sitting or dining room, often at the suggestion of parents, who considered such rooms appropriate for entertaining visitors. In some cases the interviews were conducted simultaneously with either a parent and young person or, more usually, two parents at once in different rooms. Significantly, where an interview took place in the kitchen, it was either with the mother, when both parents were being interviewed, or the young person, if the interviews were with the young person and a parent. (The higher-status person got the sitting room.)

In a few cases, interviews were conducted outside the home. This was mainly in order to keep the interview secret from another family member. For example, one mother and daughter did not want the father of the family to be interviewed for fear, they said, he would 'take over'.

Analysis

Just as our research methods employ quantitative and qualitative approaches, so, too, does the analysis of the different data sets. In general, we have used data from different sources for different purposes. The questionnaire survey was used to provide descriptive and contextual data of a quantitative nature, especially concerning young people's health behaviour and items governed by parental rules. By contrast, the analysis of the interview study of household members aims to focus on the interpretative understanding of household processes, especially the ways in which parents and young people negotiate relationships.

In the household study, we have undertaken analyses of the data sets relating to the different samples of mothers, fathers and young people, and also an analysis at the household level. With respect to the latter – the daunting task of dealing with data spanning 64 households – we have systematically searched for patterns, on a household-by-household basis, in respect of our theoretical ideas. It is not, however, possible to present this systematic analysis in full because of space constraints. Because of this, it is important to stress that cases should be seen as representative of other cases not presented, rather than merely as 'illustrations' of the quantitative data.

In some parts of the analysis of the household study, we have grouped the households according to parents' ethnic origins. We have contrasted those households in which both parents were born outside the UK with those in which both parents are UK-born or one parent is UK-born and the other is not. Since the parents who are not UK-born come from various different countries, it is not legitimate to treat them as a uniform cultural group. However, at an abstract sociological level, we have considered that households in which both parents were born outside the UK (the majority in Asia and the Middle East) have in common the fact that family roles and statuses are ascribed; it is parents who confer upon young people new responsibilities, especially towards others. By contrast, for households containing one or two UK-born parents, young people's roles and statuses are achieved; young people are ideally freed from parental interference in their acquisition of new roles and statuses. This is especially relevant to cultural definitions of adolescence: the ways in which parents treat young people's transitions to adulthood, that is, as a 'positional' status which is assigned according to collectively held norms or as a 'personal' status which individual young people renegotiate for themselves (Bernstein, 1971). In the 'ascribed status' group, we have placed 19 households consisting of parents born outside the UK – 11 of Asian origin, four from the Middle East, and four from Africa, China, southern Europe and North America.[11] The 'achieved status' group contains 45 households in which young people's parents are UK-born (39), and six households where one parent is UK-born and the other not. Social class as well as culture defines the transition to adulthood so that working-class transitions tend to be ascribed rather than achieved in accordance with young people's entry to the labour market.

In the presentation of the questionnaire survey data we have used percentages and, while claiming that our survey of young people is only representative of the population of young people in the particular London borough in which it was carried out, we have applied the chi-square test of significance where appropriate. We follow convention in referring to anything with a probability of less than 0.05 as 'significant'. In the presentation of the household interview data, we have referred to proportions (although we have also given percentages in places for ease of interpretation). Moreover, although the household sample is representative of the questionnaire sample, we have not applied ideas of statistical inference. In tables the row or column percentages may sum to 99 or 101 per cent because of rounding. In some tables where base numbers are small, actual numbers are reproduced in square brackets as percentages have not been calculated.

Outline of the book

In the next two chapters (2 and 3), we examine parents' and young people's accounts of adolescence and parenthood. Chapters 4, 5 and 6 are devoted to themes concerning health – definitions of health and illness, health status and practices and health-related behaviours. In Chapter 7, we turn to the issue of parental control of young people and examine what both parties have to say about norms and 'household rules'. Chapters 8 and 9 take up the theme of negotiation in relation to particular topics under the general heading of health – negotiations over food, sex, smoking, drinking alcohol and drugs. Chapter 10 examines the quality and nature of the relationships between young people and parents, focusing especially on the ways in which parents exert control. Chapter 11 attempts an overview of the whole study, and tries to draw out some of the major research and policy implications.

Notes

1 A comparison of young people's financial circumstances as shown in the Young Europeans Survey (European Community, 1989) confirm that young people aged 15–19, whether employed or studying full-time, increasingly rely on their families as sources of income.

2 Because of the different distribution of women in the labour force, occupation does not have the same meaning in class terms for women as it does for men (see, for example, Crompton and Mann, 1986). In general, it has been shown to be preferable to use housing tenure, income group or some other indicator of material resources in locating the class position of women (see, for example, Oakley and Rajan, 1991, for a discussion). However, we looked at mothers' occupations in analysing our data in order to compare the relevance of these with those of fathers, and to allow comparison with the findings of other studies.

3 We aimed to include schools with pupils from a range of ethnic backgrounds rather than those dominated by one particular ethnic group. The following gives schools by fifth-formers' ethnic origin:

| | Ethnic origin | | | | |
| | Asian | White | Black | Other | |
School	%	%	%	%	Base
All	18	64	11	7	838
1	11	78	7	4	126
2	18	65	14	2	169
3	31	44	12	13	196
4	6	71	14	9	145
5	19	63	10	8	72
6	16	72	4	8	130

4 In 1990, 8 per cent of boys and 8 per cent of girls aged 11–15 were in independent schools in England and Wales. However, since state school pupils are disproportionately more likely to leave school at 16, the proportion of young people aged 16 and older in independent schools rises considerably – to 16 per cent of girls and 20 per cent of boys (Central Statistical Office, 1993).

5 Our occupational classification of high- and low-status jobs is based on the Registrar-General's extended classification of 11 groups, as used in the *Women and Employment* survey (Martin and Roberts, 1984). The first four categories, equivalent to the Registrar-General's socioeconomic groups I and II, are classed as 'high-status', and the rest – Registrar-General's III non-manual and manual, IV and V – as 'low-status'.

6 There are no significant differences by social class between the ethnic groups in either the state schools or the private schools.

7 The following table shows mothers' occupational status by young people's ethnicity, school and housing type:

| | Ethnicity | | | | School | | Housing | |
| | Asian | White | Black | Other | State | Private | Rented | Owner-occupier |
Mothers' occupational status	%	%	%	%	%	%	%	%
High	21	25	28	23	17	48	8	28
Low	58	56	55	40	62	34	62	54
Not employed	21	19	17	37	21	18	31	18
Base	136	500	77	62	586	194	134	610

$p < 0.05$ $p \ll 0.0001$ $p \ll 0.0001$

8 The following table gives interview response rates by school:

School	Mothers % (n/N)		Fathers % (n/N)		Young People % (n/N)	
State						
1	45	(9/20)	19	(3/16)	50	(10/20)
2	84	(16/19)	53	(10/19)	70	(14/20)
3	41	(7/17)	36	(5/14)	53	(9/17)
4	53	(10/19)	25	(4/16)	63	(12/19)
Private						
Boys	100	(5/5)	80	(4/5)	80	(4/5)
Girls	50	(5/10)	33	(3/9)	50	(5/10)

9 As noted above, it would have been preferable to use an indicator of material resources such as income, but we did not have this information.

10 The household occupational breakdown is as follows:

20 with fathers or single-parent mothers in manual occupations;

17 with fathers or single-parent mothers in managerial occupations;

11 with fathers or single-parent mothers in professional occupations;

6 with fathers who are shopkeepers;

5 with fathers or single-parent mothers in clerical or sales occupations, and 1 policeman;

5 with no parent in employment (father retired or absent and mother not in employment).

11 The North American parents come from small-town America, and are members of a fundamentalist Christian church; they hence have strong moral views which have some correspondence with those of the Asian and Middle Eastern parents.

2 Meanings of adolescence

In this chapter and the next, we look at the ways in which young people and their parents view the experiences of being a teenager and a parent at this stage in young people's lives. The material we draw on in the chapter comes from the household interviews. Parents and young people were asked general questions at the beginning of the interviews, a point by which they had scarcely begun to reflect on the issues or to contextualize their responses within their own experiences. It seems that young people are less likely than parents to respond to such general questions, and more likely to refer directly to their own experiences and situations. Young people and parents were also asked to consider the context in which young people grow up – its constraints and its possibilities. We asked them to consider how young people's lives are specifically affected by gender, race and class differences.

What are the general normative assumptions of parents and young people in the study concerning the nature of 'adolescence'? To what extent do these reflect what Davis (1990) calls the 'hyperbolic' media presentation of young people as dangerously unruly and conflictual? In our study, parents' and young people's comments about adolescence fall into three main categories: teenagers' behaviour in the wider society; behaviour at home; and what we have called 'emotionality'.

Teenagers in society: negative stereotypes?

In the view of adults, teenagers have a bad press, while in teenagers' eyes adults are perceived more favourably. Parents were asked 'Do you think adults generally like or dislike teenagers as a group?' Nearly two-thirds of parents (49 out of 76) suggest that teenagers are generally disliked. By contrast, young people asked 'Do you think teenagers generally like or dislike adults as a group?' were more charitable about adults. One-third were totally positive, while around half mentioned negative as well as positive aspects – such as adults being 'old fashioned' and 'thick' because 'they don't know about compact disc players and computers and videos'.

Teenagers are less likely than parents to generalize, and they prefer to judge and be judged on an individual basis. They focus on the reactions of adults as parents, friends and teachers to them and their relationships, and describe these reactions as generally good. As one young woman says, it is not a question of stereotypical teenagers or stereotypical parents:

> You hear so many sort of clichéd things about rebelling and not wanting to be with adults, and I don't think you can generalize cos a lot of people I know want – enjoy – being with their parents, and can get on with adults ... Most of the adults I know anyway are sort of, they're not staid, if you see what I mean. (Anna Gibb)

The idea that young people pose a threat to the status quo is not new. As Douglas (1966) notes, minorities and those on the margins of society are considered 'potentially dangerous and polluting'. None the less, parents distinguish between teenagers as a generality, on the one hand, and their own teenagers, on the other:

> If the minority display anti-social behaviour, then the majority gets labelled – tarred with the same brush. (Sandra Purcell's father)

William Lovelock's mother points out that teenagers' bad image, especially with older people, generally reflects badly and unfairly on them and their parents.

> I think they're all tainted as far as older people are concerned, unfortunately by the publicity that the ones who do cause the aggravation seem to get. Most people say 'Oh, the youth of today!' I get cross sometimes, because when you've got teenagers you tend to think that's reflective on you as well. And when you've brought them up and done your best for them – in the same category as the trouble-makers – I get a bit upset then, and think that people shouldn't generalize all teenagers in one group. My son brings some lovely friends home here.

Parental explanations for the negative image of youth focus on the 'generation gap'. A father says 'They've been complained about (by adults) from time immemorial'; and a mother believes that 'Adults forget what it's like to be young.' One father, a policeman, is constantly reminded of this in his job:

> I have been called out by a lot of adults over the years to a lot of noisy kids. Therefore, you could say that parents don't like teenagers. The truth is that adults don't like their privacy and their silence and their peace being interfered with. It's always those bloody kids, isn't it? On some occasions it's absolutely true ... It's people's attitudes. I think people can become very intolerant. (Colin Clark's father)

Just as parents' and young people's accounts distinguish between 'good' and 'bad' teenagers, so they also distinguish between intolerant and tolerant adults; nearly a quarter of parents (17 out of 76) note that parents with teenage children are more positive towards teenagers, especially

compared with older people. A number of fathers see themselves as particularly sympathetic towards teenagers, having been teenagers themselves
in the 1960s:

> They cannot tell us anything. (Anna Gibb's stepfather)

Daryl Conlon's father, an archetypal 1960s man, says that his son finds
him 'outrageous' rather than the other way round:

> He's more conservative than ever I was. He thinks I'm outrageous as a
> father. I'm one of the sixties children ... He says 'Get your hair cut, Dad
> ... You embarrass me' or I shouldn't do outlandish things ... Thatcher's
> children are very right-wing, very dogmatic, very narrow minded.

Young people do not speculate about the reasons for youth's unpopularity with adults. Parents are more sensitive to the issue. According to one
of the mothers, negative perceptions of young people are fuelled by adults'
envy of youth, as adults become increasingly aware of ageing and their
own mortality:

> ... a jealousy from the older generation because hearing the younger ones,
> they have got the energy, they look good ... We think that when we get
> older that things are going to be easier and smooth. Now that I am the
> older generation ... I mean, you look at the younger people ... basically
> they are fresh and they are young and they don't have any responsibility.
> They are free. (Sheila Summers's mother)

Indeed, youth is positively described by young people, especially as they
sense its finiteness. One young woman, now in full-time work, describes
her earlier teenage years in terms of freedom:

> They're the best years really, enjoy them while you can ... When you're
> older and you've got kids you might not be able to go out on a Friday night.
> It's things like that, you know, like your friends knock at the door, and
> 'Coming out tonight?' 'Yeah.' And you get your shoes on and go.
> (Alison James)

Although parents exempt their own teenagers from negative stereotypes, they none the less see young people's unpopularity in society to be
largely of their own making. Frequently mentioned as accounting for
young people's poor image is their public behaviour, notably 'hanging
around in groups', behaviour which is said to be offensive and frightening,
especially to elderly people. Loudness, aggressive behaviour and disrespect
– 'pushing and shoving at bus stops' – are said to offend adults. A mother
observes:

> I believe adults, speaking from experience – I've run several youth clubs in
> the borough – do not understand young people because they feel isolated
> from them – the way they talk, the way they dress ... Young people today
> speak more freely. I think the older generation probably feel that the
> younger people have no respect for elders. (Margaret Nelson's mother)

Young people themselves also mention these kinds of teenage behaviour as threatening, though rarely in response to questions eliciting general perceptions. Many tell stories of other teenagers menacing and even mugging them. Several describe the phenomenon of male gangs, and one young man admits to being ringleader of a gang which regularly clashes with other gangs in the area. Because of his position as gangleader and his large size, he says, other boys come to him for protection – 'like a daddy in prison'. He and his dozen or so mates meet in the park most evenings:

> We hang about on a pathway where we sit. And like, a lot of people are scared of us down there. People don't want to walk past that alley at eleven o'clock, because they think we're going to stab them. But we wouldn't do that! (Amin Choudry)

Another stereotypical teenage behaviour, again particularly mentioned by parents as giving young people a bad name, is their sometimes outlandish or scruffy appearance. In practice, only a fifth (12 out of 56) of young people claim definite allegiance to a particular dress 'style'. Two middle-class young women say they mix with 'gothics' and dress in black when they go to venues. Another young woman, Emma Kerr, stresses the importance of wearing the right clothes 'if you want to be accepted', though music preferences are considered to be just as important – 'heavy metal or sixties stuff'. She says her mother laughs at her clothes, especially a pair of fringed shorts, and accuses her of looking like the child prostitute in the film *Taxi Driver*. Tracksuit bottoms and large expensive trainers, described by one young woman as an 'Afro-Caribbean look', are also said to amuse parents: 'My dad takes the mick out of my trousers . . . and my trainers, cos I paid eighty pounds for 'em.' But her clothes do not create any serious friction; her parents, she says, accept it as fashion, equivalent to their 1960s 'flares and platform soles', and do not interpret it as a sign of rebelliousness. The 'Indy' look is another fashion mentioned; this is described as 'DMs [Doc Martins boots] and black jeans'.

Some teenagers are as critical as their parents of specific types of group dressing, and dismiss the slavish following of fashion as showing a lack of individuality:

> I don't really like tracksuit bottoms and all that . . . Why can't they look individual? Why can't they be different? . . . And then there's those people who try to be too different, I don't mind them, it's just that sometimes what they wear is just totally outrageous . . . I just like to look smart, I don't like to look scruffy. I always like to look respectable. (Chenglie Wang)

Teenagers at home: connectedness versus independence

Some of these issues concerning the way young people and parents perceive and relate to one another are taken up again in Chapters 7 and 10. But in terms of general perceptions, parents are more likely than young people to mention stereotypical behaviours which, according to the paradigm of psychological development in adolescence, young people are expected to exhibit: rudeness, rebelliousness, having no respect and refusing to listen to adult advice. Parents born outside the UK, who view status as ascribed rather than achieved, are particularly likely to mention the ways in which young people push against parental conventions, though, as we shall describe, they do not see this as intrinsically part of adolescence. The first comment is from a mother of Nigerian origin and the second from a mother of Iraqi background. In both cases, they are perturbed by the 'waywardness' of young people, and their refusal to accept the 'truth' – namely that adults know best.

> They find it difficult to accept the truth. Because they want to have their way. They know it is true, but because they want to have their way, they're not ready to take it . . . I think what you need to do is to speak to them, explain better . . . (Ukande Osunde's mother)

> I don't like this age. You have to look after them all the time, be with them, make sure they don't make mistakes. . . . From 15 they start becoming very active and they want to do everything, try everything. Their mind is not what they think it is. They think they can do everything, but it's not [true].
> (Judith Gabriel's mother)

Some young people whose parents were born outside the UK talk in general terms about respecting their elders – parents, relatives, and teachers:

> I think I get on quite well [with adults] because we are brought up to respect our elders and so, you know, we make more effort. (Farrukh Aziz)

On the other hand, some young people think that their families and communities lack understanding of their situation, which some describe in terms of being squeezed between two cultures:

> English people can more or less do as they like and the Asian girls, they get pressured, especially with arranged marriages. I totally disagree with arranged marriages . . . I've hit that on the head . . . so my parents say I have to get married to someone of my own religion . . . And now I'm involved with this Malaysian guy [who is] a Catholic. . . . If my dad knew I was going out with someone he would kill me. (Sai Kumar)

A number of young people of non-UK parentage are censorious of the attitudes and behaviour of some of their peers. A young woman of Asian background differentiates between obedient students like herself, who do their A levels and those who do the Certificate of Pre-Vocational Education.[1] Another young Asian woman says that some pupils

> have such a bad attitude to the teachers. . . . They just insult them so badly . . . And the thing that annoys me most is that they're intelligent, and they're wasting it, and I have to work for what I want to do.

These two young women are unusual among Asian-origin young people in their alienation from their parents, particularly their fathers.

Teenagers see resistance to parental control as a normal part of every-day life, rather than to do with their own development. For young people with parents born in the UK, this is referred to as part of the 'natural' process of growing up:

> If at some point you don't get fed up with your parents you'd never leave.
> (Carole New)

Central to normative notions of adolescence are parents' and teenagers' ideas concerning how much general independence parents ought to allow young people at 16. Since there are many dimensions to the notion of independence, considered in later chapters, we only touch upon the issue here. In terms of general norms, we asked parents and their young people whether they agree or disagree with the idea that 'young people should be free to lead their own lives and make their own decisions' at 16. Surprisingly, more parents (35 out of 80, or 44 per cent) than young people (17 out of 54, or 31 per cent) agree with this idea, though more parents than young people disagree and the rest are ambivalent. Among parents not born in the UK and their children, there is predictably greater disagreement than obtains with UK-born parents and their children.

In addition, we asked young people and parents about the desirability of young people developing their own ideas or following those of their parents. Again, young people are rather more conservative than parents, saying they ought to follow their parents' beliefs, at least partially, although parents born outside the UK and their young people are more likely to say they should be at least partially in agreement. However, when young people and parents are asked how much they share similar ideas, the differences are rather less marked. Over a third of both parents and young people of non-UK origin suggest that their beliefs are similar, with only a small proportion (less than a fifth in both UK-origin and non-UK-origin groups) declaring little or no overlap.

Also relevant are young people's and parents' ideas concerning young people's independence. These include the desirability of young people leaving home (at any age), parents giving them financial support, and parents being supported by them in old age. While attitudes to these issues may not shed light on ideas about adolescent independence *per se*, they are indicative of the broader issue of connectedness with kin – the extent to which children are considered by their parents ever to become independent of family ties. In so far as families in non-Western cultures are expected to remain connected, the idea of adolescence as the process by which individual independence is achieved is unlikely to have a great deal of currency.

Parents and young people differ little in attitude to young people leaving home, with a roughly equal distribution between those who are positive, non-committal, ambivalent or negative. In general, parents from non-UK backgrounds are less likely to favour the idea than those of UK origin, and, as we note in Chapter 7, some consider that parental encouragement contributes to the phenomenon of homelessness among young people. A father of Egyptian origin comments:

> Here young people can leave home ... [In Egypt] accommodation is not available, and you are expected to keep in touch with your family. You only leave to go abroad or to get married ... Here you can get a job or walk out the door. The household and his parents are forgotten. It is very hard for me to accept that in a year or two he might be gone. (Michael Hammoud's father)

Compared with UK-origin parents, parents not born in the UK are more likely to favour continuing ties of material support and obligation, especially the idea of giving considerable financial help to their young people when they set up house. They are also more likely to be in favour of their young people giving them support in their old age. The account of a Moroccan stepfather serves as an example, since, in the context of his own upbringing, he finds the notion of independence strange:

> Well, you never become independent in that way. I mean you always have respect for your parents and you always think your parents are everything. I know children who are married, and they are under the same roof as their parents. They work and they take care of their parents. We will never ever chuck our parents out and put them in a home, for example. That doesn't exist in our society. Even if he is not related, a little smell of the blood in the family – we do take care of our old ones. We are never going to put them away. (Theo McGuiness's stepfather)

Young people's general assessment of their current independence *vis-à-vis* their parents is best captured by the question 'Do you consider yourself to be an adult?' A quarter of young people say they are adult, half claim to be 'in between', and a quarter are 'not adult'. Interestingly, young people with parents born outside the UK are more likely to describe themselves as adult; they associate adulthood with responsibility rather than independence, and adolescence is accorded less significance in their parents' cultures.

For some young people adulthood is portrayed in terms of what teenagers are *not* allowed to do and defined in terms of the legal rights attached to being 18; excluding them from adult status are laws about not being able to vote, drive a car, go to pubs or certain types of clubs and films. Others equate adulthood with positive rights to join the labour market and to be financially responsible. In one case, a young woman mentions giving birth and deciding to bring up her child without a partner. Others describe feeling grown up because they have experienced family bereavement (in two cases the death of the father). Not surprisingly, young people have more to say about their current status being not quite adult. But most young people, especially working-class young people whose parents were born in the UK, describe this 'in between' status positively – just under half see it as wholly positive and just under half as both positive and negative. Adolescence is described as the antithesis of responsibility and is akin to childhood – the freedom to 'muck about', 'mess around' and 'have a laugh', to watch children's TV and to go on the swings in the park.

Young people were also asked about the transition out of childhood. Significantly more girls and more working-class young people describe this as a sudden, rather than a gradual, change. For young women the onset of menstruation as a biological 'marker' is undoubtedly important here.

Teenagers as emotional beings: a time of emotional turmoil?

Psychological models of adolescent development, as we saw in Chapter 1, place a good deal of emphasis on the notion that adolescence is inevitably a time of emotional turbulence (Erikson, 1968). We were interested to discover if young people and parents agree with this, and if it matches their own experiences. Rather fewer young people (23 out of 53, or 43 per cent) than parents (48 out of 84, or 57 per cent) agree with this portrayal in general terms. On the other hand, parents agree that adolescence has not been so very difficult for most. Under a fifth of parents (16 out of 83) mention 'a great deal' of difficulty for young people, and under two-fifths (32) 'some difficulty', with rather more parents of daughters (28 out of 39, or 72 per cent) than of sons (20 out of 44, or 45 per cent) saying that their young people's adolescence has been difficult. Young people's assessments of their own adolescence are nearer to the stereotype than are those of parents; over a quarter (15 out of 54) admit to a great deal of difficulty, and just under half (25) to some difficulty.

Young people link their emotions – 'moody', 'depressed' and 'ratty' are some of the words used – to specific situations. Teenagers are emotional, not because they are necessarily going through a psychological 'stage', but because they are having to renegotiate relationships, particularly with parents, at the same time as making new peer-group relationships, frequently with the opposite sex. Adolescence thus becomes a time of emotional upset, when difficulties with social relationships occur and have to be coped with. Examples mentioned by young people include situations where parents are inflexible about allowing them more freedom, especially about going out at night; the break-up of their parents' marriages and problematic relationships with step-parents; 'bitchy' friends and bullying; falling in love and breaking up. One young woman comments that labelling teenagers as 'emotional' and 'moody' is a way in which adults avoid confronting young people's legitimate grievances; by identifying young people with the irrational, their point of view can be conveniently ignored:[2]

> I suppose everyone does a bit of the old tantrums, arguments with their parents and the emotional stuff. But I don't think I do that any more than my mother does. I'm not being funny, right? But we both have a problem of yelling and screaming and arguing. But because I'm a teenager – an adolescent – it's like, 'This girl is being a typical adolescent.' But arguments

tend to be because the teenager wants to grow up and the parents don't
really want them to, because it's their little child you know. (Andrea Dewar)

Another middle-class young woman in a dual-career household says that
she had to be independent from an early age:

I had to become more of my own person and do stuff by myself – organize
things for myself.

She has not experienced any particular emotional trauma since the start
of adolescence.

Those who link teenage trauma to parental restrictiveness include several
young women whose parents were born outside the UK, and whose
struggles for independence are met by their parents' accusations about
the 'abnormality' of their behaviour – 'something must be wrong with
you':

I mean, I throw a couple of tantrums now and then, all people at my age do
that, I suppose, it's part of growing up. (*That's not been a particular difficulty?*)
No – we don't find it difficult, it's just people older than us. You know, they
think it's a major problem, 'Must get them seen to.' 'They need a
psychiatrist', or something. I'm not kidding! (*Who's said that?*) Well, it's just
like sometimes they think I'm crazy, they think, 'You're mad', I don't know
why. It's like people saying 'You're mad.' I'm not mad, I'm normal. . . . My
dad sometimes complains 'Why are you dressed like that?' (*How would he like
you to dress?*) Oh, cute little dresses and bows in my hair. (Judith Gabriel)

Another talks about her parents branding her as 'moody', someone who
shows her temper too easily, or has a tantrum when she does not get her
own way. She finds this portrait totally unrecognizable:

I don't mean to anger them – but they don't agree with what I say.

Sai Kumar's assertiveness about expressing her contrary opinions is interpreted by her parents not simply as the rebelliousness of youth, but as
individual psychopathology. She feels caught between two cultures and
understood by neither, and says of her adolescence:

'It's not the best time in somebody's life . . . I wouldn't go back to save my
life.

Nasreen Mohammed attributes her problems to the lack of 'any real
communication with my parents . . . I was always a solo act'. For this
reason, she tends to censor her conversation with her parents, especially
her mother:

I could only talk to her about things which I thought she would find
acceptable. But that means there's always a kind of barrier between you. You
can't really talk about something which she wouldn't find acceptable . . . the
traditional thing is for the girl to be just like her mother . . . If I'm in love
or whatever, I couldn't talk about that, because they would find it
unacceptable for me to feel certain emotions before a given time! Hey,
check the calendar, maybe next year! It's quite funny, but a bit sad really.

The tendency towards self-censorship by young people of non-UK parent-age when communicating with parents emerges as a major theme else-where in the book (Chapters 9 and 10).

Parents born outside the UK are inclined to interpret their young people's non-communicativeness and moodiness as an individual character-istic rather than as a general feature of adolescence; this explains in part why they find the norm of emotionality in adolescence unfamiliar. None the less, proportionately fewer such parents (9 out of 21, or 43 per cent) than UK-born parents (39 out of 62, or 63 per cent) report that their young have experienced difficulty. The fact that the term 'emotional tur-moil' was not understood by some parents, notably those with a different cultural view, is not solely a linguistic problem, since we usually rephrased the term in the interviews. For example, Sandeep Kumar's father still sounds perplexed, even after the interviewer's elaboration:

> There might be some problem, but I don't think people mention about these things. Probably they just take it as it comes, you know. I'm not quite sure.

Many parents and young people who subscribe, both generally and in practice, to the idea of adolescence as a period of emotionality, use differ-ent words to describe the phenomenon. Fathers especially prefer to speak of 'a time of change', or a time of 'confusion' and 'inconsistency', and emphasize the cognitive and physical aspects of the 'betwixt and between' status of adolescents as 'neither adults nor children':

> He's going through a funny stage. He's not quite sure what he thinks about things half the time himself . . . It's thrown him into confusion.
> (Jeremy Talbot's father)

Mothers also talk about the 'betwixt and between stage', and are particu-larly likely to mention the hormonal and other physical changes which happen in adolescence. Unlike fathers, they mention that young people may be 'upset for no reason', or they attribute their daughters' mood swings to menstruation. Only one young woman mentions mood swings related to her menstrual cycle.

There are other gender differences among young people here. For example, and as noted earlier, young women are more likely than young men to describe the change from child to teenager as abrupt rather than gradual (13 out of 26 young women against 5 out of 27 young men). Young men's comments tend to deny a link between adolescence and turbulent emotions. Rather, they see any emotional disturbance as related to the fact that life is difficult, especially in making the transition to adulthood:

> I think of it [adolescence] as the first emotional time of your life, rather than the only one. Because I mean, it's not as if you just like get out of your teenage years and then it's just plain sailing all the way through.
> (Jeremy Talbot)

The context of adolescence: constraints and possibilities

Despite parents' negative perceptions of young people as a category and their attribution of blame to young people themselves, they say that life today is tough on young people. Young people are more likely than parents to dwell on the positive possibilities which life offers them.

Parents and young people were asked whether they thought it harder or easier to be a teenager today than in the parents' teenage years. The majority of parents, especially mothers, consider it harder now, with most parents (75 out of 81, or 93 per cent) agreeing that young people have a greater number of largely external pressures upon them. Between a half and two-thirds (50 out of 85) say that life is harder, a fifth (17) that it is both harder and easier or no different, and under a fifth (15) that it is easier (three say they do not know).

Not surprisingly, young people find the generational comparison difficult. Of those who express an opinion, rather more young people than parents think life is easier now and only a few say it is harder. In contrast to parents who think that young people have to grow up 'too quickly', young people see 'getting older younger' in a positive light. Those whose parents were UK-born are particularly likely to believe that youth is and ought to be a time for enjoyment: 'We're supposed to enjoy it.'

> I know I get away with a lot more than my mum did . . . I can do more and tell my mum everything. I know if my mum did the same things I did and told her mother, she wouldn't have got away with it . . . But I think parents are so much more easy-going now anyway, even if they don't want to, they feel that they should be. (Anna Gibb)

Young people whose parents grew up in the East and Middle East lack this sense of liberation and, although some do not feel deprived, others are clearly distressed at their chaperoned lives. One young man, Chenglie Wang, says his parents

> don't consider fun to be allowed at all, practically . . . I mean, life's not really worth living if you don't have any fun, right?

Only a recent unchaperoned visit to relatives in Hong Kong awakened him to a sense of his own independence. Even so, these young people are quite clear in their minds that their lives are an improvement on those of their parents who grew up in countries where religion and custom greatly restricted their lives and particularly those of their mothers.

The pressures of the market

The values of individual freedom and choice are central to the ideology of a market society, but for teenagers the pressure to consume may create considerable constraints. While few young people mention consumerism and the growth of teenage markets as a pressure, several parents, mothers in particular, mention the way the clothing industry creates a demand among young people for designer clothes (several singled out expensive trainers for which they are expected to pay). In the context of peer pressures to conform to fashion, consumerism is seen to be pernicious:

> There's so much competition to be a teenager today ... If you haven't got the right trainers or the right tee shirt, you don't fit in. If they come from a poor or hard up family, I've heard they're upset because they can't get the money off their parents. (William Lovelock's mother)

> It's buy, buy, buy. Everything is done to get their money out of them, and sometimes it's rubbish. I don't like the way the clothes are made for the kids. It's here today and thrown off again later. They charge such a lot for gimmicky things. (Alec Sargent's mother)

Some parents, especially those of working-class origin, see material plenty – more pocket money, more possessions, more opportunities for holidays and leisure activities – as benefiting young people. This is particularly the case when they reflect upon their own materially disadvantaged teenage years:

> It has to be easier because it's a more affluent society. My dad never gave me pocket money in my life.

Several young people, particularly those with parents born in poorer countries, or those whose parents' working lives began early, also contrast their advantages with their parents' impoverished childhoods.

Nowhere for young people to go

Several mothers note that young people at 16 have few opportunities to meet together outside the home. They lack organizations such as youth clubs, and they are at risk of violence, including ethnic friction, when they enter public places. Parents contrast the lack of external freedom of their young with their own experiences. A mother talks about her own youth, when it was considered acceptable for young people to explore local beauty spots:

> I mean we used to cycle a lot. You could go out for the day to the woods and things like that ... I mean you couldn't send your own children up to Barrowden Hill now, because you'd be afraid. So I think, you know, it was more freedom ... You weren't worried about going out, and now when they go out you stop and think, where are they going? (Jo Saunders' mother)

Another mother describes a similar lack of freedom which originates in childhood – the relocation of children's activities from the street to the home:

> Where I was brought up, it was all open air. We played in the street – street games. I was hardly ever in. There wasn't much TV ... But [my sons] haven't been allowed out in the same way because it's not safe. The road is totally awful. And there's the fear of sex crimes, so you warn them. Luckily there's two of them. They were always together ... No, they haven't had

much freedom. They're stuck in the house more than I was. So I think you find more aggression playing computer games, because they're more enclosed. (Jeremy Talbot's mother)

Though young people do not spontaneously mention in their interviews the limited opportunities to explore their own external environments, answers to questions in the survey suggest that they see the wider physical environment as a live political issue. Forty per cent rank 'the environment' among their three greatest worries for the future, less than the percentage listing the death of themselves or a close relative and fear of unemployment, but more than those citing nuclear war, health risks (AIDS, cancer, heart attacks), and parental divorce.

Education and employment pressures

Education is the item most frequently mentioned by young people as making their lives hard. They describe feeling like 'guinea pigs' in taking the relatively new GCSE examinations, with their emphasis on continuous assessment. While middle-class young people are particularly likely to mention the 'competitiveness' of the school environment as a pressure, a working-class young woman from a state school speaks about having to cope with poor teaching and an absence of teachers:

I mean, school work can be a pressure. I mean, the worst thing in our school was the fact that they give you course work that you've got to do within two years, and in the last six months before your exam they give you five lots of course work that they should have done within the previous year, which is atrocious. And not having teachers being able to teach you. We had one teacher who had ten nervous breakdowns. One couldn't teach the maths class, so I had to be put down a set because he couldn't teach. We had eight people for Spanish. All the people who were in my class, we all just suffered through our exams and our school. (Stella Wheeler, former state school pupil now in employment)

Several parents who sent their children to private schools mention that they did so in order to give them a better base from which to compete in education and employment. Middle-class parents are mindful of their need to maintain the position of their young people within the social class system. As one mother puts it:

But they have to work very hard now to achieve what their parents are achieving.

A mother, herself pursuing educational courses to raise her own occupational chances, comments on the difficulty that this creates for young people; she implies that mothers ought to be concerned with their children's opportunities, rather than their own. However, educational pressure is not necessarily seen as having the desired effect in terms of preparing young people for work. Daryl Conlon's father, who left school at 15 and built up his own company without the aid of formal education, says:

> More emphasis [today] on marks and results ... not so much on using
> common sense and nous to get around, and guile and cunning ... It's so
> much structured so the child has to follow certain rules. If he can't follow
> them, he's lost ... It breeds children who are very clever ... guys with PhDs
> working on motorways ... with no ability to adapt what they know to life.

A stepmother who was born and brought up in the United States contrasts
the extra-curricular activities available to young people in the USA with
the situation in the UK today which, she argues, has resulted from financial
constraint and the underfunding of state education.

Several young people mention the high rate of youth unemployment
which has prevailed in the UK during the 1970s and 1980s. The experiences of those leaving education are therefore in stark contrast to those
of parents, most of whom entered the labour market in the 1960s, a
period of full employment. One young woman is aware of the impact of
these changes:

> In the 1960s you knew you could get a job ... You just decided what you
> were going to pick and went off and did it. Today it's quite different.
> (Anna Gibb)

The changed occupational chances of young people are starkly reflected
in the fates of those young people in our study (15 out of 56) who left
school at 16 and did not succeed in getting work immediately, or, when
they did, found poorly paid unskilled manual jobs under youth training
schemes, which frequently ended in redundancy.

Family pressures and possibilities

A small number of parents refer to inadequacies within the family when
discussing the difficulties confronted by young people. The most striking
comment here came from a mother who belongs to a Christian fundamentalist church. Young people, she suggests, have it hard because parents
do not restrain them enough, due to a general decline in moral values
and lack of home-centredness, as mothers vacate the home and join the
labour market:

> I think there's a lot of demands, so much presented to them from the moral
> point of view ... Like on TV ... it's if you haven't had sex by the time
> you're 16 you're really weird ... There's so few examples of family-centred
> things any more. I mean, both parents work ... I mean, people are just
> gone all the time. I don't think they have much example of family life ...
> The moral fibre is just totally lacking ... It shows in the statistics. I mean, so
> many of my children's friends [come from] single-parent homes ... It's not
> the freedom that children really need ... It's just that for us there was some
> type of restraint, you know. I mean, *The Graduate* was the most risqué movie
> of the time and, you know, there's just no limits at all, and when you take
> limits away ... by nature, we don't like limits, and by nature you go just as
> far as you can go ... I feel sorry for them. (Philip Stevens's mother)

By contrast, other parents born outside the UK say that the teenage years of their young people are easier than their own were because they have a much less restrictive upbringing. Two mothers – one an East African Asian and the other from Nigeria – talk about their highly constrained upbringings:

> Easier, because when I was a teenager I couldn't speak to my parents openly like she does [to me] . . . When I was 16, I didn't know what I wanted. I was lost in my own little world, because they wouldn't understand me. They just wanted the old rules and regulations. (Soraya Khan's mother)

> They have it easier than me because until 21, I was under the umbrella of my parents. If I was going to a party, I had to give them [notice] three weeks [before] the time. Otherwise I wouldn't go to the party . . . In the holidays, I had to be in my mother's shop. She didn't pay me anything . . . We didn't have any washing machine. Everything I did by hand.
> (Ukande Osunde's mother)

Similarly, some young people whose parents grew up in the East and Middle East compare their lives favourably with those of their parents:

> It's easier now. You can get away with a hell of a lot. (*Like what?*) You can talk your parents into a hell of a lot because they've got relaxed, whereas then, you were told to sit down and you stayed sitting down, whether you liked it or not. They couldn't care less if you were happy. (Soraya Khan)

Others see their own lives as harder than their parents' lives as teenagers, precisely because their parents were not faced with conflicting models and values. A young woman whose parents grew up in Iraq says:

> That's difficult. My parents have a way of saying 'When I was young everything was like this and that.' I don't know if I could believe that. Human nature is the same. I mean, authority is always a problem with young people . . . I think I have a harder time of it. Definitely. Because my parents were brought up in Iraq, so many years ago. I have been brought up in England. And so I have problems of culture clash, very serious problems of culture clash. (Nasreen Mohammed)

Gender, race and social class

Young people and parents were asked to comment on the experience of being a teenager from the point of view of their particular gender, race and social class. Many more parents and young people think that boys have an easier time than girls than vice versa, though a substantial proportion say there is no difference (just under half of parents and over a third of young people).

Proportionately more young women than young men think that girls have it harder: girls have less freedom, since their parents worry about their safety at night, and therefore restrict their movements. Young men and women mention the risk to girls of physical violence, rape and pregnancy. Parents born outside the UK are particularly likely to mention the need to control girls' sexuality, while daughters contrast their restricted lives with their brothers' greater freedom, both inside and outside the home. Girls are not only stopped from going out at night while their brothers are free to come and go as they please, they are also required to do more housework, and may be asked to service their brothers' needs:

> Boys have it easier than girls, freedomwise and, like, work in the house as well – they don't do anything ... I mean, at one time my brother was on holiday for a week and I was at college, and he didn't do anything, and when I came home the house was in a bit of a mess and he was just watching telly all day. (Sai Kumar)

The gender struggle is still ongoing. One young woman who joined an all-male football team at school comments:

> I'm mad on football. When they used to have football clubs at school I always went along. Boys used to say 'Girls aren't any good at football, what you think you're doing?' But when I actually started playing, they saw I was pretty good – cos I played for some teams. So, like, they shrunk a bit. (Sonia Eldridge)

The view that gender makes no difference in terms of opportunities is particularly held by girls attending the single-sex private school, and by those taking A levels and expecting to go to university. For these girls, equal opportunities battles have been won already, or they were never really necessary. Several cite mothers who are successful in the professions or business. Others mention the 'equal but different' argument, and one young woman, from a Muslim family, mentions the veneration accorded to women within a male-dominated culture:

> For one thing men have got to work haven't they? Women have the choice more. People say they have not to go to work, but that's not true. Nowadays, women can work quite acceptably. But men, if they stayed at home ... their maleness would be threatened. ... I mean they don't realize in the West that, although women are perhaps, they have less freedom, in my country, it's not because they're second class citizens or not respected. In fact, I think women have a lot of respect, and so much so that they [the men] want to protect them, as much as they can. They feel the woman is sacred. And I think the women enjoy being protected. (Nasreen Mohammed)

The few parents and young people saying boys have a harder time than girls mention the pressure on boys to conform to conventional male (working-class) stereotypes of physicality, hard physical work and the provider role:

> Girls have easier jobs, like secretarial and that. (*Why's that easier?*) Sitting down, pressing a few buttons all day. Like building, they don't have to go up high buildings and that ... I don't really see much girls going on building sites. Like your job, coming here interviewing people. A man's job wouldn't really be doing this kind of work. (Amin Choudry)

Parents and young people both acknowledge racism more readily than sexism. They could talk about racism more easily, with half saying that black and Asian young people have a harder time, while the rest think that race makes no difference. A very few say whites have a harder time. The most stringent comments from parents come from blacks and Asians:

> Sometimes you go out. Everybody try to frighten you . . . Sometimes they say, 'You Indian, you Pakistani, you dead.' (Sandeep Kumar's mother)

> If you're a black boy, it's a lot harder . . . Lots of company bosses are men. They feel threatened by black boys, because they think if you're black you'll be rude or abrupt and you're going to steal from them. (Theo McGuiness's stepfather)

Among young people, whites are most indignant about racism and have more stories to tell about racist incidents involving their black or Asian friends:

> There was this girl called Debbie, and we were talking to each other a few times. She was coloured, and me mates started calling me a nigger-lover. They knew her and they were saying it as a joke, but it was stupid. (*How did Debbie react?*) She'd heard it all before. She took it as a joke and sort of laughed it off. (*How did you feel?*) I sort of like told them to shut up or something, cos it's just like immature and stupid. (*Did it stop you talking to her?*) It stopped me talking any more than I usually did cos it was just hell. (Andrew Brown)

Some black and Asian parents 'deny' racist experience. One mother simply says that she never goes out and meets people, thereby suggesting that she avoids situations in which she may encounter racism. Neena Ghosh's mother, who is of Indian origin, plays down the significance of racism, asserting its 'naturalness':

> It's hard to accept each other . . . All communities are the same: Jap to Jap, English to English, Asian to Asian.

She goes on to describe how a racist male neighbour was 'won round' through contact between the families, the women acting as go-betweens. White parents use the strategy of making racism seem exceptional by distancing themselves from it: either they themselves have no contact with black people, or their children have friends of 'all races and religions' as if, by implication, racism cannot happen in their own social circle. This argument is echoed by black and Asian young people, who claim they do not experience racism because they live in a black neighbourhood or go to multi-ethnic schools, where they have friends from different backgrounds and where teachers tend to confront racism:

> Once I was called a Paki in the middle of a class in front of the teacher. And my friend, she's English, and she turned to this person and said, 'How on earth can you say that?' She went to the teacher and told her. And the teacher was quite disgusted. (Prakash Patel)

One young woman of Afro-Caribbean origin thinks Asians suffer more than blacks because they let it hurt their feelings instead of ignoring it as she does. Asians, she says, 'stay within their family circle and ain't much fun', and are set apart by their 'goody goody' desire to work hard at school and their distinctive dress and religion. Asians thereby find it difficult to become part of the tough culture of the school, and hence are likely to fall victim to name-calling and abuse:

> I mean, everyone at school used to muck about, calling each other coloured, taking the mick out of our colour, you know, by their names, like saying, 'Oi minstrel. Come here.' But, you know, they were joking, no one ever really took it to heart. But if you say that to an Indian, they go up the wall, and burst into tears ... If anyone was nasty to me and I felt like crying, never cry in front of their faces, cos that to me is, you know, you're defeated. (Margaret Nelson)

A handful of white young people and parents complain of reverse discrimination: that blacks have preferential treatment. For example, one young woman believes that 'blacks have to put up with racism if they want to live here'. Another refuses to talk to black people since he was mugged by a black youth. A third blames black people for bringing 'problems on themselves':

> I mean, there's a lot more blacks coming into the country, and because of it they think – I don't know if it had anything to do with the way they was used for slaves – but they go round with chips on their shoulders. There's too much mugging in this area. There's blacks mugging white girls for jewellery, shooting them through the head. There's the Indian gangs in Westbank ... To be quite honest, I don't like one black person ... their attitude is that they're going to try and rule the whites. (Stella Wheeler)

Young people have very much less to say about social class differences (parents were not asked about this topic). One working-class young man confidently declares that 'teenagers are classless'. Although many deny class differences, in the questionnaire survey most answered a question asking them to place themselves in a social class group; over half (57 per cent) placed themselves in the middle class, 28 per cent in the working class, 13 per cent said they were unsure and 2 per cent placed themselves in the 'other' category. These responses reflect fathers' occupational class but have less correspondence with housing tenure or mothers' occupational class.[3] Significantly, after completing the questionnaire, several young people were overheard hotly contesting their class affiliations.

As another study suggests (Frazer, 1988), private school pupils are more class-conscious than those from state schools. A young private school girl in our study describes how she used to laugh at the 'lower class ... the casuals, which is like the Sharons and the Traceys', but now rejects her snobbish behaviour: 'They can be just as nice as other people.' Young people from private schools also suggest that they are at the receiving end of reverse class discrimination from local comprehensive pupils. They describe violent attacks and comments about their 'snobbish, public school accents' and their school uniforms:

> There's a running feud between our school and [the Comprehensive]. I've been to netball matches and they're so violent to us. And once we were out on the [High Street] with some friends and actually got attacked by some girls from the school. We were just chatting, and a girl grabbed one of my friends by the hair and pulled her back and said 'You called me a bitch!' And she denied it and in the end we just walked away. (Carole New)

Several young people interpret the class question as referring to their disposable income, noting how some can afford new clothes and new trainers while others cannot. Some also suggest that personal income inequalities lead to social differences. For example, one young woman of Asian origin says that the 'Gothics' at her school are white and middle-class and 'so posh . . . they just won't talk to you'.

Conclusion

Parental views of adolescents confirm the largely negative stereotypes current in our society. As a social category, young people are seen to receive a bad press. Parents attribute this chiefly to rowdy behaviour in public and distinctive styles of dress. This negativity about age categories is not reciprocal: young people are much less negative about adults as a collectivity. Similarly, the idea of adolescence as a time of inevitable emotional turmoil is more widespread among parents than among young people. Young people do not perceive their emotionality as part of adolescent development; rather, they see it as a rational response to difficult events and situations, such as the break-up of their parents' marriages or 'unreasonable' parental restrictiveness. But, while parents endorse the idea that adolescence is a time of emotional lability, they do not necessarily describe their own sons and daughters as having had an emotionally difficult time. Parents born outside the UK, especially those from Asian and Middle Eastern societies, generally do not hold normative views of adolescent emotionality, and are thus more likely to define any emotionality they perceive in their young people as abnormal.

Perceptions of young people's private behaviour in the home are differentiated by parents' cultural origins, especially expectations concerning the amount of independence young people should have at this age. While UK-born parents see it as 'normal' for young people to become more independent, those parents born outside the UK do not see adolescence as a time of separation from the household. These different views reflect different cultural meanings and practices with respect to kin relationships over the life course.

Though parents see teenagers' poor image as largely of their own making, the great majority report that life is tough for young people today, with most saying that it is harder than in their own teenage years. Young people are, by contrast, more likely to dwell on the possibilities life offers them.

Pressures mentioned include consumerism and the market, the lack of places for young people to spend their leisure time, the need for educational achievement, and lack of employment opportunities. Households with parents born outside the UK refer to the different cultural values held by parents and young people, though opinions differ on which generation has an easier adolescence.

The constraints of gender and race were specifically explored. Though interviewees' accounts suggest that females and black young people have a harder time, neutral and contrary views are also expressed. Social class evoked little comment, with the exception of some young people in private education who mention reverse discrimination by young people in state schools.

Notes

1 Certificate of Pre-Vocational Education courses are designed for the sixth-form pupils not taking A level.
2 There are parallels here with the cultural treatment of women. See Miller (1976).
3 Sixty-nine per cent of cases reflect fathers' social class. This figure excludes those young people who used the 'other' and 'not sure' categories, and those whose fathers were not employed, or where no information was given. Sixty-nine per cent of those claiming to be working-class were in owner-occupied housing, compared with 86 per cent of those claiming to be upper middle- or middle-class.

3 Fathers and mothers

In this chapter we draw on both the questionnaire and the household interview data to consider the broad meanings of motherhood and fatherhood at this stage of young people's lives. What does it mean to be the mother or the father of a 16-year-old? What is the division of labour and responsibility between mothers and fathers in preparing young people for healthy adult life? What kinds of cultural and social expectations shape the definition of motherhood and fatherhood, and how do these relate to the everyday experience of living with teenagers? How do teenagers see parents, and in particular the differences or similarities between mothers and fathers?

We focus in this chapter on normative views of motherhood and fatherhood. Among the many factors shaping these are parents' own experiences of being parented. Towards the end of the chapter, we look at how mothers' and fathers' beliefs and practices concerning the parenting of adolescents relate to their own remembered experiences as adolescents.

Studying parents

Fathers entered the domain of social researchers' interest in parenthood a good deal later than mothers. The mother-centredness of the earlier literature owes a good deal to the influence of psychoanalytic views of the family, according to which mothers are, and ought to be, the primary childrearers. Fathers came on the scene when the women's movement and the changes in family life of the 1960s and 1970s highlighted the need to understand the nature of men's involvement in family life (McKee and O'Brien, 1982). But, and partly as a response to these factors, much of what we know about fatherhood is patchy and informed by inappropriate research designs and theoretical perspectives (see Richards, 1982a and b). A serious shortcoming is that most research on fathers has concentrated on early childrearing. There is virtually no literature exploring fathers' relationships and experiences with young people or young people's views of fatherhood. Of 39 chapters in three recent volumes on fatherhood, for example, 36 are either concerned with fathers and childbirth, infants, or young children, or give general overviews; one chapter discusses grand-fatherhood, one stepfatherhood, and one looks at men's experiences with their own fathers (Beail and McGuire, 1982; McKee and O'Brien, 1982; Lewis and O'Brien, 1987).

Fathers were less likely than mothers to take part in our study. Of 79 fathers who were contacted, 39 per cent agreed to take part; these figures compare with 60 per cent for both mothers and young people. Access to fathers usually had to be negotiated via mothers, who often played a protective role. The most common reasons given (either by mothers or fathers) for fathers' refusals to be interviewed were that they were 'too busy' or 'not interested'. Twenty-eight of the interviewed fathers were from households in which both the mother and the young person were also interviewed; in the remaining two cases – one from a Chinese- and one from an Indian-origin household – only the father and the young person were interviewed. There were also 12 households in which only the mother and the young person in nuclear families were interviewed. These figures index not only gendered occupational roles (fathers' 'busyness' versus the presumed availability of free time in mothers' lives), but the different orientations of mothers and fathers to the responsibilities of parenthood. Whereas mothers were more likely to see participation in our research as interesting and worth the effort, fathers were more likely to perceive it as marginal to their own interests.

Fathers and mothers: the same and different

Although the focus of this chapter is on gender differences in normative definitions of parenthood, there are, of course, also important similarities. There is a common core of duties represented by the concept of 'parent-hood' to which both mothers and fathers refer directly or obliquely, as a substratum on which they base their own particular interpretations of their roles. These include: ensuring that young people are provided with the material necessities, feel cared for, and are given appropriate guid-ance to keep them out of trouble and turn them into reasonably healthy, educated, honest and conscientious citizens. The physical aspects of parenting – providing a good material environment, a good diet, and the kind of parental care that prioritizes good bodily health – are less overtly dominant concerns in parental talk about the teenage years compared to babyhood, although, as we see later in this book, these issues can become the battleground on which are acted out the competing desires of parents for control and of young people for autonomy. Foremost in parents' minds at this stage of the family life course are concerns to do with young people's activities and vulnerability to the social world outside the home. As Jim Lowe's father puts it when asked what is the hardest thing about being the parent of a teenager:

I would say making sure that they didn't get in with the wrong crowd or something like that . . . I mean . . . you can look after your children, you can tell them right from wrong, but once they're out the front door and at school and university and things, meeting other people . . . you can only advise your children, you can't dictate to them . . . I don't like dictating, being dictated to, and I wouldn't expect to dictate to my children, but all I can say is you bring up your children to the best of your abilities and then, hopefully, once they're out of your sight, you hope that they will listen to what you've told them, and that's, as far as I'm concerned, as far as you can go . . .

This 'common core' of parental duties is more sharply defined in single parents' narratives of parenting. The positions of single parents, in the space between motherhood and fatherhood, have encouraged them to reflect on what parenthood, in essence, 'is'. Clive Seymour's father, who has major responsibility for his elder son following the break-up of his marriage, accounts for his new role in terms of values hopefully inculcated – success, excellence, self-reliance – together with the responsibilities of budgetary management, providing good food, ensuring personal hygiene and social education about sex. The articulation of these basic tasks of parenthood flows from the new obligation to be mother as well as father from a starting point in which, before his wife left, areas of responsibility were strongly gender-divided.

For the most part, norms of good parenting are not gender-neutral. Parents' views about the exercise of family responsibilities, and their experiences of these, are located within a broad social context which continues to differentiate between motherhood and fatherhood in many fundamental ways. Although norms about parental behaviour have been most studied in the early phase of childrearing, where clear differences have been found (Brannen and Moss, 1991), there are reasons to suppose that cultural norms about how male and female parents should behave would hold even more strongly during the teenage years. These are the years in which young people's struggle for independence and against parental and other forms of authority gives rise to their perception as a 'social problem'. There is a long history of mothers being held responsible for containing and reversing the social problem of adolescence; in the 1990s debate about family values, this traditional view is being reaffirmed (*Guardian*, 1993). What parents should and should not do, and, within this, what it is possible for individual mothers and fathers to do, are issues much discussed in the households we studied. For example, while over half (47 out of 82) of parents think that either parents mainly or teenagers together with parents should take responsibility for the teenager's health, slightly less than half (37 out of 75) describe this state of affairs as obtaining in their own households. More fathers (14 out of 31, or 45 per cent) than mothers (20 out of 51, or 39 per cent) take this view in general and slightly more say it obtains in their own households (Chapter 4).

Table 3.1   *Gender and meanings of parenthood*

	Mothers % (n)	Fathers % (n)
Employed full-time (30 hours or more)	53 (29)	94 (29)
Fits employment round family	98 (49)	43 (13)
Fits family round employment	34 (16)	74 (20)
Conflict between role as parent and individual fulfilment	44 (24)	41 (11)
Mothers and fathers are different	82 (44)	75 (21)
Main responsibility for young person:		
mother	35 (19)	3 (1)
father	0 (0)	10 (3)
both	28 (15)	48 (14)
Negative feelings about young person leaving home	31 (16)	11 (3)
Worries a lot about young person	48 (26)	7 (2)
Influence over young person's activities:		
none	14 (6)	35 (8)
some	63 (27)	39 (9)
a lot	23 (10)	26 (6)
Effect of young person on parental relationship:		
none	54 (27)	46 (13)
positive	8 (4)	25 (7)
negative/mixed	38 (19)	29 (8)
Effect of parental relationship on young person:		
none	38 (17)	42 (11)
positive	7 (3)	31 (8)
negative/mixed	56 (25)	27 (7)
Successful in bringing up teenager	60 (32)	69 (18)

Based on total N = 55 (mothers) and N = 31 (fathers); percentages are calculated on total numbers answering particular questions.

Meanings of parenthood

The fathers in our survey were on average older than the mothers (46.8 years versus 43.1 years), and more of them were employed full-time (see Table 3.1). Differences within employment categories also obtained, with fathers working significantly longer hours than mothers (50 as compared to 41 hours). Unsurprisingly, these gender differences across the public–private divide are reflected in what parents *say* about the two domains of employment and family responsibilities. Under half of fathers, but most mothers, say they have fitted their employment around their family responsibilities. Conversely, three-quarters of fathers and a third of mothers admit to fitting their work as parents around their employment work (Table 3.1). Such patterns are, of course, heavily shaped by socio-historical processes related to childbirth and ideologies of parenthood, particularly of motherhood.

One mother of two, who worked as a childminder for 16 years and has only recently 'gone back to work' as a secretary explains the rationale behind her job choices:

> . . . if it was inconvenient for the children, I wouldn't have done it, they've
> always come first. And most of the children I've looked after have
> been teachers' children, so most of the school holidays they are off . . .
> (Rachel Pemberton's mother)

She went back to secretarial work when her son was 17 and at work himself, and her daughter was 14:

> I felt she was old enough to be left during the day for those few hours
> [and] . . . school holidays she was old enough to be left indoors . . .

This pattern of adapting work to children when children were young is described by many of the mothers. Reflecting on it, one mother thinks an underlying reason has to do with her role as wife rather than that of mother:

> I like to be around for them. [My husband] always implied that I should be
> around when the children came home from school, and then I realized it
> wasn't anything to do with them, he wanted me around when he came
> home. (Emma Kerr's mother)

If mothers tend to be defensive about their decision to work, fathers tend to be defensive about the impact of their work on the family when asked if they fit their jobs around their families, or the other way round:

> That's an awkward one to answer. . . . it's very difficult to say. You know,
> there was one time I had a contract going, that's when the children were
> younger, and my daughter said that's the first time I've seen you, Dad, for
> three weeks. I was out at six o'clock and she was still in bed, and didn't get
> home until twelve o'clock and she was still in bed . . . [but] I think we all
> have to earn a living. (Stella Wheeler's father)

> They had to [fit themselves around his job] because I've been on the
> London underground for 26 years . . . my life *is* the railway and they've got
> to fit their life around me . . . there's only one wage-earner and that's
> me . . . it may sound like I'm a bit of a male chauvinist but . . . I won't allow
> [my wife] to work . . . she does a little part-time job, but I won't allow her to
> do full-time work . . . because, one, she has enough work to do here with
> running a household, dealing with the children, she has enough on her
> plate instead of going to work and start coming home, rushing
> around . . . what's the point, when she's trying to do a 24-hour job . . . let her
> do one when the kids grow older . . . (Barry Green's father)

In the accounts of some fathers, including Barry Green's, it is precisely this emphasis on the provider role which has required them to neglect the 'being with' aspect of parenting. Reflecting on his son's current unwillingness to get a job, Mr Green says:

It is very frustrating, because all I want my sons to do is to earn the money, to get what they want so they can give it to their kids, because ... my father couldn't give nothing to me ... but I said I would give it to my children, and I have given it to the children, but *by doing that I have neglected something else.*

His son, he says, 'has had everything', a statement he immediately goes on to correct:

I'm trying to be as plain as I can ... possibly he hasn't had my love over the years ... because I was never here to give it to him ... you get what I mean ... I don't think we have ever been on holiday together ... so basically he never got nothing from me ... which, when you look back, you think ... what I'm saying is, well ... you should have made some sort of effort to do it.

The issue of employment and family responsibilities is related to the broader question of individual fulfilment versus commitment to the family, especially for mothers. Parents were asked about this in the interviews. Many mothers note, and reflect on the meaning and implications of, a conflict between the societal and personal expectation of individual fulfilment and the responsibilities of motherhood:

I would always put my children first ... sometimes I think ... like, I wasted so many years, then you know I have to start all over again ... because I have lost the confidence ... every time I go and look for a job and I get an interview and I don't go because I have lost the confidence ... (Soraya Khan's mother)

Andrea Dewar's mother calls the conflict 'quite oppressive' because:

If you're feeling a bit down in the dumps then you reflect, but everything is for other people. It's always for other people and there's no space for yourself ... but if I was to make a choice I'd much rather have children than not, absolutely.

She goes on to reflect on the tendency for this conflict to grow rather than diminish with the years:

It's very difficult to know what you want because the family are growing and the demands on you and how much you're able to provide for them are so much greater than when they were little ... and I suppose if they go to university then you have to find the money for that, so I suppose constantly, yes, you are having to put your children first, but that is something when you have a child, that's just part of it, you just have to take that on with it, there's no point in going on about it, it's just there.

For mothers, the quest for individual fulfilment is seen as linked to the timetable of childrearing. Thus, it may only be in retrospect that a conflict between this and maternal responsibility is perceived. David Monk's mother, who has three sons aged 20, 17 and 13, reflects:

I wish I had thought about it, I didn't think about it. You see when the children were younger I felt fulfilled, I felt I had done what I was expected to do, and it was only in recent years that I had become aware that they have eaten me alive. I have got no life, once they go, that's it. I mean I am not getting any younger.

The men's responses to this question of individual fulfilment versus parental responsibility tend to be more straightforward and less reflective. Asked whether he had put his responsibilities as a parent before his own wishes, Andrea Dewar's father, for example, says:

I can't say that's the case. I have seen other families where great lengths have been taken to put the children first . . . and I felt well, that's not for me . . . but I don't think anyone . . . any part of the family is in any way deprived.

Another father who, in the past, looked after children on his own for a considerable period expresses views akin to those of mothers, though his regrets are of a different nature. Asked whether he had felt there to be a conflict between his parental responsibilities and his own desires, he said:

Earlier on yes, but not so much now . . . you couldn't . . . really do anything on your own, you couldn't go out and have a good drink and then come back, you know, sloshed, pie eyed, just fall into bed, but you've got to worry about whether they're alright . . . (Andrew Brown's father)

Another father elaborates on this gendering of parental responsibility:

. . . well, it's difficult I think, for me, as with many men . . . probably we don't accept the responsibilities of home and hearth as easily as a woman, or most women do . . . I've always had a strong sense of duty, and so, you know, I would stay with that because it's something that I've created and it's my responsibility . . . but I mean there have been occasions when I wouldn't deny that I felt I would like to have more time for myself and to be doing something else . . . (Sandra Purcell's father)

More mothers than fathers say they regard the roles of mother and father as different (Table 3.1). Mothers refer to their greater feelings of responsibility, and again to the question of enhanced rather than diminished responsibility as children grow up. According to Soraya Khan's mother:

I am responsible for her, he's not here – he couldn't care less! . . . I think I have got more [responsible] as she has got older . . . because when she was young . . . I didn't worry about her, all I did was give her a bath, wash and make her do her homework and feed her . . . [now] you know, if she is slightly late, like six-thirty, and she hasn't come and I am thinking oh . . . and I am worried, I get really worried, I have to go out to the street . . . get my car and go looking for her because my husband is not here . . .

Another answers, when asked whether being a mother is very different from being a father:

Yes. Yes, it has to be . . . I try to identify with them much more, and I possibly find it easier to come down to their level now emotionally . . . I try to see things from their point of view. [Emma's father] had a very strict childhood and doesn't really seem to have had a childhood. (Emma Kerr's mother)

She went on to reflect on her husband's understanding of the concept of fatherhood:

Funnily enough, just ending this Sunday, I had a scare when I thought that I might actually be pregnant . . . and I thought my God nearly 47, this would be disastrous. It would be totally impractical . . . And shortly before I started to worry and wonder [my husband] said just out of the blue, do you know I think that I'm more ready to be a father now than I ever was and I thought oh no you're not, and you know I felt that he really *didn't have the concept.* (Emphasis added)

A question about which parent is mainly responsible for the young person elicited the view from over a third of mothers that they were; no mothers identify fathers as the most responsible people (Table 3.1). Fathers are more likely than mothers to say that both parents share the responsibility equally, or that they shoulder the greater share. Only one father assigned primary responsibility to mothers, though much of what they say points to the recognition of significant gender differences:

I think my wife has greater responsibility than me . . . just the day-to-day sort of physical mechanics of it really, of functioning, of getting to school and having your clothes right and food and just the sort of normal family existence, I suppose. (Sandra Purcell's father)

Mothers and fathers were asked whether the other parent took sufficient interest in their teenagers: over a quarter of mothers (13 out of 47) regarded their partners as deficient in this respect, but none of the 25 fathers felt the same about their female partners.

We asked parents how they felt about the prospect of their teenagers leaving home. Not surprisingly, in view of mothers' and fathers' different orientations to parenthood, and particularly gender-differentiated perspectives on the importance of 'putting children first', they give different answers to this question. More mothers than fathers feel negatively about this (Table 3.1). According to one:

[There's] the emptiness syndrome. I find the thought of being on my own with my husband quite chilling. I also find the thought of being on my own without anybody chilling. I think that's a big scare. (Emma Kerr's mother)

Andrea Dewar's mother, who has three sons and one daughter, comments:

You could ask my husband the same question and he'd say I'm like a sheepdog and I just love it when they all come home, you know when we're all here on Sundays . . . I quite miss it. I suppose I miss the female company as well. I quite miss her not coming on holiday these days . . . it's good that she's out and about, you know, I wouldn't like her to be in all the time hanging about – that would worry me as well.

By comparison with mothers, fathers are generally more ready to let go:

Well, everybody grows up and leaves home, don't they? It doesn't worry me. (Stella Wheeler's father)

I have told her several times she can leave any time she wants! (Andrea Dewar's father)

The most striking gender difference in orientation to parenthood related to worrying. Almost half of mothers say they worry a lot about their teenagers, compared with only two fathers (Table 3.1). As Mrs Dewar notes in reply to the question about which parent has more responsibility for their teenage daughter:

Worry, that's me! . . . we have different roles . . . her father would worry less about her, but if a situation arose he would probably do more than I would, I mean I'd just go frantic and run about and worry, but he will . . . do something, you know.

Or, as Soraya Khan's mother puts it:

. . . a father is different, isn't he? . . . well, many times he is not worried what is happening . . . he goes to work, comes home and that's it, he just comes home and wants to have his dinner . . . and go out again and come back again and go to bed . . . he loves the kids, he used to take them out a lot, but he doesn't have as many responsibilities as I have got because I have got Soraya on my hands . . . she is growing up, she is changing every day . . . her attitude, everything is changing, she can be in such a bad temper . . . at one minute and things are flying, and the next minute she is OK.

Asked if they worry at all, fathers tend not to elaborate on their answers, for example, Sandra Purcell's father responded:

Not over much. Just normal sort of caring, I think.

Another said:

No. I worry sometimes in a physical sense . . . her safety . . . if you are saying are you worried about what's going to happen, then no, not at all. She'll be all right. (Andrea Dewar's father)

One reason for the excess of female worrying can be deduced from answers to questions about the amount of influence parents can expect to have over teenagers' behaviour. For example, more mothers than fathers think they have some or a lot of influence over teenagers' everyday activities (Table 3.1).

In general, then, the picture that emerges is of mothers being far more closely involved in their teenagers' lives than fathers. The involvement is emotional, physical, material and moral: mothers not only feel themselves to be closer to their teenage children, they know more about what is going on, and expect themselves to be more involved. More mothers than fathers feel that the presence of a young person in the home has a negative or mixed impact on the parental relationship; similarly, more mothers than fathers describe a negative or mixed impact of the parental relationship on young people (Table 3.1). This two-way relationship is described by Mrs Dewar in the following terms:

I: Do you think having a 16-year-old affects your relationship – your own marriage – in any way?

M: Yes I do, actually. It's the time to yourself, there's none, because they're always around, and just that last hour at night or, you know . . . there's always somebody up with you, so the noise level's always up.

I: And do you think your relationship ever has any effect on her? I mean, how does she respond to the way you and your husband are?

M: Oh she does, she does, particularly the night she came in and discussed this drug business and she was upset. I think she thought that we were going to react differently, she wasn't sure if we were going to throw up our hands in horror and tell her she mustn't associate with such sorts of people and so on, and I think she was actually quite surprised at the way we took it . . . she tests the water all the time, you know, just to see how you'll take it . . . I suppose she's like all children, she never thinks that you've been young once and you've had all the same problems really, she just never thinks that.

I: How does she respond if there's any tension in your own marriage, does that bother her or not?

M: (laughs) She says –

I: Or maybe you haven't –

M: Oh no, I told you, we're a very explicit family, she says things like 'Oh for God's sake will you stop that!' and such things, that's generally what she says, it doesn't go to her heart, I mean she doesn't go tearing her hair out or anything – she says exactly what she wants to say, I kid you not.

Table 3.1 also shows one paradoxical effect of women's greater involvement with the parenting of teenagers. While women have greater responsibility over time for their children, they are also less likely than men to feel successful as parents. Even if they feel successful, they seem reluctant to claim the credit, and more concerned to identify ways in which their children are less than perfect. Mrs Dewar again:

I: Do you feel you've been successful?

M: Oh Lord, d'you know it would be a terrible question to ask because it would spark off complacency to say you'd been successful . . . something terrible would happen . . .

I: I mean do you feel you're doing OK as a parent?

M: I don't think she's been an awfully difficult child actually, I don't really think she has – she's not given us a tremendous runaround.

I: So you feel happy with the way she's turned out so far?

M: I wish she was a wee bit more . . . I'm a child of the sixties, you know, concerned about issues that weren't self-centred, you know: when we were young, we used to march and ban bombs and things, I know it's silly but –

I: Political things?

M: Yes, do you know this sort of idea that you could change the world – it would be really important! I said to her one day, who do you most admire in the world? And she said, I got such a shock, I was quite disappointed actually, she said someone who has started from nothing and has worked their way to the top! And I honestly thought she was going to say [Mother] Teresa or Gladys Aylward or something like that.

I: The Thatcher Generation! (laughs)

M: Absolutely.

Living with teenagers

In Chapter 2 we saw that most parents think teenagers have a bad press; adult society takes a generally negative view of them. One theme in this negative view is the tendency for teenagers to be generally moody, over-preoccupied with themselves, and badly behaved. Mothers and fathers do not differ from each other in their perceptions of adolescence as a time of turmoil. However, mothers are more likely than fathers to say that young people today are under pressure, and more mothers than fathers think it is harder to be a teenager nowadays (Chapter 2). As one mother puts it, conscious also of the gender difference in teenage risks:

It's harder now. Because of drugs and stuff. Especially with a girl being out at night – safety. So therefore you're saying you can't go out, or you must be taken and collected, which is harder for them because they don't like it. (Rachel Pemberton's mother)

According to these parents, the major challenge facing them as the parents of adolescents is to balance care and concern with some control over young people's behaviour. Although popular images of parenthood construct mothers as caring and fathers as controlling, exercising control seems in real life to be more a maternal than a paternal responsibility. This, of course, may well be because mothers simply have more to do with the everyday lives of teenagers than fathers. Such an interpretation is borne out in our data; for instance, in answers to a question about parental knowledge of teenagers' friends, mothers are more likely than fathers to say that they know most of their teenagers' friends – 22 out of 47 mothers (47 per cent) and 8 out of 27 fathers (30 per cent). Table 3.2 includes areas in which mothers are more likely than fathers to exercise control with respect to going out, coming home, doing homework and watching television.

The last part of Table 3.2 refers to an area of family life which attracts a good deal of discussion, confrontation and negotiation: that of household chores. Mothers are significantly more likely than fathers to say that they do most of the housework, though parents do not differ in their attribution to their teenagers of responsibility for household work. More mothers than fathers, however, are dissatisfied with the level of help young people give in the household. This is in the context of the general perception of teenagers as domestically unhelpful people. One mother replies:

Table 3.2   *Gender, parenthood and living with young people*

	Mothers % (n)	Fathers % (n)
Adolescence a time of turmoil	58 (32)	55 (16)
Young people today under pressure	96 (50)	86 (25)
Harder to be a teenager today	70 (37)	45 (13)
Parent restricts young person's going out:		
no	20 (11)	50 (15)
some	61 (33)	30 (9)
a lot	19 (10)	20 (6)
Parent restricts young person's coming in:		
no	11 (6)	26 (9)
some	66 (35)	56 (15)
a lot	23 (12)	18 (5)
Parent controls young person's homework:		
no	61 (30)	74 (20)
some	31 (15)	26 (7)
a lot	8 (4)	0 (0)
Parent controls young person's TV watching:		
no	61 (31)	86 (25)
some	33 (17)	14 (4)
a lot	6 (3)	0 (0)
Who does most of household chores:		
mother	76 (42)	45 (12)
mostly mother	7 (4)	22 (6)
both parents	2 (1)	11 (3)
mostly mother + young person/children	11 (6)	11 (3)
other	4 (2)	11 (3)
Attitude to young person's housework contribution:		
positive	20 (11)	10 (3)
OK	38 (21)	59 (17)
negative/mixed	42 (23)	31 (9)

Based on total *N* = 55 (mothers) and *N* = 31 (fathers); percentages are calculated on total numbers answering particular questions.

> I suppose for a teenager she's not doing too badly. I mean other kids don't do anything at all, especially Greek kids. (Niki Georgiou's mother)

As this mother's comment makes clear, cultural norms are also important shapers of expectation here. Young people may also be judged by comparison with their siblings:

> Well, I expect [help with housework] but I never get it . . . David is more helpful, like when I have had this bad back, he's the one that's made a cup of coffee for me or filled the dishwasher up or anything like that. [But] they like to be seen as the opposite of what they actually are. It amazes me. I think if we sat and had this conversation with David, he would probably deny half of what I've said . . . The older boy he does absolutely nothing. (*Do you*

Table 3.3   *Gender, parenthood and relationships with young people*

	Mothers % (n)	Fathers % (n)
Enjoy parenting young person	93 (51)	90 (26)
Dislike parenting young person	55 (30)	43 (12)
Parent young person takes after:		
mother	31 (15)	26 (6)
father	22 (11)	39 (9)
both	29 (14)	26 (6)
neither/other	18 (9)	9 (2)
Parent young person gets on best with:		
mother	51 (24)	39 (10)
father	4 (2)	23 (6)
both	28 (13)	31 (8)
neither/other	17 (8)	8 (2)
Parent young person is closest to:		
mother	65 (34)	50 (12)
father	8 (4)	21 (5)
both	23 (12)	25 (6)
neither/other	4 (2)	4 (1)
Change in closeness with mother recently: yes, closer	43 (15)	13 (2)
no, same	51 (18)	67 (10)
yes, less close	6 (2)	20 (3)
Change in closeness with father recently: yes, closer	9 (2)	18 (3)
no, same	74 (17)	47 (8)
yes, less close	17 (4)	35 (6)
Thinks young person thinks s/he has a good relationship with parent:	77 (33)	79 (19)
Young person discloses:		
to parent	49 (27)	21 (6)
yes, but not to parent	7 (4)	28 (8)
no	33 (18)	41 (12)
no need/other	11 (6)	10 (3)
Young person turns to parent with:		
health problem	67 (28)	41 (9)
school problem	74 (39)	56 (15)

Based on total N = 55 (mothers) and N = 31 (fathers); percentages are calculated on total numbers answering particular questions.

get cross about that sometimes?) Yes I do. I resent it. I don't actually voice it, but I resent it, because he thinks he's at work now, he's got to be waited on hand and foot, but I try to point out we are all working, and why should I have to be the only one? (David Monk's mother)

Table 3.3 moves from these more general aspects of living with teenagers to features of parents' and teenagers' personal relationships. Women's greater responsibility for the parenting of children and young people is associated with more reporting of both positive and negative experiences connected with parenthood. Most mothers and fathers say they have enjoyed being the parent of the survey teenager; but slightly more mothers than fathers report disliking this experience.

Answers to questions about which parent the young person most resembles, gets on best with, and is closest to, reveal a tendency for mothers and fathers to give preference to themselves rather than each other. More fathers than mothers think that their children take after, get on best with and are closest to them. Similarly, more mothers than fathers consider that it is mothers rather than fathers that the young people take after, get on best with and are closest to. Asked about recent changes in parent–adolescent relationships, significantly more mothers than fathers say that their children have grown closer to them recently, whereas fathers are more likely to say either that there has been no change or a decline in closeness with mothers. The pattern is the same for recent changes in closeness with fathers: fathers are more likely than mothers to report that their young people have grown closer to them recently. Mothers and fathers are equally likely to say that they think their children think they have a good relationship with them. Underlying these apparently gender-symmetrical patterns is, however, a basic difference: that between mothers and fathers in their perceptions of teenager disclosure. Forty-nine per cent of mothers (27 out of 55) compared with 21 per cent of fathers (6 out of 29) say their teenager has disclosed to them. This is manifested in a range of different issues, including those to do with health and school problems (Table 3.3). For instance, more mothers (28 out of 42, or 67 per cent) than fathers (9 out of 22, or 41 per cent) say that their young turn to them with a health problem. This gender gap actually underestimates the extent of differences between mothers and fathers as perceived by young people, 75 per cent of whom in their questionnaire answers say they talked to their mothers about a health problem in the last year; the comparable figure for fathers is 52 per cent (see Chapter 10).

Mothers place more emphasis on the importance of disclosure. David Monk's mother makes it clear when she describes the quality of her relationship with her teenage son that she regards disclosure as central to a good relationship:

> Oh, it's tremendous! I have got the knowledge that they will always come to me with a problem, although David withholds it a little bit longer than the other two. At least I have got that satisfaction – that is something that I am quite happy about, I know they will come to Mum. It doesn't matter how bad, they will come to me and tell me about it . . . if they are in trouble they will come to me.

Mrs Monk is one of the mothers who says her relationship with her son has improved as he's got older; he, too, is a good listener:

Table 3.4   *Which adult do you get on best with? (Young people's questionnaire answers)*

	Females		Males	
	%	(n)	%	(n)
Mother	51	(184)	53	(249)
Father	9	(32)	14	(64)
Friend	19	(70)	16	(77)
Siblings	12	(43)	11	(51)
Grandparent	2	(9)	2	(11)
Stepmother	<1	(1)	0	(0)
Stepfather	<1	(1)	0	(0)
Other	5	(17)	3	(14)
None	<1	(3)	<1	(3)
Base		(360)		(469)

I think we've got a lot closer. We have much better conversations now, I can talk to him. Actually, I can confide in him. I have done on many occasions, then I feel guilty for burdening him with something that is not his concern, but he is a good listener, unfortunately, he shouldn't be but he is, and if he wasn't I probably wouldn't do it, but he is a very good listener. (*Who does he take after?*) I don't know, everyone says he looks like my husband, but he doesn't really act like my husband . . . it's like chalk and cheese. He's so different that I can't really recognize any of his traits. Maybe snatches of me and snatches of my husband, but basically where he gets his common sense and everything from I have got no idea. I couldn't honestly say he was like me or my husband. (*Who is he closest to?*) Me. He gets on best with me.

By comparison, it is not unusual for fathers to recite episodes in which a key objective of parenting is achieved *without* communication. Clive Seymour's father, a single parent, is concerned about his son's lack of personal hygiene; he buys deodorant for him, but 'he's a little bit of the view that it's cissy, and that sort of thing, so it sits there, unused'. When the father notices that his son has developed spots, he buys Biactol for him, and this *is* used. However, neither son nor father report mentioning the problem to the other. The entire transaction is a silent one.

This picture of mothers and fathers playing different roles in their teen-agers' lives is reflected in teenagers' responses in the questionnaire. Table 3.4 shows their answers to a question about the adult they get on best with: for over half of both young men and young women, mothers come first. Nine per cent of young women and 14 per cent of young men get on best with their fathers, 20 per cent and 16 per cent with friends, and 12 per cent and 11 per cent with siblings. The broad pattern is for mothers to be both more negatively and more positively perceived than fathers. Young men are more likely than young women to describe the quality of their relationships with their mothers as excellent. A higher percentage of young women say in the questionnaire survey that their relationships with both

Table 3.5   *Young people's perceptions of relationships with parents (interview data)*

	Mothers % (n)		Fathers % (n)	
Change in relationship with parents as got older:				
better	24	(13)	17	(9)
same: good	55	(30)	35	(18)
same: bad	15	(8)	23	(12)
worse	6	(3)	25	(13)
Perception of parent's perception of the relationship:				
parent thinks it's good	76	(41)	53	(27)
parent thinks it's mixed	17	(9)	25	(13)
parent thinks it's bad	2	(1)	6	(3)
doesn't know what parent thinks	5	(3)	16	(8)

their mothers and fathers are 'fair' or 'poor'. (These data are presented in Table 10.1 in Chapter 10.)

Table 3.5 shows information from the interviews about the ways in which these relationships were considered by the young people to have changed as they got older. There is a significantly different pattern for mothers and fathers, with relationships with fathers being more likely to be perceived as worsening. In line with this, the second part of Table 3.5 indicates that young people are likely to think that their mothers more than their fathers themselves think that the relationship is a good one: 76 per cent (41 out of 54) say that they think their mothers think the relationship is good, whereas this falls to 53 per cent (27 out of 51) for fathers. Questionnaire data (not shown in the table) suggest that, for both sexes, the feeling that parents have enough time to talk to their young people is strongly related to how the relationship with mothers and fathers is viewed in general.

The disadvantage of having a parent who does not listen, and who also does not communicate very well, is referred to by Emma Kerr's mother in her answer to the question about the extent to which she views herself as a successful mother:

I: Do you feel you've been successful so far?
M: Yes, on the whole yes. Yes, I'm very proud of both of them.
I: Do you think you and your husband share that pride in your children?
M: I think he does have some pride in them, but he doesn't really let them know.
I: He doesn't?
M: Not enough, no.
I: He doesn't feel it's good to make people feel good?
M: No, not really.
I: Do you ever try to discipline Emma these days, you know, tell her off? Would you tell her off if she was doing something you didn't like?

M: Yes, I would tell her off certainly.

I: Has that got less as she's got older?

M: I wouldn't say so, because I think that as she gets older she finds more things to do that you don't want her to do. Disciplining is a hard one, I just might say you can't go out this evening, if I was really cross about something or if I felt that she had been doing something really stupid.

I: And is your husband the same, would he tick her off or would he expect you to do it?

M: No, he would tick her off, he would tick her off for being late for school consistently. I mean, she missed the bus one day last week and she came back and asked him for a lift, and she got the lift but she was in tears by the time she got to school, but I felt, quite often I would agree with the principle, but not agree with the way he goes about it.

Being a step-parent

Within this framework of normative definitions of motherhood and fatherhood from both parents' and young people's standpoints, a particular constellation of views is attached to an increasingly common phenomenon in modern culture: that of step-parenthood (7 per cent of young people who answered the questionnaire lived with a step-parent, while five of the 64 interview households contained a step-parent). The very particular responsibilities of step-parenthood are shouldered in a culture which has its own set of myths about step-parenthood, especially stepmotherhood (Moggach, 1993). It is clear from Table 3.4 and Chapter 10 that neither stepmothers nor stepfathers do particularly well in the relationship stakes. No young men and only two young women in the questionnaire survey pick their step-parents as the adults with whom they get on best, though these findings are based on very small numbers. Only a minority report 'excellent' relationships with stepmothers and stepfathers. Young women are more likely than young men to report 'poor' or 'very poor' relationships. In some respects, the social position of step-parent would seem to override the tendency for parenting to be a gendered phenomenon: whereas, as we saw earlier, significantly more young people talk to their mothers than their fathers about health (75 per cent versus 52 per cent of the questionnaire respondents), the percentage who report talking to their stepmothers and stepfathers about health is exactly the same – 28 per cent.

In the interviews, both parents and young people mention the difficulties associated with step-parenting. Ruth Graham's parents separated when she was 3, and her mother met her new husband when Ruth was 10. The interviewer asked Ruth's mother how Ruth and her stepfather get on now, some six years later:

M: They tolerate each other. I can't say she's over the moon about him . . . They're getting on better now.

I: Was that difficult at the beginning?

M: Yes . . . They resented the fact that they didn't have me all to themselves any more . . . they were spoilt for a number of years, just being the three of us.

I: Did Ruth resent being told what to do by him, I mean would –
M: He wouldn't tell her what to do.
I: He wouldn't?
M: No way.

Ruth is asked how she gets on with her three 'parents':

R: I get on best with my mum . . . And then my dad, and then my stepdad.
I: Your dad and then stepdad? Does your stepfather realize that, and doesn't expect the same affection?
R: Oh, I don't give him any affection.

There may sometimes, however, be a commitment to believing that step-parenthood is not all that much of a problem, as in Margaret Nelson's father's case:

F: I have never been very aware of the stepfather role, because . . . though it sounds arrogant, I just assumed the father role.
I: How long ago was this?
F: Seven, eight years ago, when Margaret was a youngster, a real youngster, and I was sharing her mother's bed, she accepted me, it seemed, as her surrogate dad, in all sorts of symbolic ways . . . and I have never been hung up about my relationship with Margaret. With her elder sister I was less easy about it because she was several years older, so I was more cautious about her . . .
I: So the stepfather bit is not a problem?
F: I have never been too fussed about the stepfather bit . . .

Mr Nelson attributes this to his capacity to remain emotionally detached:

I don't know what happens in other families . . . but I am able, I think, to be more [dissociated] from some of the issues than [my wife] is. She tends to jump in very emotionally, whereas I can achieve a sense of detachment, or whatever . . . that's the male–female, logical–emotional dichotomy . . .

Emotional detachment is harder for stepmothers. Mrs Brown came into a family of a father and two sons when the boys were aged 14 and 12. Mrs Brown was asked what the worst thing was about her situation as a step-mother at the beginning:

M: The worst thing was, the way they used to talk to me as if I shouldn't be here, sort of thing, but that was the way I felt, I don't know, I think they were trying to turn us against one another, because they wasn't used to having a mother around. I mean nine years without a mum, just having dad to twist round their fingers, they can't do that with both . . .
I: How do you see yourself as a stepmother, do you think of yourself as a stepmother?
M: No.
I: You don't have a way of describing a step relationship?
M: It's a bit awkward, unless you are in that situation you can't describe it. I look on them as my own sons anyway as I always wanted more children . . . I love them, I don't love them more than my own son to be honest, I mean, my son is loved a bit more . . .

I: Would you call yourself a stepmother, do you ask them to call you your name?

M: They said to me before I came and lived here . . . They said to me 'When you and dad get married what do we call you, mum, or Mo?' I said 'It's up to you.' I can't force them into calling me mum, so they call me Mo. But in the pipeline, I have been told by my sister, they can't wait till we get married so that they can call me mum. Whether they feel insecure I don't know, because their dad and I aren't married yet . . . you can't really talk to the boys about things like that . . .

Part of the difficulty is inheriting children's difficulties in relation to the absent biological parent. Mrs Brown goes on to describe a conversation she had had with Andrew in which he admitted to a fear that she, like his own mother, would leave:

We were talking, and he said 'I don't trust you, Mo' and I said 'What do you mean?' He said 'Well, dad's told me what me mum did, walking out and leaving us as babies. You might do it.' I said 'No, Andrew.'

An additional difficulty identified by Mrs Brown is in balancing the need to behave as she would wish to in relation to the boys' father with the need to be seen by them as not simply usurping the role of their own biological mother:

I think it's sometimes difficult because I don't want him to feel that I am nagging, that I am always getting at them, but I don't think their dad should have to come in after a hard day's work and be smacked in the face with 'Oh, they've done this and they've done that.' No, if I can sort it out, I sort it out.

Parents and their own parents

Many parents describe understanding through their own experience of being parents what it was like to be parented themselves. In this sense, one's history within a family is an important influence on the kind of family one creates. This is a process that operates both on conscious and on less conscious levels. It also tends to be a highly gendered phenomenon. Some quantitative indicators are shown in Table 3.6. Fathers are more likely than mothers to recall problems in their own adolescence. Mothers more than fathers report being close to both their mothers and fathers as children and as adolescents. Mothers are also more likely than fathers to say they got on well with their mothers as children, though not as adolescents. There are virtually no gender differences in reports of getting on with fathers in childhood and in adolescence, nor in the extent to which mothers and fathers say that their own present relationships with their teenagers reflect these earlier relationships.

Emma Kerr's mother compares her own adolescence with her daughter's:

M: I think she's much more able to let her emotions go freely, and she will rage and storm and really blast if she wants to, and she's very free with

Table 3.6 *Parents' relationships with their own parents*

	Mothers % (n)	Fathers % (n)
Problems in own adolescence	44 (24)	50 (14)
Close to mother as child	70 (35)	61 (17)
Close to mother as adolescent	51 (26)	48 (13)
Close to father as child	50 (25)	36 (9)
Close to father as adolescent	38 (18)	29 (7)
Got on with mother as child	96 (49)	85 (23)
Got on with mother as adolescent	73 (38)	77 (20)
Got on with father as child	88 (43)	87 (20)
Got on with father as adolescent	78 (35)	77 (17)
Own relationship with parent similar to present relationship with adolescent	29 (15)	31 (9)

Based on total N = 55 (mothers) and N = 31 (fathers); percentages are calculated on total numbers answering particular questions.

her language, and she seems to be able to express herself and get it out of her system.

I: Does that help things at home or make things worse?

M: Sometimes it can make things more difficult, but I don't think that it's natural to bottle things up all the time, which is I think something I've done, and you get into a habit of doing it and then I, a bit like talking to you, I might bore some friend and rattle on for hours and get some of it out of my system.

I: How does your relationship with Emma compare with your relationship with your own mother?

M: I would think it's closer. I would hope so. Yes, I would hope it is. I feel that it's a very close relationship and one where most things we can talk about. I think there could be a few things that she's holding back on, but on the whole we talk a lot ...

Soraya Khan's mother reflects that the present generation's openness with their parents might be a bit of a mixed blessing:

M: I didn't have much time when I was a teenager with my mother ... because ... there is a lot of difference between our generation and this generation, because when I was a teenager we weren't open with our parents, we just sat down and kept our mouths shut, and if we had any problems we just kept them to ourselves all the time. And now here it is quite open, like when I was 13 and I was going to have my periods, I didn't know anything about it, because my mother never told me, and she didn't talk to me, and here with the schools, I was able to tell Soraya things like that because we are more open ...

I: So if you compare Soraya's teenage years with your own are there any similarities?

M: No ... nothing at all ...

I: Do you think of your adolescence as being a good time?

M: I think we were better off than this generation ... because we didn't have many problems ... they just created problems for themselves, we didn't have these problems ... honestly, I mean we were happy with what we got, we never complained ... this generation they are always complaining, even if they get everything they still complain, she is forever complaining ... so I suppose I always see it as we were better off ... because you have got more problems than we had, we didn't have any problems ...

Being a parent oneself gave Mrs Brown a new understanding of her own parents:

I: How good or bad did you say your own mother was with you at the age Andrew is now?

M: I suppose my mum was marvellous really, considering.

I: Did you think so at the time?

M: No, I thought she was an old cow. I told her so a few times, but I suppose, thinking back, seeing life as it is now as an adult and a mother and a grandmother, I think well, my mother couldn't have been all that bad, I suppose. I was worse than some of these kids were today. The boys, they try all sorts of things on, and their dad tells them 'We did this like bunking off school.' They think it's clever smoking behind the toilets and all that, but he said 'We did all that' ...

Several fathers talk at length about their relationships with their own fathers. Andrea Dewar's father talks of his own father's illness and subsequent disablement during his teenager years:

F: That's something I have spoken at some length with [my wife] about over the years. I had no relationship with my father at all. None at all.

I: Why was that?

F: I don't know, I don't know ... I'm quite different to him ... physically I don't look anything like him ... and in character I suppose one thing I inherited from him is a certain bad temper ... I have quite a short temper ... sometimes ... and he, although he doesn't have it now, my goodness if you are suffering from [illness] you are entitled to be short tempered ... but I think he had that before he had [illness] (laughs) and his father did as well ... I honestly don't know. I suppose he wasn't able to do the things that dads are supposed to do ...

I: This was after he became ill?

F: Yes, well he ... he was ill before but ... shortly after that he contracted [illness] ... so he hasn't had much of a life ... and I think he abdicated responsibility quite early on ...

I: So you didn't feel close to him?

F: No.

I: Did you feel close to your mother?

F: I suppose I must have done, although I didn't think so at the time ... we had endless rows ...

I: Was that when you were younger or when you were a teenager?

F: I think I was a teenager ... it was ... I was forced ... I suppose, to act in a responsible way at times when I didn't want to be responsible ...

I: Because of your father?

F: Yes, I felt that . . . there was some moral persuasion brought to bear to do these things – which I did – I didn't rebel against it . . . maybe that was the problem – I thought I should be rebelling, but I felt sorry for them . . . it wasn't . . . I seem to have survived. I wasn't beaten mercilessly. I wasn't starved . . . I seem to have come through it reasonably well . . . One of the things that I suppose has always rankled is that my parents have never overtly been proud of me . . . I remember when my father stopped work, he was a . . . junior manager of some sort . . . my mother had certificates [so] that she could in different circumstances have gone to university . . . my father was going to train to be a minister, so that there were certain academic aspirations that didn't come to anything . . . and then I came through and I did well at school, went to university and got a good degree, I was head boy, I was a rugby player . . . and yet one feels there is no overt . . . 'Hasn't my son done really well!' It's a daft thing, but it's –

I: Have you ever talked to them about it?

F: No, I haven't, it's too late now.

Mr Dewar goes on to compare his own adolescence with his daughter's:

Andrea is much better off . . . I think we do have a reasonable relationship . . . I have deliberately . . . listened to her and tried to understand . . . and given her that bedrock that I felt I didn't have . . . of a dad you could go and talk to and maybe confide in . . .

However, parental views of what constitutes a 'confiding' relationship may not match those of young people (Chapter 10).

Family values?

Fathers tended to demonstrate in the interviews a concern with presenting a public face of the family as a happy, successfully functioning unit. This is connected to two other aspects of fatherhood; the role of fathers as 'protectors' of mothers and children, and the inhibitions of the masculine role as regards disclosing problems. The rhetoric of protection comes over very clearly in the interview with Colin Clark's father, who is, co-incidentally, a police officer:

If you want society to work, you've got to live within its rules. If you expect society to defend and protect you, you must therefore be there to protect the society. You can't have one without the other. You can't expect things unless you put things into them . . . I would like Colin to turn out a good citizen . . .

Accompanying this is an account of family routines in which the descriptive narrative (what 'really' happens) is mixed with an idealist-romantic representation (what 'ought' to happen):

I: What kind of relationship do you have with Colin? You said very early on that you were friends.

F: We're mates. That's not that mates don't put their point of view and that's not that mates don't express themselves . . .

I: Probably, very difficult to answer, yes . . .

F: (Mumbles)

I: He isn't the kind of person?

F: No . . . It would be nice to get into him in the sense of really see what ticks and that would be nice, but it will never happen.

In their interviews, fathers were less likely overall than mothers to mention problems reported either by mothers, by young people or by both, for example, young people's health problems (see Chapter 5). Related to this, their replies to many questions tended to be truncated compared to those of mothers, and, in some couples, their interviews were shorter.

These gendered differences in parental concerns are linked to the wider differentiation of masculinity and femininity as cultural concepts and experiences. Men are not expected to be sensitive to personal problems and difficulties, or to discuss these, in the same way as women. Within families, these specialisms are expected of mothers rather than of fathers. Parents in our interviews were asked a number of questions designed to tap their characterization of their own families and households, and to probe moral concepts of family structures and relations. These questions asked parents to assess their own households as the same or different from others, and to judge their relative closeness, open or closed nature, and the extent to which the family as a unit tended to put on a 'united front' against the external world. Fathers are more likely than mothers to describe their own households as the same as others, and as presenting a united front to the rest of the world. On the other hand, mothers, responding perhaps to their own greater emotional involvement in internal family relations, are significantly more likely than fathers to describe their families both as emotionally close, and as open to the rest of society.

This tendency for fathers to present their families as happy, functioning social systems, closed off from the outside world, is evident in the responses of Stella Wheeler's father to the questions about household descriptions:

I: What are the first words that come into your head if I ask you to describe your family?

F: The first words that come into my head to describe this household? To be quite honest I'm very proud of them.

I: Anything else, the second thought?

F: I'm proud of them and I love them, what else can I say?

I: Do you feel you're the same or different from other families that you know in general?

F: I think we're a closer-knit family than most families.

I: Closer than a lot of others?

F: I think so and I think I'm getting, you know, I think that the children all say, even Stella said it, we've got a nice home, we've got a spacious place. You know I mean I think that we could say, we are a very happy family.

I: Would you describe yourselves as united or divided?

F: United, I would say.

Conclusion

Considerable differences between fathers and mothers in beliefs and practices relating to parenthood coexist with underlying similarities. A major theme common to paternal and maternal narratives is the struggle of young people towards some notion of independent adulthood, on the one hand, and parents' concerns to control and shape this process, on the other. An underlying fear is that parents will not get the balance between care and control right, and will so alienate their sons and daughters that they will remove themselves altogether from parental control. In their responses to this fear, and in many other aspects of the general challenge of parenting in the teenage years, mothers and fathers differ. As we will describe in Chapter 10, while mothers emphasize the importance of facilitating communication with their young people, and through the 'duty' of worrying are constantly reflecting on and redefining the nature of the relationship, for fathers such manifest anxiety tends to be seen as a sign of weakness – the very 'antithesis' of masculinity. Fathers in general appear less flexible and thoughtful in their dealings with young people.

Both the differences between mothers and fathers, and their common core of concerns, are manifested in parents' answers to a question about 'the hardest thing' about being the parent of a teenager today. David Monk's mother:

> *I*: Thinking over everything you've said, what would you say is the hardest thing about being the parent of a teenager?
> *M*: Oh, doing the right things for them I think, because you can often make mistakes but you can't correct . . . I think I make a lot of emotional decisions that are wrong, I make them emotionally, rather than . . . I think I should talk to the children a lot more about decisions that they make, perhaps I sort of think they're older and they can . . . because David's not really grown up, he thinks he is, they all think they're grown up, but they're not, they're not mature . . . I think I would like to go back and start again and give them a lot more of me and help them a lot that way . . . but I don't think they've come up too badly out of it all . . . they seem to be quite adult, especially David, he doesn't seem to have lost anything for it, I think, I don't know, there's lots of things I'd like to change . . .
> *I*: You don't regret . . . ?
> *M*: I regret not talking to them more . . . but you try, you think you're doing the right thing.

Similarly, another mother with one daughter mentions 'worry'.

> The worrying of when she's late or something, you know, worrying about the most important, you know I'm always worrying. If something comes into my head when she's out and I think, Oh my God, what's she up to? Has somebody raped her in the street or something, you know, it always worries me, it worries me, yes.

4 Definitions of health

This chapter and the next two are devoted to issues related to young people's health. All three draw on data from the questionnaires and the household interviews. In this chapter we consider the importance parents and young people place upon health, the meanings they attach to it, their definitions of young people's state of health and, lastly and most significantly, the extent to which the health of young people aged 16 is the responsibility of parents rather than of young people themselves.

Experts' conceptualizations of health

Concepts and practices regarding health in developed societies are dominated by the professional ideologies and organization of medicine (Freidson, 1970). These emphasize illness rather than health, and the treatment of disease rather than the promotion of positive health. The underlying model of both illness and health is a mechanical and individualistic one; that is, people's embodiment as separate biological organisms is regarded as more important than their enselvement as social beings. Features of individuals, rather than aspects of the social and material environment, tend to be stressed as relevant to their health and illness states.

The medical frame of reference has also tended to dominate the arena of health education. Much of the activity in this field, which has grown enormously over the last 20 years, has taken an individualistic perspective. Traditionally, health educators attempt to teach individuals to make healthier choices about the way they lead their lives. The emphasis is on the ability of individuals to control their own health, rather than on the environment as shaping and constraining this (Research Unit in Health and Behavioural Change (RUHBC), 1989). The key concept in health education is the individual's attitude to health, which is seen as central in bringing about behavioural change. As Graham (1979: 165) notes, this paradigm implies that 'more responsibility, as reflected in more responsive lifestyles, will be sufficient to effect major changes in health'.

Competing with the assumptions underlying the traditional health education model is considerable epidemiological evidence about the social determinants of health and illness. In the UK, this evidence has been phrased mainly in terms of social class inequalities arising from the unequal distribution of high-quality housing, jobs, money and other material and cultural resources (Department of Health and Social Security (DHSS), 1980; Marmot *et al.*, 1984, 1987). Social class continues to be among the most significant predictors of morbidity and mortality in the UK, with evidence of widening inequalities in recent years (DHSS, 1980; Marmot and McDowell, 1986; Whitehead, 1987; Smith *et al.*, 1990). On the publication of *The Health Divide* (Whitehead, 1987) the Chief Medical Officer, Sir Donald Acheson, is quoted as saying:

> While to specialists in public health the most attractive points of initial attack are health promotion initiatives to reduce risk factors such as smoking, poor diet and physical activity, there is a limit to the extent to which such improvements are likely to occur in the absence of a wider strategy to change the circumstances in which these risks arise by reducing deprivation and improving physical environment (Acheson, 1991).

The 'lifestyle' approach to health has been criticized by sociologists of health and illness for its philosophical assumptions of individualism, which obscure the social and material conditions in which individuals live. However, it does reflect the way in which market forces increasingly translate health into an item for consumption. The notion of individual 'choice' over health-related behaviour leads, moreover, to blaming the victims (Davis, 1979; Graham, 1979; Pill and Stott, 1985, 1986; Naidoo, 1986). This critique of the 'lifestyle' approach has extended to gender as another source of health inequality: in particular, the ways in which women carry the onus of responsibility for health within the household, often at the expense of their own mental and physical health (Graham, 1984).

However, along with the definition of health as a personal responsibility within the control of the individual, a new focus has developed on the self-production of well-being. Well-being itself is conceptualized as having numerous components which 'empower' the individual. The World Health Organization (WHO, 1946) definition cites mental and social well-being as well as physical functioning. Others have added to this the dimension of 'fitness' (Downie *et al.*, 1992). A more 'social' definition of health has highlighted the need to consider the ways in which people themselves conceptualize health and illness, and the kinds of belief they hold about the importance or otherwise of health, and about the factors responsible for staying well and becoming ill. What people believe about health has been shown to influence not only their health-related behaviours, but the extent to which they see health professionals and medical practices as relevant to disease prevention and health promotion (Cornwell, 1984; Oakley, 1992).

Health beliefs also appear to reflect material inequalities. Those who have fewer material resources are more likely to see health as outside their control than are those with greater resources (Blaxter and Patterson, 1982; Pill and Stott, 1986). Research in France found that positive definitions of health, expressive of personal well-being, were much more likely to be held by more educated non-manual workers and the financially more secure (d'Houtaud and Field, 1984). Health for manual workers was more a means to an end than an end in itself. Research in a working-class area of London has shown the importance of 'coping' to lay definitions of health; being healthy is about being able to carry on with one's ordinary everyday activities (Cornwell, 1984). Lay understandings of health and illness represent a complex mix of biological, psycho-social, cultural and environmental factors (Blaxter, 1990). Blaxter (1990: 17–31) describes ten different concepts which emerged in a representative survey of adults: these included not being ill, being fit, having energy, having a healthy lifestyle, being happy, and coping with relationships. In this study, age and gender shaped these definitions, with young men especially defining physical fitness as crucial to health, and young women identifying energy and the ability to cope mentally and physically. Women of all ages found the questions on health more interesting and gave fuller answers than did men. There is also an important moral component in health, which affects the way people talk about health (including to researchers). Being healthy is better than being unhealthy; that is, the admission of ill health is both a technical and a moral statement about oneself as an individual.

These expanded understandings of health and illness have forged a new language of health 'promotion' as distinct from that of health 'education', and have led to a new emphasis on the need for a healthy public policy (Smith and Jacobsen, 1988; RUHBC, 1989). However, there is no necessary correspondence between research findings and policy or practice. Many health education policies and programmes have continued to place the main responsibility upon the individual to lead a healthier life. This includes health programmes directed at young people.

Young people are one of the healthiest social groups, as judged by indicators such as mortality and hospitalization rates. People in the 15–24 age group have lower mortality rates than any other adult age group in most developed countries (WHO, 1989). Young people do, however, have distinctive health problems; accidents account for some 60 per cent of deaths; deaths from suicide and external violence are also increasing as causes of death, especially for young men. For young women, pregnancy poses a particular hazard; aggregated data show that the risk of death during pregnancy or delivery in women aged 15–19 is between 20 per cent and 200 per cent higher than in older women (Hein, 1988; WHO, 1989). The main rationale for the plethora of health education interventions targeted at young people does not derive from these statistics but, rather, from the clustering of health-risk behaviour observed to occur with increasing frequency in the teenage years. Smoking, alcohol consumption, drug-taking, and unprotected sexual activity are all singled out by adult

health educators as of particular concern. Some health education interventions aim to put across a message about the risks of these activities,
while others are aimed at the inculcation of life skills and the enhancement of self-esteem, assertiveness and problem-solving (Tones, 1983; Collins,
1984; Nutbeam *et al.*, 1991). The growth of self-esteem is supposed to
equip the young person to resist not only peer-group pressures to participate in 'risky' health-damaging behaviours, but also other risks such as
those associated with lack of employment and spending leisure time in
'dangerous' places.

There is a striking lack of information about how young people
themselves view health, health care, or the benefits and hazards of different
practices relevant to health. Few studies, for example, have explored what
young people think about the health care on offer to them, and there are
few data on young people's health beliefs in general (see Hein, 1988,
for a discussion). One group of studies shows how children move from
simple, internalized understandings to more abstract physical, psychological
and functional explanations of health and illness (Natapoff,1978; Millstein,
1981). A large group of studies seeks to explain why young people engage
in apparently unhealthy behaviours such as smoking. One influential model
in the USA has been provided by Becker's (1973) 'health belief model'
which relates individual 'compliance' with preventive health strategies to
a number of predisposing attitudes and to rational 'cost benefit analysis'.
Yet other work suggests that young people have absorbed health education messages, but behave differently. Thus, work on anti-smoking campaigns suggests that young people's beliefs are less important explanations
of behaviour than social factors such as stress, sociability, and concern
about major environmental dangers such as pollution and nuclear war
(Knight and Hay, 1989; Sharpe and Oakley, 1991; Solantaus, 1991; Oakley
et al., 1992). A study carried out in the USA found that teenagers defined
health chiefly in terms of activity and energy and the capacity 'to do what
I want' (Levenson *et al.*, 1984). Health was viewed as being able to take
one's body for granted. This study compared young people's views about
health with the views ascribed to them by doctors, teachers and school
nurses, and found that young people considered health more important,
felt more responsibility for their health and avoided risky behaviours
more than adults perceived them as doing.

It is also notable that young people and their health are rarely considered within the family context. An exception concerns an American study
of children's use of home medication, which suggests that neither the
beliefs of mothers (fathers were not included) nor those of children are
good predictors of children's behaviour (Iannotti and Bush, 1988).

In this chapter we take a processual approach in terms of understanding health beliefs – the ways parents and their young people construct the
notion of health, the importance they place upon health, the degree and
nature of the responsibility entailed, and the different meanings attributed
to 'being healthy'. At the same time, we also take account of the structural

Table 4.1 *Perceptions of importance of health by household members*

	Health is			
	very important % (n)	quite important % (n)	unimportant % (n)	Total Base
Young women	32 (8)	56 (14)	12 (3)	25
Young men	41 (12)	48 (14)	10 (3)	29
Mothers	70 (37)	28 (15)	2 (1)	53
Fathers	29 (8)	57 (16)	14 (4)	28

determinants of health in terms of gender, social class and culture. Current sociological approaches as they apply to youth and the study of young people's health, and which we have adopted in this study, aim to integrate social structural explanations with those emphasizing self-determination (Jones and Wallace, 1992). A linking concept between the individual actor and social and material contexts is provided by the concept of citizenship, a crucial element of which is health (Marshall, 1950). Young people accrue citizenship rights and responsibilities, while their access to these rights continues to be determined by structures of inequality such as social class, gender and race (Jones and Wallace, 1992).

The importance of health

How important is health to mothers, fathers and young people? Are there systematic differences between parents and young people in the priority accorded to health? Table 4.1 shows the distribution of responses in our household interview study. Mothers are most likely to say that health is 'very important' to them, followed by young people, especially young men. Fathers are least likely to say it is very important.

Social class also makes a difference here, with middle-class parents and young people more likely to say health is very important than are those of working-class background. Ethnic background appears to make less difference. Furthermore, less than half the pairs of mothers and young people and fathers and young people interviewed within the same households have the same perceptions of the importance of health.

The questionnaire findings concerning the importance of health *vis-à-vis* other issues do not, however, reflect these gender differences, and suggest that health has a lower priority than happiness, love and family relationships. Young people were asked to rank (first three choices only) 'the most important things in life to you'. Health was included along with future job security, happiness, success, peace of mind, money, friends, love and happy family relationships. Most young women and young men put happiness in their first three choices. For young men, love comes next closely followed by health, while young women give health a slightly lower priority, below love and happy family relationships.

Table 4.2 *Definitions of being healthy provided by household members**

| | Parents | | | | | | Young people | | | | | |
| | Mothers | | Fathers | | Both | | Females | | Males | | Both | |
Health definition	%	(n)	%	(n)	%	(n)	%	(n)	%	(n)	%	(n)
No illness	35	(19)	33	(10)	35	(29)	24	(6)	10	(3)	17	(9)
Fitness	11	(6)	33	(10)	19	(16)	24	(6)	59	(17)	43	(23)
Healthy lifestyle,												
e.g. diet	19	(10)	10	(3)	15	(13)	32	(8)	10	(3)	20	(11)
Emotional well-being	6	(3)	7	(2)	6	(5)	8	(2)	14	(4)	11	(6)
Having energy	9	(5)	–		6	(5)	4	(1)	–		2	(1)
Ability to cope	6	(3)	–		4	(3)	–		–		–	
Body functioning	6	(3)	7	(2)	6	(5)	–		–		–	
Appearance	4	(2)	–		2	(2)	–		3	(1)	2	(1)
Ability to work	4	(2)	10	(3)	6	(5)	–		–		–	
Don't know	2	(1)	–		1	(1)	8	(2)	3	(1)	6	(3)
Base	54		30		84		25		29		54	

*The table shows only the first answers given to the question, 'What does being healthy mean to you?'

What does being healthy mean?

Table 4.2 shows the answers given in the household study to the question 'What does being healthy mean to you?'

Agreement within households concerning definitions of being healthy is the exception rather than the rule. Gender and age across households are significant differentiating factors, however. Compared with young people, parents are more likely to emphasize negative statements of health, notably not being ill, while more young people (particularly young women) dwell on healthy lifestyles and fitness (particularly young men). Mothers are more concerned than fathers about lifestyle, including diet; like young men, fathers emphasize fitness.[1] Six young people give emotional or psychological well-being as their chief indicator of health, twice the proportion of parents. These definitions of health are very similar to those found by Blaxter (1990), despite the somewhat different age range of our study group.

Given that absence of illness is the most common definition of health, we might predict that illness would emerge as a significant threat to health. But in an open-ended interview question, aspects of lifestyle – smoking, drinking, lack of exercise and poor diet – together with environmental problems – pollution, traffic – figure more prominently than illness as threats to health. Table 4.3 gives the figures. However, young people are more likely than parents to mention diseases such as cancer, heart disease and AIDS.

In a fixed-choice question in the questionnaire survey, the effects of particular diseases (AIDS, cancer and heart attack were listed separately)

Table 4.3 *Types of threats to health reported* by household members*

Type of threat	Fathers %	(n)	Mothers %	(n)	Young people %	(n)
Lifestyle	42	(13)	34	(16)	19	(36)
Environment	32	(10)	28	(13)	25	(13)
AIDS, cancer and other illnesses	13	(4)	17	(8)	33	(17)
Stress	10	(3)	21	(10)	6	(3)
Health services	3	(1)	–		–	
Base	31		47		52	

*Only the first-mentioned threat to health has been coded.

Table 4.4 *Items reported by young people as among the three most worrying things about the future**

	Females %	Males %
Death of self or close relative	51	61
Unemployment	51	40
Destruction of the environment	41	38
Nuclear war	33	38
AIDS	29	33
Violence	20	23
Cancer	14	26
Heart attack	9	3
Base	362	481

$p < 0.0001$
*Percentages include items mentioned as first, second or third choice and so do not sum to 100.

are rated as personally less threatening than death (of self or close relative), unemployment, destruction of the environment or nuclear war by both young men and women. Table 4.4 shows the figures for young men and women separately.

Health risks may be seen as within the individual's control or independent of it. We asked in the interviews whether health is a matter of individual control, luck, or a mixture of both (Table 4.5); the replies suggest that around half of parents and young people think that the state of one's health is subject to both control and luck, in keeping with the findings of other researchers (see, for example, Furnham and Gunter, 1989). Young men and fathers are more likely than young women and mothers to mention control. Young women are more likely than young men to mention luck.

Fathers, like young people, think that serious illness in particular is beyond an individual's control, especially because of genetic factors. Mothers give various examples concerning the role of luck. Some of these responses are from women who follow the Islamic religion. Aspects of

Table 4.5 *Perceptions of individual control over health versus luck by household members*

	Parents			Young People		
	Mother	Father	Both	Females	Males	Both
	% (n)	% (n)	% (n)	% (n)	% (n)	% (n)
Luck	15 (8)	14 (4)	15 (12)	20 (5)	3 (1)	11 (6)
Control	28 (15)	33 (9)	29 (24)	32 (8)	52 (15)	43 (23)
Mix of both	57 (31)	54 (15)	56 (46)	48 (12)	45 (13)	46 (25)
Base	54	28	82	25	29	54

health said to be within individuals' control include the following in decreasing order of importance: diet, smoking, 'looking after yourself' (women), personal attitude (women), controlling stress (women), exercise, weight and alcohol consumption. A few interviewees mention specific links between smoking and cancer and between cholesterol and heart disease.

In the questionnaire survey, 88 per cent of the young people disagree with the concept that staying healthy is a matter of luck, with only 5 per cent claiming that luck plays its part. A further 7 per cent are uncertain. However, only 58 per cent agree that if anything goes wrong with their health, it is their own fault. The remainder are equally split between those who are uncertain and those who believe that problems with their health are not their own fault. There are no differences between the sexes here.

Evaluations of young people's health

Parents paint a generally positive picture of their young people's health. Three-quarters of mothers and over four-fifths of fathers say that the health of their sons or daughters is good. Similarly, around three-quarters of parents consider that young people are happy with themselves and their bodies. Young men are marginally more likely than young women to say that their health is good. This sex difference emerges more strongly in parents' accounts; parents of young women are more likely to rate the health of the latter as 'less than good' (14 out of 40, or 35 per cent) compared with parents of young men (5 out of 46, or 11 per cent). These findings can be partly explained by the fact that young women do have a slightly higher incidence of long-standing and recurrent illnesses, and visit the doctor more frequently than young men (see Chapter 5). Young women also worry about their health more than young men, are more likely to claim they are unhappy and/or stressed, and are less satisfied both with themselves as people and with their physical appearance.

Young people's assessments of their health are less favourable than those of their parents. In the questionnaire survey only a third of female pupils and around two-fifths of male pupils rate their health as good. During the household interviews, rather more young people (around three-fifths) rate their health as good. The numbers of parents and young people reporting the latter's health as 'not so good' or 'bad' are small – three parents and three young people at interview. These discrepancies between the questionnaire and interview data in young people's evaluations of their health are interesting. The passage of time could account for some of the difference; so, too, could the need to present interviewers with a morally acceptable 'public' assessment of one's health status.

While assessments of young people's health do not vary by ethnic origin, there are significant class differences. In the questionnaire survey, those whose fathers are in higher-status occupations are more likely than those with fathers in lower-status occupations to rate their health as good (see also Chapter 5).[2] These findings are replicated in the interviews in parents' but not young people's assessments.

There is general consistency between the 28 pairs of parents who were interviewed in the same households concerning their perceptions of young people's health status. (We exclude here those households in which only one parent was interviewed.) Much less agreement exists between parents and young people. Of the 48 households where the young person and at least one parent were interviewed, agreement between parent(s) and young person occurs in 29 cases. Of these, young people and parents from 22 households claim that the young are healthy (15 young men and seven young women), while in the remainder both parties say that the young people are not so healthy (five young women and two young men).[3]

While the majority of parents' and young people's evaluations of young people's health status agree, young people's and parents' evaluations of young people's health do not consistently reflect young people's illness conditions, emotional state or the nature of their lifestyles. Below, we take a more detailed look at three groups: those in which there is consensus between a parent and a young person concerning the state of the young person's health (the 'healthy' and the 'unhealthy' groups of young people), and the group in which there is no consensus.

'Healthy' teenagers

Most young people in this group are still at school (18 out of 22). The young women are middle-class (including four with dual-career professional parents), while the 15 healthy young men include five from working-class backgrounds. Most live with two parents (20 out of 22).

Being described as 'healthy' is not the same as *being* healthy, however. Parents include as 'healthy' those young people who suffer from allergies and have recently had glandular fever, tonsilitis and other illnesses. Similarly, a good health evaluation is not compromised by accidents. One father mentions that his 'healthy' son is always breaking his nose: 'He's a normal boisterous boy.' Another 'healthy' young man has had many accidents playing rugby, including one recent incident when it was suspected that he had broken his neck, and had been fitted with a brace. Nor do parents necessarily attribute good health to the fact that young people are non-smokers, or do not drink alcohol or take drugs. Moreover, though some parents describe teenagers as 'moody', 'depressed', or 'stressed', these definitions do not seem to affect their overall judgement of young people's health status.

'Unhealthy' teenagers

Those teenagers who consider their health less than good, and whose parents agree, include five young women and two young men. Five have working-class parents and four (all young women) are in the labour market. The latter four have achieved considerable independence. All are sexually active with older, long-term boyfriends with whom they spend their leisure time; one left home but returned after a difficult period of unemployment. Three are smokers. This group reports a variety of conditions. In one case, the young woman suffered from fainting fits, a potassium deficiency and debilitating period pains. Another suffered with asthma and migraines, while a third attended a psychiatric clinic after a suicide attempt. The fourth talked at length about her high blood pressure, irregular heartbeat and sickle-cell anaemia, conditions which her parents play down in their interviews, emphasizing instead their daughter's poor lifestyle – 'smoking, sedentary behaviour, getting up late and eating at the wrong time'.

In some instances, the young person omits reasons for a poor health evaluation. A young woman who made a suicide attempt does not mention the incident in her interview, but claims that lack of exercise and the 'wrong' food make her unhealthy, a situation that she has no intention of changing: 'You should eat what you want and if it's the wrong food, tough, you've got to pay for it.' Another young woman mentions feeling stressed because a school-mate committed suicide, while her mother only refers to a recent serious dental problem.

Illness is a significant feature of several of these households. In one, the mother was recently treated for cancer, and withdrew significantly from household work. Her teenage sons consequently cater for themselves, taking little account of nutritional standards. Both mother and son identify diet as the main reason for poor health and lifestyle.

Discrepant evaluations

In this group, parents are more inclined to define the presence or absence of serious or significant physical illness as central to health (see Chapter 5 for the implications concerning going to the doctor). Thus, in the absence of illness, parents may 'overestimate' their children's state of health, while young people mention a poor lifestyle and stress as contributing to their 'less than good' state of health.

Eight young women and five young men give less positive definitions of their health than their parents. The young people mention poor lifestyle (lack of fitness, smoking, poor diet) and stress or accidents, rather than illness. In some cases, the parents do not know about the young people's behaviour, notably secret smoking and emotional distress.

Five young people define their health positively, in contrast to their parents' negative definitions. One young woman mentions allergies and glandular fever, while her mother regards these as a sign of 'a weak constitution'. Similarly, asthma and recurrent headaches are downplayed by two other teenagers, while their parents link these complaints to childhood and a low resistance to illness.

Who takes responsibility for young people's health?

The questions asked in the household interviews included both normative and practical dimensions of responsibility for health. However, it should be noted that the two questions were asked sequentially, and this probably led some respondents to elide the two issues.

Over half (30 out of 54) of all the young people who responded to the interview question think they ought to be responsible for their own health at this point, with 22 mentioning sharing the responsibility with parents and only two citing the parents alone. Parents' views in the interviews are similar to those of the young people, with over half (47 out of 82, more fathers than mothers) agreeing that young people should be responsible for their own health at 16, a fifth (16 out of 82) claiming it should be a shared activity, over a fifth sole parental responsibility (18 out of 82), and one mother saying 'it depends on the person'.

The young people were also asked to comment on the normative issue in the questionnaire survey: 'My parents should be responsible for keeping me healthy.' Half of those asked agree that their parents should be responsible, with no significant differences by sex, ethnicity, type of school, social class or household composition. Thirty-four per cent disagree, while 16 per cent are not sure. As with other issues, there are some discrepancies between the questionnaire and interview data. Of the 49 young people who answered the normative question in both the questionnaire and the interview, 13 have moved to believing that young people rather than their parents should be responsible for their own health. (Seven were unsure in the questionnaire, but by interview, three say that the responsibility should be shared, three that they alone ought to be responsible and one that the parent ought to be responsible.) Again, these discrepancies in answers could reflect a change in opinion over time, or the fact that the relative anonymity of the questionnaire compared with the face-to-face situation of interviews elicited different representations of health.

Compared with their responses to the normative question, fewer young people claim to be responsible for their health in practice (21 out of 47), though some find it difficult to state categorically that their parents are in control. Several young people confess to not being 'responsible enough', while not claiming that their parents are in charge. Control mainly by parents is cited by more than half the young people (26 out of 47). (Boys are equally divided between parents and self, and girls are more likely to mention parents.) The remaining young people manage to answer the question in normative terms only.

Again, compared with their responses to the normative question, fewer parents say that young people have assumed responsibility for their own health in practice (37 out of 75), with the rest saying responsibility belongs to the parents (27 out of 75) or is split between parents and young people (11 out of 75). Only two fathers claim sole responsibility for the health of their teenage children, compared with over a quarter of mothers who are, in turn, significantly silent about fathers' lack of responsibility in this sphere. (Significantly both these fathers are or had been single parents.)

For the majority of parents and young people, 'responsibility for health' refers to the young person's body. 'It's my body, I should look after it . . . It's up to you whether you stay healthy or not.' Young people mention being responsible for eating healthily, keeping fit, and making GP appointments; several note that the efforts of parents to dictate health-maintenance practices are likely to be in vain: 'They can't force you to eat certain foods', 'They can't pressurize you to do sports.' However, responses to these questions are generally remarkably brief, with one exception, in which a young man sees being healthy as good luck rather than a result of his taking charge of his health:

> Well, I don't keep myself healthy to keep myself healthy. (*Can you explain that?*) Well, I like to compete – athletics, play rugby, ride my bike 18 miles a week, which is just socializing, that last bit because I live out here . . . But I also play the saxophone, which is very good for the lungs. (Justin Young)

Parental concern with health responsibility focuses upon young people within the domain of the household specifically; personal cleanliness, eating well and getting plenty of sleep are all mentioned. These matters are seen as either the teenagers' responsibility, or they are shared between them and parents, with the parent, usually the mother, keeping a watching brief and only intervening when neglect is obviously having negative repercussions.

A specific instance of a young person taking responsibility concerns deciding whether to eat beef during the food scare about bovine spongiform encephalopathy (BSE):

> It's up to him now really . . . I buy food for him but there was that scare about beef, he refused to eat it. He said 'I've put enough work into my brain. I'm not having it pickle.' (Michael Hammoud's mother)

For other mothers, especially those not born in the UK, adolescent responsibility means a moral duty to be self-sufficient, so as not to draw too heavily upon family resources:

> *Mother*: I think she can look after herself, I mean, she's not a young girl any more. I have got the other two to look after as well.

Daughter: I should take responsibility for my own health, cos I'm old enough. I shouldn't drop everything on [my mother]. She's got enough problems of her own without having to feed me, 'You're going to eat this today.' (Soraya Khan)

In so far as responsibility is shared between young people and parents, effectively mothers, young people expect them to intervene when there is a problem:

I think it's something that's shared. I mean, if I had a problem with my health then my parents would be worried ... They think we should all do a lot of exercise, not a lot, but enough. I'm careful about my diet and everything, and I mean, if I do have a problem then I tell my parents and we sort it out together. (Aruni Kathiresan)

Many mothers who are still mainly responsible for young people's health feel that their young people should be taking more responsibility for themselves:

He ought to be growing into that. But that's what they don't think about. I think it's the parent ... It's usually the mother who stops off work when they're ill, sees to their diet, stops them from staying out all hours. (Jim Lowe's mother)

One of these mothers is particularly conscious of the need constantly to 'encourage' her son into healthy habits such as getting plenty of sleep:

Teenagers think they know everything, but there's so much healthwise they could learn ... I was brought up to think sleep was basic. I tend to encourage my son to get a couple of early nights. I encourage him to get a milky drink before he goes to bed. (William Lovelock's mother)

What goes on outside the household is seen, especially by mothers not born in the UK as being beyond their control. Setting a good example and providing a 'sound foundation' are all they can hope to do:

If you just had a couple of parents that were couch potatoes and vastly overweight and just sat there all the time, that wouldn't be a very good example, and it would be hard for the child to break out. (Emma Kerr's mother)

An extreme case of maternal responsibility concerns a young man who does very little for himself (he refused to be interviewed). His mother notes that responsibility has to lie with 'the parents because it's not something that matters much to teenagers', and she describes 'organizing' him in terms of providing a 'good diet', providing clean clothes, making sure he washes and cleans his teeth:

He gets very irritated by that. I still ask him ... I confiscate his clothes every night so he has to put clean ones on from day one. (Steven King's mother)

Although only two fathers claim sole responsibility for their teenage children's health, fathers are more likely to mention cleanliness, especially with respect to sons. One man, until recently a single father, 'drums' it into his son that he must wash because 'nobody likes people who stink', and the other, currently a single father, describes having to 'prompt' his son about being 'smelly' and lazy about personal hygiene.

Conclusion

The findings of our study confirm those of others in showing the lack of correspondence between different aspects of people's approaches to health. An evaluation of health as important does not necessarily mean that one behaves in ways that would be approved by health educators. Perceiving oneself to be generally healthy is compatible with having a range of illnesses and complaints; in this sense, notions of health embody ideas about everyday functioning and about 'normal' illness that are not represented in narrow medical definitions. In terms of how they approach health, our study shows that young people are not intrinsically different in these ways from other groups in the population.

Replies to a locus-of-control question suggest that health is believed to be a product of both individual control and luck, with young men and fathers more likely to mention control than mothers and young women. Health is considered 'very important' by mothers and less so by fathers and young people. Health is also more likely to be seen as important in middle-class households. To parents, being healthy means mainly not being ill; young people are more likely to mention lifestyles and fitness, with young women being more likely to mention the former, and young men the latter. Threats to health reflect these definitions, although both parents and young people also mention broader social and environmental factors affecting health. In a fixed-choice survey question put to young people, the major 'killer diseases' are considered less important health issues than death, unemployment, destruction of the environment and nuclear war. These findings are in line with other studies in which young people are asked about the issues that concern them. For example, in a study of young people in Austria, England and Finland, Solantaus (1987) found that English young people were more concerned than those in the other two countries about work and unemployment (the unemployment rate in England at the time the study was carried out was about twice as high as in Finland or Austria). A third of the young people in the English and Austrian samples worried about nuclear war; the figure was more than three-quarters for Finnish youth. In a British study carried out in 1985, 60 per cent of 15–16-year-olds regarded the problem of waste from nuclear power stations as 'very serious', and significant proportions of young people expressed concern about other environmental health issues (Davies, 1987).

Evaluations of young people's health are structured by gender and social class. In line with illness patterns, which we discuss in the next chapter, young men and parents of young men are more likely to say that young men's health is good compared with young women and the parents of young women. Those in high-status occupations are more likely to rate young people's health as good, compared with those in low-status occupations. Within households, mothers and fathers agree on the health status of young people. They tend to be more positive than the young people themselves. Evaluations of health status do not always neatly match up with reports of illness, or with assessments of lifestyles and emotional state.

Our study explored the locus of responsibility for young people's health in both normative and practical terms. On the normative question as to who *ought* to be responsible for young people's health, more than half of the young people who took part in the survey agreed that parents should be responsible, while at interview (several months later) more than half of the young people thought that they should be in charge, a view shared by a similar proportion of parents. The practice of responsibility is a little different, with fewer young people claiming to be in control in practice than in theory, claims which are reflected in parents' accounts. Asked what responsibility for health refers to, parents and young people focus on young people's bodies – diet, fitness, personal cleanliness and sleep. In so far as parents are described as responsible, mothers are the principal actors. Many mothers are concerned that young people do not take sufficient responsibility for their health. In this, and other ways, as we saw earlier, the parenting of young people is marked by strong gender differences which repeat many of the themes established for early parenthood.

Notes

1 These latter findings correspond with dietary behaviour. Young women eat a healthier diet than young men. Young men are more likely to have done sport and to describe themselves as healthy. (See Chapter 6.)
2 A similar relationship holds with respect to mothers' occupations, but only for young women.
3 'Healthy' is defined as 'good' health, while 'not so healthy' includes health being defined as 'quite good', 'not good' and 'bad'. This replicates a regular question from the annual *General Household Survey* (OPCS, 1991: 300).

5 Young people and illness

In this chapter, we examine the evidence from the questionnaires and interviews concerning the illnesses reported by the young people in the study and their contact with health services. We look at illness patterns and contacts with GPs by gender, social class and ethnic origin, and their satisfaction (or otherwise) with the health services. Drawing on the parents' and young people's interviews, we examine what happens in the household when young people fall ill, the extent to which parents intervene, and the ways in which young people themselves take control.

The questionnaire data

Reported illness

The level of illness reported by young people over the preceding year is high: 39 per cent report a long-term and/or a recurrent illness. Young people describe a wide range of conditions. As indicated in Table 5.1, there is a high incidence of allergies, including asthma and hay fever, together with muscular/skeletal problems. Ear, nose and throat infections are also frequently mentioned. Two per cent of the sample report serious illnesses such as diabetes, epilepsy and sickle-cell anaemia.

Another indicator of health problems is contact with the health services. In the survey, 9 per cent of young people report having been hospital in-patients in the past year, while 35 per cent have attended out-patient or casualty departments. In total, over 62 per cent of out-patients visits were the result of accidents, 4 per cent each for ENT problems, dental treatment and minor operations such as ingrowing toenails; approximately 25 per cent were for tests, check-ups and treatment for a variety of conditions – diabetes, asthma, skin disorders, dietary problems. With respect to GP consultations, 16 per cent of young people claim not to have visited the doctor in the past year, while 14 per cent say they went five or more times. Those reporting a long-term or recurrent illness are more likely to have been to the doctor frequently over the past 12 months.[1] Young people with

Table 5.1 *Young people's long-term and recurrent illness conditions reported in the questionnaire, by sex*

	All		Females		Males	
	%	(n)	%	(n)	%	(n)
None reported	64	(542)	60	(219)	67	(323)
Asthma	6	(54)	6	(21)	7	(33)
ENT, skin	7	(60)	8	(29)	6	(31)
Muscular/skeletal	7	(55)	7	(24)	6	(31)
Headaches, nausea	4	(36)	4	(15)	4	(21)
Hay fever	4	(31)	4	(16)	3	(15)
Misc. pains	3	(24)	3	(10)	3	(14)
Misc. serious	2	(20)	3	(11)	2	(9)
Period pains	1	(9)	2	(9)	–	–
Glandular fever	1	(7)	2	(6)	0	(1)
Stress	1	(5)	1	(2)	1	(3)
Base		843		362		481

$p < 0.05$

asthma and ENT problems are particularly likely to visit frequently, as are those with more serious illness.

Illness and social class

Social position is significantly associated with patterns of health and illness in virtually all countries which collect the relevant statistics (Williams, 1990). These social class differences obtain from before birth right through the life cycle. As we saw in Chapter 4, young people's reports of the state of their health ('good', 'fairly good' or 'not good') vary by their social class origins, with young people whose parents work in high-status occupations more likely to report 'good' or 'fairly good' health, than those whose fathers are in low-status occupations.[2] Those young people who, at the time of the survey, were expecting to leave school at 16 to join the labour market, are less likely to report good health and more likely to report poor health than those expecting to stay in full-time education.[3] Most of these young people are likely to enter manual or low-status non-manual employment. Indeed, by the time the household study was carried out, 15 young people had left full-time education: four had found clerical work; two shop work; five skilled, two semi-skilled, and one unskilled manual jobs; and one was unemployed.[4] Several of these young people reported accidents at work or stress-related illness connected with employment or unemployment.

Reported illness in the questionnaire survey does vary significantly by social class. Of those with fathers in high-status occupations, 43 per cent reported some long-term or recurrent illness compared with only 35 per cent of those whose fathers were in low-status occupations. However, hospital in-patient and out-patient attendance is significantly higher for those with fathers in low-status occupations than for those whose fathers are in higher-status occupations. Frequency of visits to the doctor shows no significant difference by fathers' social class but differences by housing tenure are significant, with 19 per cent of those living in rented accommodation reportedly visiting the doctor five times or more in the past year compared with only 13 per cent of those whose parents are owner-occupiers.

One reason for the inconsistent relationships between class, on the one hand, and health status and reported illness, on the other, is the lack of correspondence between people's reports of illness and perceptions of their health status (see, for example, Cornwell, 1984). Some illness is regarded as 'normal'; definitions of health status take into account 'coping' and everyday functioning, rather than simply the occurrence of diagnosed illness.

Illness and gender

The sex of the young person is the main factor associated with differential reports of illness in our study.[5] Significantly more young women (14 per cent) than young men (8 per cent) say that their health is 'not good', and more young women than young men worry about their health (14 per cent claimed they worried 'a great deal', compared with 10 per cent of young men). In this context, it is interesting that slightly more young men than young women rated their lifestyles and diets as 'unhealthy'.[6]

Reports of illness bear out these sex differences, with 10 per cent of young women reporting long-term illnesses and 38 per cent recurrent illnesses, compared with 7 per cent and 37 per cent, respectively, of young men. Table 5.2 shows a similar picture for contact with the health services. Significantly more young women than young men say they visit their GP frequently. Even those young women who report no significant illness are more likely than young men to have visited the GP frequently in the past year (14 per cent of women and 6 per cent of men having been five or more times). Slightly more young women (10 per cent) than young men (8 per cent) have been hospital in-patients in the past year. The reasons for hospital admission are sharply sex-differentiated. Of the 33 young male in-patients, 14 were there as a consequence of accidents, compared with six of the 33 young women. Seventeen young women were hospitalized for surgery, compared with 15 young men, and ten young women went in for observation or non-surgical treatment, compared with four young men. No differences were found with respect to out-patient visits (36 per cent of young women and 35 per cent of young men), but more out-patient visits due to accidents were made by young men (72 per cent) than young women (51 per cent). Substantial differences by sex are shown in Table 5.2 in the use of prescribed medicines, reported by 20 per cent of young women, but only 8 per cent of young men.[7] Young women are also more likely than young men to take 'over-the-counter' medicines, notably iron tablets, vitamin pills and painkillers.

Table 5.2 *GP visits and hospital admissions reported in the questionnaire survey by sex of young person*

	All %	Females %	Males %	
No. of GP visits in past year				
None	16	12	20	p < 0.001
1–2	47	46	48	
3–4	22	23	22	
5+	14	18	11	
Hospital treatment				
in-patient	9	10	8	ns
out-patient	35	36	35	
both	6	7	5	
neither	62	62	63	
Use of prescribed medicine	13	20	8	p < 0.001
Base	839	362	477	

Examining the role of gender throws some light on the complex rela-tionship between reported illness and perceived state of health noted above. While young people who report a long-standing or recurrent illness or who have been referred to hospital in the past year are more likely to rate their health as 'not good', compared with those who report no illness (14 per cent as against 7 per cent), this is less true for young men than young women. Young men who report illness appear to be more optimistic than young women about the general state of their health. For example, among young people with asthma, 18 of the 33 male sufferers in the survey reported their health as 'good', compared with four of the 21 female asthmatics. Similarly, although there is some association between reported illness and frequency of visits to GPs, this is stronger for young women than for young men. Additionally, with respect to asthma and the 'serious' illnesses noted in Table 5.1, more young women than young men with such illnesses went to the doctor frequently. Use of primary and secondary health-care services are linked; of those who have been to hospital as either in-patients or out-patients, young women visit their GP more frequently than do young men.

So far we have been discussing physical illness. There are, of course, links with psychological problems of various kinds, and this is an area in which there are well-established gender differences in adult health and illness patterns (Verbrugge, 1985). In the questionnaire survey, illness in the form of a long-term or recurrent health problem is disproportionately found among those who report feeling dissatisfied with life, especially females (Table 5.3). Illness is also more likely to be reported by those who say they would like more information on what to do about stress and about depression. These young people are more likely to be female than male. Our questionnaire data also show that painkillers are more likely to

Table 5.3 *Percentage reporting illness and desire for information on stress and depression by satisfaction with life, and by sex*

	Young women satisfied with life			Young men satisfied with life		
	usually %	rarely %		usually %	rarely %	
Reporting illness	38	52	p < 0.05	33	37	ns
information wanted on:						
stress	61	84	p < 0.005	50	63	ns
depression	52	80	p < 0.001	43	61	p < 0.05
Base	190	61		252	72	

be used by young women than young men, whether or not they report a long-term or recurrent illness. Forty-eight per cent of young women and 30 per cent of young men said they had taken painkillers in the last week. Among young women there is a tendency for use of painkillers to be associated with smoking and drinking alcohol, an association less marked for young men.

Illness and ethnicity

There are no significant differences between ethnic groups in their assessments of health, lifestyle and diet. Similarly, the degree to which the groups worry about their health is not significantly different. However, more Asian and black young women (20 per cent) claim to worry 'a great deal' about their health, compared to only 12 per cent of white and 6 per cent of 'other' young women. More white young men and black young men (12 per cent) than Asian young men (3 per cent) never worry about their health. In contrast, significant differences occur in the reporting of long-term or recurrent illness, with 57 per cent of black young women and 53 per cent of 'other' young women reporting illness, compared with only 35 per cent of Asian and 41 per cent of white young women. No significant differences emerge among the young men. Again, no differences are found in the frequency of GP visits over the previous year, although 31 per cent of black young women have been five times or more, compared with only 17 per cent of both white and Asian young women. Asian young men are the most frequent visitors to the doctor; 18 per cent have been five or more times, compared with 8 per cent of white young men. White young men were the least likely to have been over the past year; 21 per cent reported no visit, compared with 15 per cent of the Asian young men. While 17 per cent of black young women reported the highest rate of hospital in-patient visits (this compared with 9 per cent of white and 8 per cent of Asian young women), 38 per cent of white young women had attended as out-patients, compared with 19 per cent of Asians and 31 per cent of black and 'other' young women. With respect to illness and ethnicity, therefore, Asian young women appear to have less illness and to consult GPs and to use hospital services less than other groups. The latter findings are related to their particularly low rate of out-patient accident admissions (only 4 per cent).

Satisfaction with health services

There are no significant differences by sex, housing tenure or social class in the degree of satisfaction expressed by young people with their doctor in the questionnaire. Overall, 64 per cent of young people are satisfied with their doctor, 11 per cent are dissatisfied and 17 per cent unsure. The remaining 8 per cent claim never to use their GP. Further, there are no significant differences in how well they think their doctor understands them although they are less positive on this point, with only 34 per cent believing that their doctor understands them most of the time. Almost 40 per cent report that the degree of understanding depends upon the problem involved, but 12 per cent assess their GP as rarely understanding young people. Private school girls are less positive than the girls at the state school, with 28 per cent unsure whether their doctor understands them, compared with only 11 per cent of the state school girls.

Overall, only a quarter express satisfaction with the school nurse, but 37 per cent claim never to use the service. As might be expected, there are significant differences between schools since responses are affected by both the availability and the personality of the nurse in each school. Well over 40 per cent of the private school girls express dissatisfaction, compared with only 9 per cent of the state school girls. In one state school over 60 per cent of the pupils claim never to use the nurse, compared with around only 20 per cent at another.

The household study

Young people's illness in the family

The household interviews took place some six to 15 months after the questionnaire survey. Differences between data from the questionnaire survey and the household study may therefore at least in part be explained by the time difference.

If we include those with any illness, nearly half the young people in the household sample (25 out of 56) experienced either a significant illness, an accident or were referred to hospital either as an in-patient or out-patient in the past year. Compared with the questionnaire survey, the household sample reveals similar rates of long-term and/or recurrent illness reported by young people (38 per cent and 35 per cent, respectively). A comparison of out-patient hospital use between the survey and the household study shows consistent rates of 35 per cent and 37 per cent, respectively.

Any under-reporting of illness by young people in the household study is offset by their mothers' reports. Twenty-seven out of the 55 mothers (49 per cent) report recurrent or long-term illness among the young people, compared with 12 out of 31 (39 per cent) fathers.

Negotiating illness in the family

The sociological perspective on health and illness has highlighted the notion of an illness 'career' (Locker, 1981). Symptoms are identified and, if an illness is defined, some action to ameliorate it may be taken, such as using an 'over-the-counter' medicine, or seeking a doctor's opinion and prescription. Although the process of symptom or illness identification is theoretically distinct from the decision to take action, in practice, and in people's accounts, the two are often closely associated. We discuss these pro-cesses with respect to the conditions under which parents either intervene in, or leave their children to manage, their own symptoms and illnesses.

One feature of the sick role as described in traditional medical sociology is the exemption from normal roles and activities. This may serve to reduce individuals' freedom and autonomy (Parsons, 1958). Taking on the sick role also entails the right to be cared for by others. In the case of young people, especially those in the process of gaining some independence from parents, being ill and accepting the role of sick person may thus temporarily entail being restored to the dependent status of childhood. While some young people at 16 may take on more of the responsibility for their own health than others, sickness is likely to iron out some of these differences. And while some parents allow their children to take charge of their own diet and bodily health, they may be less likely to do so when ill-ness strikes. These considerations mean that relationships between parents and their young people may require sensitive negotiation.

In order to explore household negotiations concerning young people's illness, we asked household members about the last time, within a spe-cified period, the young person was ill. Where interviewees could not remember recent illness or where none had occurred, the interviewers questioned them about any significant recurrent or long-term health conditions they had mentioned earlier. In 60 households an illness episode involving the young person was reported. In the other four households only the young people were interviewed, and they mentioned no illnesses.

Most common among the illness episodes described in the interviews are colds, flu and sore throats. These represent over one-third of the total mentioned. In addition, there are ten cases of infections, nine cases of accidents to limbs or limb problems, five allergies, five cases of fainting or concussion, five cases of migraine, and four skin conditions. The 12 episodes classified in the miscellaneous category include three of period pains, one eating problem and a grumbling appendix.

Reporting illness

As we observed earlier, young people are less likely than their mothers to report their own illnesses, but more likely to do so than fathers. Only one of the 55 mothers did not mention an illness, in contrast to nine of the 31 fathers and six of the 55 young people. Four of the young people and the one mother who did not mention an illness said that there had been no illness in the past few years; most of the fathers simply said they could not remember.

We asked interviewees to recall, if possible, an illness which had occurred in the past six months. Three-quarters of mothers mentioned illnesses within the previous six months, and the rest within two years. Young people are less likely than mothers to mention recent illness episodes. In accordance with the questionnaire data, there are marked gender differences between young people in recent recall of illness. Almost three-quarters of young women and only a third of young men mentioned conditions which had occurred within six months.

'Diagnosing' illness

Noticing symptoms is the first point in the individual's illness career. Nearly three-quarters of young people, notably more young men than young women, say they themselves first noticed something was wrong. But they also testify in their accounts to their mothers' role in picking up the signs when they are unwell.

Mothers report themselves as highly sensitive to noticing signs of illness in their sons and daughters. When mothers say, 'they are pretty obvious', they mean that these signs are obvious to them. Since mothers have intimate knowledge of the health histories of their children from birth onwards, and carry out most of the routine care of children throughout childhood and youth (see Chapter 3), it is perhaps not surprising that they have become so attuned. Fathers also say that mothers are efficient at noticing young people's illness. An instance of a sensitive mother is Jim Lowe's mother. Suspicious that her son has long suffered an allergy to particular foods (those high in additives), she attributes her son's symptoms – mood swings and hyperactive behaviour – to his diet. She now watches this carefully:

Last year after he'd been to scout camp, after he came back he was diabolical. I said 'Have you been buying anything you shouldn't have done?'

By contrast, fathers' accounts of themselves in terms of identifying illness in their 16-year-olds suggest less sensitivity and expertise. As already noted, nine of the 21 fathers interviewed could not recall an illness; if they did mention something, few were able to comment further. As Peter Greenway's father says:

My wife would tell you that. I wouldn't know. I should know. But it's something I don't really take in.

When children reach the age of 16, many mothers try to carry out illness surveillance without young people noticing. Mothers often feel tempted to intervene, but fear the reproach that they are 'fussing'. Nasreen Mohammed's mother is worried that her daughter may be becoming anorexic, and says that

> I keep an eye on her without her knowing, though I can't help myself sometimes. I interfere.

Talking about her daughter's suppressed anger and general unhappiness, Catherine Sheppard's mother notes:

> I can see signs sometimes that something is bugging her and she won't let it out. But, however much you try, you mustn't keep on.

For one mother, herself severely disabled, symptoms and illness are such major preoccupations that she feels she can divine them in advance:

> I told [my daughter] she was due to have a migraine.

For many women, noticing children's illness is part and parcel of being a 'good mother'. Fathers agree with this definition of motherhood. A UK-born father of four children whose wife, in accordance with his wishes, is a full-time mother, says:

> She knows from the kids when there's something wrong healthwise ... She's got that little thing ... which clicks and tells there's something wrong with one or the other ... She has got that sort of there, which I don't. She can always tell, because she brought most of the kids up. (Barry Green's father)

As Voysey (1975) and Locker (1981), among others, argue, sensitivity on the part of mothers to signs of illness in their children has a symbolic as well as a practical value. It constitutes an important criterion of the provision of 'proper care' by which others judge mothers, and hence mothers judge themselves.

With respect to 16-year-olds, mothers' sensitivity to young people's illness is structured by the normative climate in which they carry out their role as carers, namely the requirement that young people acquire independence from them. Mothers worry about their children whatever their age, but because of the requirement on young people to become independent in adolescence, mothers are especially likely to worry about 16-year-olds. Indeed, as we saw in Chapter 3, worrying is one of the most gender-differentiated aspects of parenthood; nearly half of the mothers (26 out of 54) say they worry 'a lot', compared with only two fathers (out of 30). However, mothers also feel constrained to conceal how much they worry, since young people are inclined to interpret the display of too much maternal concern as a threat to their liberty. A mother whose son was recently knocked off his bike describes how she tries to persuade her son to use a cycle helmet. She adds: 'I don't like him to know I worry, but I do.'

Though mothers are quick to notice illness in their sons or daughters, the process of diagnosis is interactive, and involves both mother and child. A young person 'lets on' by verbal or non-verbal cues (see Davis, 1963) that s/he is feeling unwell. A mother picks up the message and may respond or act upon it in a number of ways. She may enquire 'What's wrong?' and interpret the forthcoming information in the context of the young person's health history as a specific sign that she or he is ill. As one mother says: 'He goes off his food, so I know there's something wrong with him.' Next, mothers may label the condition by specifying some form of treatment, such as prescribing a home remedy or suggesting that the young person go to the doctor.

From the young person's standpoint, 'letting on' may also be directed towards gaining some form of legitimation of the illness, and justification for taking on the sick role. The young person feels s/he has the right to be cared for and, in some cases, more importantly, the right to be exempted from everyday activities such as going to school. For example, one young man complains that his claims to illness are not always received sympathetically by his parents. In this case, the parents consult the doctor in order to discover if the young man's claim has a legitimate foundation:

> I told them I was ill, but sometimes we say it to get out of school. So I was taken to the GP's [by my mother] and he said I had gastric flu.

Lay solutions – cosseting and taking tablets

On the basis of symptom diagnosis, mothers and young people discuss a range of treatments, which include home remedies as well as going to the doctor (though one is not necessarily a substitute for the other).

In the interviews, parents and young people often move from discussing what happened with respect to a particular illness to what 'normally happens' when the young person feels ill. One reason for this may be that they cannot recall the precise details of the situation under discussion. Another may be that this provides an opportunity to construct a convincing narrative about the way in which the household and its internal relations function with respect to illness and the care of young people when they are ill. The fact that the move from the particular episode to the general behaviour is most striking with respect to home remedies supports the latter interpretation. Just as mothers are sensitive to noticing illness symptoms, so they are also the principal administrators of home remedies such as painkillers:

> She went to bed, and I gave her some Beecham's powders and hot lemon . . . But it wasn't sort of wait on her hand and foot. (Ann Kennedy's mother)

> If I'm really feeling sick, I always lay in bed and get my mum to waken me and bring me aspirins and glasses of water and that kind of thing . . . And she'll pop in and say 'Do you want anything?' And just carry on as normal. (*It's your mum who does this?*) It's usually because my dad's – it's, you know,

it's usually during the day that I'm ill and my dad's usually at work.
(Jane Richards)

The following account is given by a mother of four sons. She extends her
task beyond the dispensation of painkillers to watching over the sick
16-year-old when he is asleep.

> (*Will he get medicines by himself?*) Yes ... but I say 'Don't forget medicine.
> Take it.' You know, you are a mother. You can't stop. (*Does he like you to take
> care of him?*) When he is ill he likes somebody to. But when he is not, no.
> Sometimes even in the night I go to his bed and I see how he is going on.
> And if the blanket is off, I put it on. Yes. I tell him I come to his bed in the
> night. He say 'Oh, mummy, I sleep, I didn't sleep. After that I did sleep.
> I didn't hear you.' (Abrahim Samuel's mother)

The questionnaire data indicate marked gender differences in the use
of medication, with young women significantly more likely than young
men to make use of it. Though the majority of young people taking tablets
do so in consultation with parents (54 per cent of those taking non-
prescribed medicines), when young men take tablets they are more likely
than young women to refer to their parents. Thirty-four per cent of young
women either take their own tablets or use the family stock without
consulting their parents, compared with only 23 per cent of young men.
Evidence from the household interviews also suggests that young people,
especially young men, generally refer to their mothers when they are
considering taking a tablet:

> (*Would he help himself to a paracetamol?*) No. He'd say 'I've had a headache
> for a couple of days. What shall I do?' I'd say 'Well, do you think you need
> a hot drink or a paracetamol when you go to bed?' And he'll say 'Yes' or
> 'No'. But he's not – he doesn't take tablets. He'll only take them if he's
> desperate. (Peter Greenway's mother)

Parents are particularly conscious of the dangerous properties of many
medicines. Mothers continue to be mindful of these with 16-year-olds.
Thus, it is not surprising that even those young people who say that they
help themselves to tablets seek parental 'permission', albeit in a subtle,
rather than an overt, way. Not all parents are able to articulate reasons;
Mrs Monk's account is one of the exceptions:

> If there is anything like diarrhoea he will tell me that and I will recommend
> something for that. He also tells me if he is taking a paracetamol, because
> that is out of the cupboard. It was stressed to all of them, and the younger
> one is not allowed to take tablets without coming to me. He will tell me,
> 'I am taking a couple of paracetamol. I have got a headache.'

Not going to the medicine cupboard without permission is a clear rule of
the household which is imposed by 'responsible parents' to protect their
children. When young people are allowed to become more independent
and begin to take responsibility for themselves, this rule requires some
renegotiation. Making a public announcement that one is about to take,

or has just taken, a tablet, may be interpreted as a carry-over from childhood. On the other hand, it may constitute an intermediate strategy, whereby the transition from childhood dependence towards adult independence is managed. Again, instances of this phenomenon tend to concern young men rather than young women. A father says of his son:

> I'm sure he took a Panadol . . . In the night he might go and get one himself. But in the morning, he said 'I feel terrible, I need a Panadol or something' . . . that would be the course of events, rather than him just going down and dosing himself. (Justin Young's father)

In some cases, the permission is obtained *post hoc*:

> He might have taken a couple of Panadol . . . He has asked. I mean, if I'm here he asks me. But I don't check the cupboard to see whether they've taken them when I get home. I just expect them to be still there. Most of the time he will say 'Oh, I've had a couple of Panadol' . . . He has actually said to me a couple of times when I've been home, 'Oh, I've had a headache so I took something. Is that all right?' (Adrian Alexander's mother)

These parental comments need to be interpreted in the context of parents' concern with representing themselves both to us and to themselves in the interviews as 'responsible parents'.

Medical solutions – deciding to go to the doctor

The next stage in the young person's illness career is the decision whether the condition 'merits' the attention of the doctor. Again, mothers tend to make the suggestion. Of the 40 households in which young people and/or parents mention a visit to the doctor with respect to one of the illness episodes described above, over two-thirds of the mothers (28 out of 40) report, or are reported by the young people (in a few cases by fathers), to have made the suggestion to consult the GP. In only three of these instances is there disagreement between the account of the young person and the parents, with the young person omitting to say that the mother made the suggestion. Only two fathers are mentioned as having suggested that their children consult the doctor. (One of the cases, concerning a problem with the son's sexual organs, is discussed below.) Nine young people, supported by their parents' accounts, say that the decision to go to the GP was theirs alone. A somewhat protective mother talks about 'getting' her son to the doctor:

> I'd get him to the doctor's if I think he's getting chesty or got an ear infection . . . I watch his temperature if it's his ears, or anything a bit odd. I'd get him to the doctor's if he wasn't well. (Jeremy Talbot's mother)

In many cases, mothers and young people describe arriving at a rapid consensus about going to the doctor. Decisions concerning 'normality' versus 'illness' can be difficult to make (Locker, 1981). The following accounts are those of Adrian Alexander and his mother:

Mother: I've actually said to him, 'It's time you went [to the doctor] and got that [virus] sorted out, and while you're there mention so and so.' He asks me because I'm a nurse, you see. 'What shall I do about so and so?' And I say, 'Well, I don't know. You'd better go and see a doctor.'

Son: I think [going to the doctor] is sort of a joint decision. 'I think it's time you went to the doctor's.'

In a few cases, there is evidence of the young person seeking to consult the GP against her or his mothers' wishes. A young Asian woman wants to visit her GP for a skin condition in order to get a particular drug, which she believes will clear it up. Her mother disapproves of orthodox medicine in this instance, and the daughter makes her own decision, ignoring her mother's wishes.

There are also cases where the young people decide to go to the doctor without telling their mothers. Two daughters (of UK-born parents), who decided to go to the GP for the contraceptive pill, only confided in their mothers afterwards. The mothers then insisted on accompanying them to the doctor on follow-up visits.

The interviews with the young people suggest that fewer young people make the decision about going to the doctor (16 out of 43) than go to see the doctor unaccompanied (26 out of 43). Making the decision oneself does not, therefore, necessarily lead to going alone to the doctor. In respect of particular illness episodes, three young people who made their own decisions to go to the GP went accompanied, though the mothers waited outside the consulting room.

Making the appointment with the GP

Following the decision to go to the doctor, usually an appointment has to be made with the GP.[8] According to the questionnaire survey, more young people say that 'the last time' they went to the doctor their parents made the appointment (58 per cent) than say that they made the appointment themselves (24 per cent). The results from the household study show that, by the time of the interview some months later, a higher proportion of appointments are 'usually' made by young people.[9]

Mothers' accounts of who usually makes the young person's appointments suggest that a third (15 out of 43) are made by young people, and over half by mothers (25 out of 43); the rest say 'it varies'. Fathers' accounts suggest that the responsibility lies either with the young person (7 out of 21 cases), or with mothers (8 out of 21), or that 'it varies' (6 out of 21).

Since negotiating the gatekeeping role of the doctor's receptionist can demand considerable skill, parents rather than young people may prefer to make the appointments. Young people do not often refer to difficulties here, though a young man suggests that he is aware he lacks the appropriate skills:

[My mother] makes the appointment cos like, I don't know how to make the appointment because I haven't got the phone number or anything.

Table 5.4 *Who makes young person's GP appointment, and whether accompanied to GP by parent, by sex of young person (young people's accounts)*

	Questionnaire survey		Household interview	
	Females %	Males %	Females % n	Males % n
Appt. made by self/ to GP alone	15	22	33 (7)	23 (5)
Appt. made by self/ parent accompanies	5	4	5 (1)	– (0)
Appt. made by parent/ to GP alone	14	20	10 (2)	18 (4)
Appt. made by parent/ parent accompanies	44	36	14 (3)	5 (1)
No appt. needed/ to GP alone	6	7	10 (2)	27 (6)
No appt. needed/ parent accompanies	9	4	5 (1)	– (0)
Varies or not sure	7	8	24 (5)	27 (6)
Base	361	473	21	22

$p < 0.005$

Going to the GP alone

Going to the doctor alone may be considered an important milestone for young people in the process of gaining independence. Our questionnaire data show that in the fifth year 44 per cent of young people visit their doctors alone; significantly more young men (51 per cent) than young women (36 per cent).[10] Some months later, in the interview data, the proportion has grown – just under two-thirds of young people (15 out of 22 young men and 11 out of 21 young women) say that they go to their doctors alone 'on most occasions'. Age is a discriminator here: younger teenagers are more likely to be accompanied. Reports from both the young people and their parents in the interviews suggest an increase in unaccompanied visits around the age of 15–16. There are significant sex differences here, with more young men than young women going alone at younger ages.[11]

We might expect to find links between young people going to the doctor alone and making their own appointments. The questionnaire survey shows some association, although only a minority of young people in the fifth year at school – 15 per cent of young women and 22 per cent of young men – are both making their own appointments and going to the GP alone. The majority (more young women than young men) have parents who make the appointments and accompany them to the GP (Table 5.4).

Going to the doctor alone is more common the greater the number of visits in the past year.[12] This finding is unsurprising, since those who go to the doctor frequently will be on average older at their last visit, that is, aged 15–16. Moreover, frequent visits to the doctor may be for follow-up or routine checks, and it can be argued that these are less likely to require the presence of parents. Parents are more likely to accompany young people with respect to the *onset* of illness, especially significant illness. As the questionnaire data indicate, young people visiting the doctor for significant illness are likely to be accompanied by parents.[13]

The fact that more young men than young women go alone to the doctor and at an earlier age needs to be considered in the context of the sex of the parent who typically accompanies them, namely the mother. A mother is more likely to continue to accompany her daughter as she gets older than she is to accompany her son. Indeed, many of the instances of mothers and daughters going together centre on female health issues such as painful periods, going on the contraceptive pill, and (suspected) pregnancy. In three cases, two involving the pill and one a pregnancy, the mothers insisted on accompanying the daughters, rather than the daughters desiring their mothers' presence. By contrast, mothers of sons are more likely to consider it 'inappropriate' to accompany them by 16, and young men resist their mothers' presence for similar reasons. Some mothers suggest that sons ought to consult their fathers over certain problems, notably to do with male sexuality. In one case, a stepmother describes what happened when her stepson developed a 'spot on his willy', a revelation that was 'blurted out' by the younger brother:

> I thought 'He's not going to show me.' He showed his dad, and his dad said 'You'd better go to the doctor.'

In a second case, the son told his mother about a small lump on his testicles. The mother describes how she referred the son to his father:

> He came straightaway and spoke to me about it, and I said to him obviously, if he was worried, the doctor was the right place to go, but it would probably be better if he talked to his father about it first . . . I said to him that we would go to the doctor with him, but would he prefer his father rather than me in that particular instance? And he did so, and his father went with him.

Going to the doctor alone for follow-up visits or non-significant health problems is also related to parents' normative values concerning the nature of adolescence, and the consequences of these values for their relationships with young people. As we discuss in Chapters 7 and 10, some parents are more favourably disposed than others towards to the idea of young people having independence at 16. In those households where the parents are more favourable, the mothers endeavour to create strategies of communication with their young people; these function both as a way of keeping their young people close to them emotionally, and also as a means of exercising influence over them. Young people who do *not* discuss health issues with their mothers are significantly more likely to be using the health services independently of parental help.[14]

Relevant also to the issue of mothers accompanying their daughters to the GP is the sex of the doctor. If the doctor is male, which is more commonly the case, the mother may act as chaperon to her daughter, and as an intermediary between the doctor and the daughter. In one such case, a young Asian woman says that she prefers to be accompanied, because she wants her mother to speak on her behalf and she feels uncomfortable with a male doctor.

An examination of the data on illness episodes suggests that mothers who accompany their young people to the GP's surgery may frequently wait outside the consulting room. This poses a difficulty in interpreting the exact meaning of 'going alone' to the GP. Waiting outside the doctor's consulting room represents, for mothers, a compromise or intermediate strategy. It is most likely to occur in respect of minor illness conditions or follow-up visits and allows young people a degree of independence to see the GP in confidence. Confidentiality is a characteristic of doctor–patient relations which most young people favour unreservedly (55 per cent in the survey and 91 per cent in the interviews). At the same time, the mother stations herself to receive information concerning the medical encounter directly the young person emerges from the consulting room. Evidence from young people also suggests that the strategy is arrived at through their own resistance to their mothers' presence at the consultation.

In one instance a UK-born mother was banished by her daughter to the waiting room when the health problem was relatively trivial. When the matter was more serious – the daughter wanted the GP to prescribe the contraceptive pill – she did not tell her mother. However, when the mother later found out, she insisted on accompanying her daughter for a further visit to the GP. In the following quotation, the daughter describes 'what normally happens' and how she came to exclude her mother:

[Normally] I go alone unless I had a temperature or something ... or unless my Mum was determined to come with me ... [When the doctor says] 'What's wrong with you?' I'll open my mouth, and my Mum will tell him for me, which is why I don't let her go anywhere near a doctor with me ... By coincidence I go when she wants to go as well [for her own problem]. So she sits there and waits. And then, when she wants to see the doctor, I go and wait for her outside. (Anna Gibb)

In being excluded from the doctor's consulting room, some mothers fear missing out on important information concerning their children's state of health; either the young people do not ask the doctor the 'right questions' or they do not ask questions at all. Sometimes they fail to pass on any information gained. A mother who accompanied her son to the doctor when he dislocated his knee joint describes the lack of feedback if he goes alone:

[I would go in to the GP] if it was something that I thought he wanted me to go in ... (*What about his knee problem?*) Oh, yes I would then ... I would feel it would be better if I managed it, or I wouldn't get to know what had

been said, because he wouldn't tell me. It's not that I wouldn't think he was
capable of dealing with it himself. It's just that I wouldn't get any
information. (Steven King's mother)

Those young people who report going into the doctor's consulting room
on their own include those who have left school and started work.[15] This
is not to say that young people who are accompanied necessarily want
their mothers to be there, rather that the employed group are generally
more successful in banishing them. The point is nicely illustrated by the
case of a young man who damaged his hand at work, which involved going
to the local hospital to have it stitched. The mother describes her son's
determination to go to the hospital on his own. The young man in question
is silent on this matter, except to say that his mother 'normally' makes GP
appointments for him and, contrary to the typical practice, accompanies
him 'unless it's something serious':

> He phoned me and said 'I'm just going to the hospital' . . . He phoned, he
> said, to see if his sister was here – the one who has the car. I said 'No, she's
> gone out. Why?' He said he'd split his hand. He was so calm. I said 'Jan's on
> lates.' So I said I would get the bus and meet him at the end of the road.
> And he said 'No, no. It's all right.' I said 'No, I'll come up, cos it's nice to
> have someone' . . . When I got [to the hospital], he was still waiting to go in.
> He had no money on him, so it was just as well I went up. (Jo Saunders'
> mother)

Fathers are rarely involved in young people's visits to GPs. If they do
become involved in health-care encounters, they do so largely through the
agency of mothers and under rather specific circumstances, notably when
the illness is serious and where new relationships with health professionals
(for example, with the staff of hospital casualty departments) have to be
negotiated. In these situations, fathers are often called upon to act as
official spokespersons for the family; alternatively, they simply act as car
drivers, taking their young people to the hospital.

Paternal involvement in non-routine visits to health professionals is
characteristic of the households of parents not born in the UK. Maternal
involvement is also common in these households, in that mothers often
accompany their daughters into the doctors' consulting rooms.[16] A
mother is asked why the father took the son to the hospital when he was
concussed in the school playground. In reply, she says:

> If it's anything major we (both parents) went with them. Let's put it like
> that.

Some mothers born outside the UK spoke English less well than the
fathers, a factor which may account for the emphasis on the fathers' role
in making contact with the health services. However, even where language
is not a problem, a division of labour exists by which the non-UK-born
mothers deal with intra-household matters and fathers negotiate relationships with the external world. A mother from the Middle East whose

daughter developed a mouth infection needing urgent treatment is asked why her husband rather than she took the daughter to the dentist. In reply, she refers to her status of mother-at-home and the exclusive burden of household work, thereby implying that the negotiation of the world outside the household is not her role but the father's:

> If I go with her, half the day is gone and I have so many things to do in the house.

But instances of serious problems when fathers accompany their young people to hospital are not confined to families of Asian or Middle East origin. For example, a UK-born retired council worker, born and brought up in West London, describes how he offered to accompany his son on his hospital follow-up visit in connection with a fainting fit. His son did not, however, take up his father's offer.

Conclusion

The extent to which young people and their parents report the former's illness varies significantly by sex, with young women more likely to be ill. Young women also use both primary and secondary health care more frequently than young men. The reported health problems of young men disproportionately involve accidents.

Our data are comparable with those from other sources and national surveys. For example, according to the 1989 *General Household Survey* (OPCS, 1991), long-standing illness was reported for 21 per cent of males and 16 per cent of females aged 5–15. The same source gives an average of three GP consultations per year for those in the age range 5–15, with hospitalization as in-patients reported for 7 per cent of males and 5 per cent of females. Most studies of accidents report roughly twice the rate for young men as for young women (see, for example, British Medical Council, 1990).

While it may appear that at 16 going to the doctor is the young person's preserve, this assumption needs to be contextualized in the household within which young people's illness 'careers' develop. In common with other studies of parental health care (Graham, 1984; Mayall, 1986), our study finds that mothers play a key role in the care of young people's health problems. Particularly crucial is mothers' role in identifying the early signs of illness, and in prompting young people to seek treatment for their conditions. Moreover, in the case of serious or significant illness, mothers accompany their children, and especially their daughters, to the doctor. Where illness is relatively minor or involves follow-up GP appointments, parents and young people negotiate intermediate strategies. These enable young people to exercise autonomy in managing their own illnesses. For example, young people help themselves to medication in the home at the same time as making a public announcement that they are doing so. Or, in the case of follow-up visits to the doctor, young people may attend the GP's surgery alone or go into the consulting room while their mothers wait outside.

Fathers' role in young people's illness is marginal and limited to exceptional circumstances. Their role is often managed by mothers. Fathers born outside the UK especially are required to act as public spokespersons when young people have accidents and/or need hospital treatment. In addition, fathers are called on where their sons have problems relating to their male bodily identity.

A number of factors to do with gender, culture and social class differentiate negotiations concerning young people's ill health in the context of the household. On the one hand, young women appear to be more autonomous than young men when it comes to treating their own illness, while, on the other hand, young women are more likely than young men to be accompanied by their mothers on visits to the doctor. Relevant here is the gender combination of the parent and child – mothers and daughters. Culture is also important; parents born outside the UK are more likely than UK-born parents to chaperon young people on visits to the doctor, especially daughters. Labour-market status is significant, with young people more likely to attend the GP alone when they have left school, in contrast to those who remain in full-time education.

Notes

1 The following table lists reported long-term or recurrent illness by frequency of visits to GP:

	Young women %	Young men %
With no reported illness		
Frequency of visits to GP		
Not at all	16	23
1–2 times	52	51
3–4 times	18	20
5 or more times	14	6
Base	207	308
Some reported illness		
Frequency of visits to GP		
Not at all	6	14
1–2 times	39	42
3–4 times	31	26
5 or more times	24	18
Base	155	169

$p < 0.05$

2 Differences are significant with respect to fathers' occupations for young men and young women, but only for young men with respect to mothers' occupations.

3 The following table shows young people's education/employment plans by reported state of health (questionnaire survey):

| | Reported state of health | | | | |
| | good | fairly good | not good | not sure | |
Intending to:	%	%	%	%	Base
Stay in education	41	48	9	3	691
Go to work	32	50	15	4	130

4 Nine of their fathers were in manual occupations, and most of the mothers in lower-status non-manual employment.

5 Young people who are only children and those with two or more jobs while still at school report significantly higher incidence of illness than do those with siblings and those not working. Illness prevalence does not appear to be related to young people's activities, such as going out often at night, or habits such as smoking, drinking and drug-taking.

6 Differences are small, however. More young men (33 per cent) than young women (25 per cent) thought that their lifestyle was healthy. On the healthiness of diet, 20 per cent of boys and 17 per cent of young women thought their diet unhealthy; 10 per cent of both sexes thought their diet 'very healthy'.

7 Data on prescribed medicines are derived from the answers to specific questions about the contraceptive pill, medication for asthma, diabetes, valium, anti-depressants, and certain 'other' medicines. We have assumed that these were prescribed.

8 Fourteen per cent of the questionnaire sample and a quarter of the interview sample say their GPs have no appointments systems.

9 The young people's accounts with respect to their last illness produce slightly lower proportions of young people saying they made their appointments themselves (9 out of 32).

10 With respect to visits to the dentist, there are similar sex differences (51 per cent of young men go unaccompanied, versus 36 per cent of young women).

11 According to the interview data, nearly half of the young people say that they first went alone at 15–16 (19 out of 41), and slightly fewer between the ages of 12 and 14 (17 out of 41). However, more young men than young women say that they started to go alone aged 12–14 (13 out of 21 compared with 4 out of 20). As to the parents' accounts, more mention 15–16 than other ages as the age of change.

12 Fifty-four per cent of young women in the questionnaire survey who had been to the GP five or more times in the last year went alone on their last visit, compared with only 16 per cent of those who had not been in the past year. For young men, the equivalent proportions are 67 per cent and 36 per cent respectively.

13 In the questionnaire survey, 63 per cent of young women and 56 per cent of young men who reported having a recurrent or long-standing condition were accompanied by their mothers on GP visits.

14 Of those who had discussed their health with their mothers in the past year, 22 per cent had made their own appointments, compared with 30 per cent who had not. Similarly, 43 per cent of the former go unaccompanied to see the GP compared with 49 per cent of the non-discussers.

15 Eight out of 19 of those who went alone to their GP had left full-time education, compared with none (out of 18) of those whose mothers waited outside the consulting room (and 2 out of 14 of those whose mothers went into the consulting room with them).

16 Differences on this issue are not significant, with 68 per cent of the female 'other' group, 60 per cent of the female Asian group, 59 per cent of the female white group, and 52 per cent of the female black group saying that their parents go with them to the doctor. The figures for the young men are as follows: 'other', 50 per cent; Asian, 40 per cent; white, 50 per cent; and black, 27 per cent.

6 Taking risks

Although young people are one of the healthiest groups in the population as judged by mortality and health service use, there are other aspects of their health which provide an important focus for adult attention. Experimenting with risky behaviours of various kinds is probably part of growing up. But the easy availability of cigarettes, alcohol and 'recreational' drugs, combined with changes in sexual mores, presents young people in developed societies today with a whole new range of risks. The extent to which young people engage in these behaviours has become a major concern to those with a personal or professional interest in young people's health. Not only are drinking, smoking, drug-taking and some forms of sexual behaviour in themselves a risk to health, but the tendency of these risk-taking behaviours to cluster counts as an additional hazard (World Health Organization, 1989).

Examining patterns of these health-related behaviours is part of any study of young people's health. It is, however, essential to frame the focus on risks within the general context of the meanings of health to young people, and the material and cultural resources for health provided by their families and wider environments. This social context provides many of the clues to why young people behave as they do. Cigarette smoking, for example, as we shall show later in this chapter, is related to parental and peer-group smoking, and takes place in a society which continues to permit the advertising of cigarettes in public places. Indeed, young people have been shown to be particularly susceptible to the influence of cigarette advertising (*Observer*, 1992). Similarly, while young people are the target of considerable health education efforts designed to improve their diets, particularly with a view to reducing the later incidence of heart disease, diet is only one among many factors implicated in the aetiology of heart disease (Fox and Cameron, 1989).

In this chapter we describe young people's health behaviour in respect of 'risky' activities. We look at participation in these activities in relation to a variety of structural factors including gender, ethnicity, household composition, type of school and social class. In the last section of the chapter we discuss the 'clustering' of risk behaviours, and the factors associated with this.

Sexual activity

No direct questions were asked about sexual activity in the questionnaire survey, with the exception of the use of the contraceptive pill, which was included in a list of medicaments. Only 5 per cent of young women (17 white young women, one Asian and one black) report being on the pill. Sexual activity was covered in the household interviews, and here nearly two-fifths of the sample (22 out of 56) reported having already had sexual intercourse. Thirteen of these young people were below the 'legal' age of 16. Three of these young women and three of the young men, responding to a specific question, said that they consider themselves to be currently at risk of catching AIDS. Over half of those who have had sex had not used a contraceptive on the first occasion of having sex. Of the 16 who report using a contraceptive on the last occasion, nine used condoms, five took the pill and two (both young women) relied on coitus interruptus.

Diet

Researchers in the USA and Britain have noted that children and young people are adopting less 'socialized' and more 'individualized' food practices, taking snacks and informal meals rather than participating in the formal, 'sit-down' meal that takes place at regular intervals in the home (Fox and Cameron, 1989; Gardner Merchant, 1991; Perry, 1991). These findings suggest that young people and children are exerting increasing control over their diets. We examined some of these issues in the questionnaire survey, including whether young people eat regular meals, if and where they eat lunch during the school week, and their consumption of snacks and confectionery. We also look at other dietary changes made by young people, such as the adoption of vegetarianism. Lastly, we examine the quality of their diets in terms of their consumption of a range of 'healthy' and 'unhealthy' foods.

Regular meals

Gender appears to be the most striking influence on the behaviour of young people with regard to eating regular meals. Young women eat fewer regular meals than young men. Around a quarter of young women skipped breakfast, proportionately twice as many as young men. Nineteen per cent of young women, compared to 12 per cent of young men, skipped lunch at least three times. Breakfast, if taken, can be eaten by family members at different times, and most students are at school during lunchtime, so the evening meal, which is generally the meal that is most in the control of parents, is the meal most frequently taken. Seventy-one per cent of young

Table 6.1   *Frequency of meals eaten by young people in previous week by sex (per cent)*

	Breakfast		Lunch		Evening meal	
	Females	Males	Females	Males	Females	Males
Never	25	12	5	2	4	1
1–3 times	20	16	14	10	10	5
4–6 times	14	14	21	15	15	13
Every day	41	58	60	73	71	81
Base	357	476	360	473	360	472
	$p < 0.0001$		$p < 0.0005$		$p < 0.001$	

women and 81 per cent of young men report eating an evening meal every day during the past week. These figures are shown in Table 6.1.

One-tenth of all young women had no breakfast in the previous week and missed lunch up to three times, compared with 4 per cent of young men. Less than a third of young women, compared with 47 per cent of young men, consumed breakfast and lunch every day. Young women from the private school, compared with young women from the state schools, are the most abstemious about meals; only a third ate breakfast every day in the previous week, compared with 42 per cent of the state school young women, and half ate lunch regularly, compared with 62 per cent of the state school young women. By contrast, young men in the private school are the most regular meal-takers.

In addition to gender, material resources appear to play a part in how often young people eat regular meals. Those whose fathers are economically inactive (because of unemployment, sickness or retirement) are significantly less likely than those with employed fathers to take meals. By contrast, maternal employment status, parental occupation and housing tenure have no effect on the regularity of meals taken by young people. On the other hand, having one parent working full-time and another part-time is significant: just under two-thirds of young people in this group do not miss meals, compared with 45 per cent of other groups.[1]

The conscious reduction of food intake by skipping meals and/or by eating less at meals is one way of taking responsibility for one's health. For young women, going hungry is likely to be part of being slim, and thus a means of conforming to Western normative ideas of femininity. Our questionnaire data show that for young women, slimming is associated with a low level of satisfaction with body size; 42 per cent of young women compared with 29 per cent of young men are less than happy with their shape. However, among slimmers, young men and young women are equally unhappy with their appearance. Among young people who skipped meals more were slimming (45 per cent) than among those who ate regular meals (20 per cent). Young women predictably are much more likely to have tried to lose weight in the past year compared with young men (46 per cent against 16 per cent), with 10 per cent trying to lose 14 pounds or more.

No direct question was asked about the desire to put on weight, but it is significant that some of the young people of Asian origin who were later interviewed talk of their worries about being 'too skinny', and say they eat high-calorie food in order to put on weight. They are also more dissatisfied with their body image than any other ethnic group. Forty-one per cent of young women of Asian origin are fairly or very dissatisfied with their body size, compared to 24 per cent of those of all other groups. A quarter of young Asian men, compared with 16 per cent of other young men, are similarly dissatisfied.

Snacks and lunch

It is clear that those who are skipping meals are not compensating by eating snacks. Snacks, it seems, are eaten *in addition to*, rather than instead of, meals. Of those missing meals, only 45 per cent were eating snacks four or more times each week, compared with 59 per cent of those who ate regular meals.

Eating snacks and having a midday meal are activities over which young people are likely to have considerable discretion, since they are outside the jurisdiction of parents during the school day (though some parents may have prepared a packed lunch or cooked a lunch at home). The consumption of snacks (defined in the questionnaire as confectionery, crisps, etc.) is very widespread, with 89 per cent of young women and 97 per cent of young men saying they had consumed at least one such snack in the previous week, and a quarter of females and two-fifths of males consuming at least one snack every day. Particular schools have a high take-up, presumably because of 'tuck shops' or vending machines on the school premises.

The virtual demise in schools of the 'set meal' with its guaranteed nutritional standard, and its replacement by a self-service cafeteria system, has resulted in the market-led provision of cheap 'fast' foods designed to appeal to young people and provide greater individual 'choice', though the range of foods on offer is usually quite narrow. A recent study of the school meal choices made by secondary school students finds that hamburgers top the list, with health considerations coming seventh in the reasons for choosing a meal, well behind 'favourite foods', appearance, taste and price (Gardner Merchant, 1991).

Young men in the private school and young women in the four state schools are most likely to opt for 'school lunch' (54 per cent and 42 per cent, respectively), although, overall, packed lunches from home are almost as popular. In neither of the private schools do the students buy their lunch from shops outside school and, unsurprisingly, in view of the wider catchment areas for private schools, they are unlikely to go home for lunch. In contrast, a quarter of young men in the four state schools buy their lunch from a local shop (rising to 51 per cent in one school) and 5 per cent return home.[2] Again, there are wide variations between individual state schools, with 59 per cent of young women and 62 per cent of young men in one school having school lunch, compared to only 24 per cent and 20 per cent, respectively, in another.

Vegetarianism

An increasingly common way in which young people exert control over their diets, and also initiate change in the diets of their families, is to become vegetarian. Seven per cent of young people in the survey describe themselves as vegetarians, and 16 per cent describe themselves as semi-vegetarian (meaning that they avoid red meat). In keeping with the finding that young women are more likely than young men to exert control over their diets, they are also more likely to be vegetarian. One-third of young women abstained or only occasionally ate meat, and they are twice as likely to be fully vegetarian as young men (11 per cent as against 5 per cent). Some young people are moral converts to vegetarianism, while others, for example devout Hindus, are vegetarian for religious reasons. A young person who makes an individual decision to be vegetarian in a meat-eating household is in a very different position from one in a religious household where vegetarianism is practised by the whole family. Young people of Asian origin are most likely to be vegetarian; this may in part explain the high rate of vegetarianism we found in our study. Twenty-five per cent of Asian young women are totally vegetarian, and a further 35 per cent are semi-vegetarian (the comparable figures for white young women are 7 per cent and 21 per cent, and, for white young men, the group least likely to be vegetarian, 4 per cent and 8 per cent).[3]

Quality of diet

The quality and type of food eaten is important to health. Current health education guidelines in the UK recommend eating less energy-rich processed food, less fat, sugar and salt, and eating more wholefoods such as wholemeal bread, cereals, fruit and vegetables. These are the kinds of nutritional guidelines issued by bodies such as the National Advisory Committee on Nutrition Education (Health Education Council, 1983), and the DHSS Committee on Medical Aspects of Food Policy (DHSS, 1984). The NACNE report recommends, for example, a reduction of fat intake from the present average of 38 per cent of total energy intake to 30 per cent; a reduction to 20 kg of sucrose per head per year from the present 38 kg; and a trebling of fibre intake. These dietary recommendations are based on debates about the relationship between food and the aetiology of specific diseases, particularly the link between heart disease and diets high in saturated fat and salt, and low in fibre.

In order to examine the quality of young people's diets, we constructed

Table 6.2   *Unhealthy food scores by healthy food scores*

Unhealthy food scores	High	% (n)	Low	% (n)	Total % (n)
		Healthy food scores			
Low	Group 1	33 (267)	Group 3	22 (177)	55 (444)
High	Group 2	20 (155)	Group 4	25 (198)	45 (353)
Base					797

diet 'scores' based on the kinds of food young people say they eat 'most days'. We took items of food consumption which have been identified by nutritionists and government reports in the last ten years as either encouraging good health or impeding it, and we allocated numerical scores according to the young person's consumption of the 'healthy' items and avoidance of the 'less healthy'.[4] It should be noted that no attempt was made to include *all* food items, and neither was the quantity of food eaten taken into account.

The distribution of young people according to the 'healthy' food score varies significantly according to gender, father's occupation and household composition, with young women, middle-class young people, and those in two-parent households scoring significantly higher. Those obtaining the highest score include over a quarter of the young women, compared to 17 per cent of the young men; over a quarter of those with fathers in non-manual work, compared to 18 per cent of those with fathers in manual jobs, and 12 per cent of those whose fathers were not at work; and just under a quarter of those with two parents, compared to 15 per cent of those in single-parent households. The proportions are almost exactly reversed for those young people who eat none of the healthy items.[5]

When it comes to the 'unhealthy' food scores, the generally high consumption of such foods by this age group is striking: almost three-quarters eat at least one 'unhealthy' item most days. Like 'healthy' foods, the distribution of unhealthy food scores is associated with class and gender, with fewer young women and young people whose fathers are in non-manual jobs eating these items on a regular basis.[6] By contrast, 50 per cent of young men consume two or more unhealthy items per day such as chips, cakes/biscuits and fizzy drinks. Those whose fathers are unemployed are most likely to consume these items frequently.

The scores for the regular consumption of the 'healthy' and 'unhealthy' foods are combined in Table 6.2 to give an overall picture of young people's diets. Group 1, with high scores on healthy food and low scores on unhealthy food, is the largest and healthiest group and accounts for one-third of young people; those in this group eat two or more of the healthy items most days and one or none of the unhealthy sweet or fatty foods. Conversely, the 25 per cent of young people in group 4, the second largest group, are the least healthy, eating only one or none of the three healthy food items and anything between two and five of the sweet or fatty foods. Groups 2 and 3 represent those young people who eat a mixture of healthy and unhealthy items, and those who eat neither, respectively.

As we have already seen, patterns of eating are heavily influenced by gender and class. Almost half the young women (44 per cent) but only a quarter of the young men are located in the healthiest group and, conversely, the least healthy group includes 18 per cent of the young women but 30 per cent of the young men.[7] When type of father's or mother's occupation is taken into account, middle-class young women are found to have the healthiest diets; over half are in group 1, compared with a third of middle-class males and working-class females, and only a fifth of working-class young men. The positions are reversed with respect to the unhealthiest group; over a third of young men whose fathers are in manual occupations or are non-employed are in this group, compared to a tenth of the middle-class young women. Group 3, those who score low on both healthy and unhealthy foods, differs significantly from the other groups in ways which suggest that this group is materially less well off than the others. For example, 18 per cent have no family car compared with 10 per cent in group 1, 9 per cent in group 2, and 12 per cent in group 4; in addition, 44 per cent of those living in households with one parent in part-time work, and over 30 per cent of those with no parent in employment fall in this diet group.

School type, which is associated with social class, also distinguishes between the unhealthy and healthy: 66 per cent of private school young women are in the healthy group and only one out of 70 pupils is in the unhealthy group; these figures compare with 39 per cent and 22 per cent, respectively, for the state school young women. For young men the differences are less marked but still significant. Even controlling for fathers' class, there are still significant differences for both young men and young women by school type, with private school pupils whose fathers are in high-status occupations more likely to be in the healthy eating group, compared with similar pupils in the state education sector.

There are links between diet and ethnic background, with 'other' and Asian young men significantly more likely to be in the healthiest diet group than white and black young men. Conversely, less than 20 per cent of Asian and 'other' young men are in the unhealthiest diet group, compared with 42 per cent of black young men and 33 per cent of white young men. Taking gender and household composition together, those young women who live with their lone mothers are less likely than those who live in two-parent households to be in the healthy group.

The quality of food ingested is related in part to the practices of dietary control we discussed above. Those young people in the unhealthy group are most likely to be eating snacks every day. Moreover, students who take a packed lunch to school, or who eat breakfast, lunch and evening meal on a regular basis, tend to be in the healthiest diet group compared with

Table 6.3   *Smoking habits by sex, ethnicity and type of school*

Sex, ethnicity and school type	Base	Never smoked %	Past smoker %	Current smoker %		Mean number smoked Yesterday	Past week
All females	353	32	38	30	p < 0.0001	6.8	34.7
All males	463	42	40	17		6.8	39.2
By ethnicity							
Asian	144	65	25	10	p ≪ 0.0001	4.1	19.4
White	522	32	40	28		7.7	41.0
Black	85	31	47	22		4.5	25.3
Other	60	35	50	15		2.6	13.3
By education							
Females							
state	282	32	38	30	ns	7.5	36.8
private	71	35	37	28		3.6	26.0
Males							
state	339	42	42	16	ns	8.6	45.9
private	124	43	35	22		3.2	26.6

those who have the school lunch provided or who regularly skip meals. Membership of the healthiest diet group is statistically related to being vegetarian.

Young people's perceptions of the quality of their diets may, however, bear little relationship to their content. Of the young people who are in the unhealthiest diet group (group 4), 55 per cent judge their diets to be 'very' or 'quite' healthy, and another 9 per cent are not sure. In particular, three-fifths of young men rated as having poor diets appear to disagree; they have positive perceptions of what they eat. Only the perceptions of those with the healthiest diets (group 1) are in keeping with their actual diet scores.

Smoking[8]

Smoking among young people is increasingly a female rather than a male activity. Thirty per cent of young women and 17 per cent of young men in our questionnaire survey report that they are current smokers, while 42 per cent of young men and 32 per cent of young women claim never to have smoked. On the other hand, slightly fewer young women (38 per cent) than young men (40 per cent) describe themselves as experimental smokers, that is, as only having smoked once or twice, or having smoked regularly in the past. The figures are given in Table 6.3.

There are very marked differences between the ethnic groups in our study with respect to smoking. Only 10 per cent of Asian young people currently smoke, compared with 28 per cent of whites, 22 per cent of blacks and 15 per cent of the 'other' group. Within ethnic groups, only among whites are there significant differences by gender, with twice as many young women as young men smoking.

School type makes little difference in smoking rates for young women, but 22 per cent of young men at the private school currently smoke, compared with only 16 per cent at state schools. Taking the mean number smoked yesterday, both sexes say they smoked 6.8 cigarettes. Among private school pupils, 40 per cent of young women and 44 per cent of young men smoked only one or no cigarettes yesterday compared with 16 per cent of young women, and 7 per cent of young men in the state schools (not shown in table). With respect to ethnicity, the 'other' group smoked the least, averaging 2.6 in the past 24 hours, compared with 4.1 for Asians, 4.5 for blacks, and 7.7 for whites. These differences by sex, school and ethnicity are repeated when cigarette consumption over the past seven days is examined. However, a comparison between smoking rates reported for yesterday and those reported over the past seven days yields considerable inconsistency. In 25 per cent of cases, the number smoked over the week is less than the daily average over the past week, and in 68 per cent of cases the number smoked yesterday is above the previous week's daily average. There are two ways of interpreting this; either cigarette smoking among young people is not a regular habit, and varies from day to day, or there is a tendency for young people to underestimate their weekly rate. These two explanations are, of course, not mutually exclusive.

There are some interesting variations in smoking rates by household composition. Smoking is lowest overall among young people living with both parents, and highest among those living with lone fathers (though the number in the latter group is very small). Smoking among young women appears to be more 'responsive' than smoking among young men to differences in household composition, with the lowest rate (25 per cent) in mother–father households and the highest rate in lone-father households (five of the six cases).

The known association between the smoking habits of young people and parental smoking (see, for example, Baric, 1979; Murray *et al.*, 1983; Green *et al.*, 1991; Sharpe and Oakley, 1991) is statistically significant for young women but not for young men in our study. Smoking is marginally more prevalent among those reporting one or both parents smoking (29 per cent) than among those who report neither parent smoking (20 per cent). However, 47 per cent of young people who smoke (44 per cent of young women and 51 per cent of young men) have parents who are both non-smokers. There is also evidence of a reverse relationship in some households – parental smoking promotes strong anti-smoking feelings among young people, and therefore makes their taking up smoking less likely (see Oakley *et al.*, 1992).

Parents do not necessarily know about young people smoking: 26 per cent of young women and 34 per cent of young men say that their parents are unaware of their smoking, while 19 per cent of young women and 20 per cent of young men say that they do not know whether their parents know. Fifty-six per cent of young women who smoke and 46 per cent of young men say that their parents know about their smoking. Only a very small proportion of both sexes (6 per cent) say that their parents are in agreement with their smoking, while 12 per cent say they 'sometimes' agree; the largest group (39 per cent) of young people have parents who are said to disagree, while the rest 'don't know' or say their parents are unaware of their habit.

Social class overall, as measured by maternal or paternal occupation, is unrelated to young people's smoking, although there are some differences by housing tenure. There are no differences in the smoking habits of young people by the employment status of their parents. On the other hand, there is some link between young people's own access to income (through pocket money and paid work) and whether they smoke: mean average income is higher for those currently smoking than for non-smokers. Forty per cent of young women who have regular paid jobs smoke, compared with 21 per cent of those with no job, but there is no difference for young men. Plans for the future also show association with smoking rates. In the state schools, 26 per cent of young women and 10 per cent of young men intending to stay in full-time education smoke, compared with 54 per cent of young women and 32 per cent of young men intending to enter paid work or employment training at the end of the fifth year. Not only are smokers more prevalent among those who are planning to leave full-time education, but they also smoke more heavily. Young men average 48 cigarettes a week compared with 30 for those staying in education, while girl leavers average 38 a week compared with 32 for those intending to remain in education.

Evidence from the survey suggests that teenage smokers are aware of the health risks associated with smoking. When asked to think about their futures and which three items from a given list they worry about, 28 per cent of smokers include cancer as one of their worries, compared with only 17 per cent of non-smokers. (By contrast, there are no differences between smokers and non-smokers concerning worries about death and AIDS.) Furthermore, non-smokers are significantly more likely than smokers to assess their way of life as healthy: 30 per cent of female non-smokers and 36 per cent of male non-smokers describe their lifestyles as healthy, compared with 14 per cent of female smokers and 20 per cent of male smokers.

Alcohol consumption

In the questionnaire survey, we asked young people on how many days in the previous week they drank any alcohol. The results are shown in Table 6.4. Over one-half of young people had consumed no alcohol. In contrast with smoking, there is little difference between the sexes, with 52 per cent

Table 6.4 *Number of days on which alcohol was consumed in the previous week by sex, ethnicity and type of school*

	Number of days last week alcohol drunk					
	0	1	2–4	5 or more		
	%	%	%	%	Base	
Females	52	27	19	2	347	ns
Males	54	22	21	3	446	
Asian	78	16	6	0	141	$p < 0.0001$
White	44	28	25	3	506	
Black	56	24	19	1	84	
Other	65	20	15	0	59	
State	55	24	19	2	604	$p < 0.01$
Private	45	24	26	4	189	

of young women and 53 per cent of young men having had no alcohol in the previous seven days.

Young men who reported drinking alcohol did so more frequently than the young women who drank; differences are not significant, however, with 27 per cent of young women having alcohol on only one day compared with 22 per cent of young men. Only 2 per cent of young women and 3 per cent of young men had alcohol on five or more days. Young men also consume more alcohol than young women: the average for young men is 6.6 units over the week compared with 4.9 for young women. Only 9 per cent of young women consume more than 7 units in the week compared with 16 per cent of young men. If units are related to the number of days in which alcohol is taken, then 22 per cent of young men and 24 per cent of young women average only one unit per alcohol-drinking day. At the other extreme, 21 per cent of young men and 12 per cent of young women average 5 units or more per drinking day.

Most male drinkers choose beer, lager or cider (77 per cent) compared with less than a third (32 per cent) of females. Wine is more popular with young women, 48 per cent having drunk some wine in the past week, compared with 38 per cent of young men. (Nineteen per cent of young women drank wine only, compared with 10 per cent of young men.) Overall, 64 per cent of the drinking young men drank only beer, lager, cider or wine, compared with only 31 per cent of young women, the latter favouring wine, ordinary and fortified, and spirits.

With respect to ethnicity, the white group are more likely than other groups to have consumed alcohol: 56 per cent had drunk alcohol in the past week, compared to 44 per cent of blacks, 35 per cent of the 'other' group, and only 22 per cent of Asians. Similarly, whites took alcohol on more days than the other groups, with the Asians having alcohol on the smallest number of days.

Social class makes some difference to the chances of young people reporting drinking alcohol. Those with fathers or mothers in high-status occupations are more likely to say they drink. School type makes a difference, too, but only for young men, with 59 per cent of private school boys drinking, compared with 47 per cent of state pupils.

In general, drinking alcohol appears to be highly associated with drinking at home and with having parents who also drink alcohol. Among those parents who were interviewed, most mothers (41 out of 55) and all but one father drank occasionally or regularly. The great majority of young people who consumed alcohol in the past week report drinking at home (81 per cent of young men and 84 per cent of young women). Consistent with this finding is the fact that over half the drinkers had not been to a pub in the previous week (54 per cent of young women and 56 per cent of young men). Moreover, those who drink a lot (15 units or more) or who drink moderately (3–7 units) also drink at home.

Not only is drinking alcohol associated with drinking at home, it is also associated with parental knowledge and, to some extent, their agreement. Over half of those who consumed alcohol in the past week (56 per cent of young women and 53 per cent of young men) say that their parents always know about their drinking, while a further 30 per cent of both sexes say that their parents sometimes know. Only around 8 per cent say that their parents never know. Not surprisingly, few parents are said to disagree with young people drinking (7 per cent) and a further 59 per cent are said to 'sometimes agree'.

Drugs

Young people were asked in the questionnaire which drugs on a given list[9] they regarded as dangerous or safe, which they had been offered, which they had used and whether they knew anyone who took any of the drugs on the list. Around 25 per cent of young people said they had used one of the drugs, with the percentage slightly higher for young women than young men (see Table 6.5). Half the drug use reported in the questionnaire data was confined to cannabis, with over 20 per cent of both sexes, and 29 per cent of private school pupils, having tried this. If those who have tried *only* cannabis are excluded, then only 13 per cent of young women and 11 per cent of young men have experience of using other drugs. Only 15 individuals in our sample of 843 young people have tried cocaine or heroin.

Table 6.5 shows that gender does not appear to discriminate with respect to either being offered or using drugs. But as regards ethnicity, whites and blacks are more likely to report being offered drugs (43 per cent and 46 per cent, respectively) than Asians (24 per cent) or the 'other' group (34 per cent). On drug use, whites top the list, with 28 per cent having tried one of the drugs listed, compared with 24 per cent of blacks, 22 per cent of the 'other' group, and only 11 per cent of the Asians. There are no significant differences by gender within the ethnic groups.

Table 6.5 *Percentages ever offered or using drugs, by sex and type of school*

	Females %	Males %	Females v Males	State %	Private %	State v Private
Offered drugs	38	40	ns	35	53	$p \ll 0.0001$
Solvents	7	7		7	6	ns
Stimulants[a]	9	8		8	10	ns
Cannabis[b]	34	35		30	49	$p \ll 0.0001$
Hard drugs[c]	10	8		7	15	$p < 0.001$
Hallucinogens[d]	16	19		15	25	$p < 0.005$
Used drugs	25	24	ns	22	31	$p < 0.05$
Solvents	3	3		4	< 1	$p < 0.01$
Stimulants	5	2		3	3	ns
Cannabis	21	22		19	29	$p < 0.005$
Hard drugs	3	1		2	1	ns
Hallucinogens	5	6		5	7	ns
Base	362	481		640	203	

[a]Amphetamines, barbiturates and tranquillizers.
[b]Leaf, oil and resin.
[c]Natural and synthetic.
[d]Heroin and cocaine.

Over half of the private school pupils (53 per cent) had been offered drugs, compared with only 35 per cent of state school pupils; private school pupils are also more heavily involved in drug use: 31 per cent compared with 22 per cent of state pupils. No significant differences are found by gender within the two types of school. There are significant differences by household composition, with those living in lone parent or step-parent households reporting a higher incidence of drugs being offered and of using drugs than those living with both biological parents (33 per cent against 21 per cent). There are significant differences, too, by mothers' occupational class but not by fathers', with 48 per cent of state school pupils with mothers in high-status occupations reporting that they had been offered drugs, compared with only 33 per cent of those whose mothers are in low-status occupations. Twenty-seven per cent of the former had also used drugs, compared with 21 per cent of the latter.

Do health-related activities cluster?

The correlations between smoking, alcohol use, drug-taking and poor diet are shown in Table 6.6. Smoking and drug use are the most highly correlated at 0.6, with somewhat lower correlations between alcohol and smoking, and between alcohol and drug use. The sex of the young person makes little difference to the strength of these associations. With respect to diet, there appears to be little association between unhealthy diet and other behaviours, although for young men alcohol and diet are statistically linked.

Table 6.6   *Correlation between poor diet, smoking, drinking and drug use*

		Poor diet	Smoking	Alcohol
Smoking	Female	0.12		
	Male	0.11		
Alcohol	Female	0.05	0.47**	
	Male	0.12*	0.34**	
Drug use	Female	0.05	0.60**	0.39**
	Male	0.02	0.61**	0.38**

*$p < 0.01$; **$p < 0.001$

Table 6.7   *Patterns of smoking, drinking alcohol (in past week) and use of drugs (ever) by sex and type of school (per cent)*

	Females			Males		
	All %	State %	Private %	All %	State %	Private %
No smoking, drinking or drugs	42	43	41	43	46	36
Smoker only	3	3	3	1	2	0
Alcohol only	21	21	20	27	26	27
Drugs only	3	3	3	3	4	2
Smoker and drinker	9	10	6	4	4	4
Drinker and drug-user	4	3	8	9	7	14
Smoker and drug-user	2	3	–	3	2	5
All three	15	14	20	9	8	13
Base	353	282	71	463	339	124
		ns			$p < 0.05$	

The ways in which young people combine the different activities of smoking, drinking alcohol and trying drugs can be seen in Table 6.7. Just under half of young people engage in none of the activities (43 per cent overall, but rising to 69 per cent of Asian-origin students). The next largest group confine themselves to drinking alcohol only (27 per cent of the young men and 21 per cent of the young women), with the only other substantial groups either engaging in all three activities (9 per cent of young men and 15 per cent of young women) or, in the case of young people in private schools, drinking and taking drugs (14 per cent of the males and 8 per cent of the females). Smoking is highly correlated with other activities; only 2 per cent of young people overall are 'only smokers' and 3 per cent have only tried drugs. In other words, the activities traditionally regarded as 'risky' items in the health behaviour of young people do tend to cluster.

In view of this clustering of 'risky activities', we have combined the data to produce four separate groups of young people: the non-risk-takers, and the groups involved in one, two or all three activities. Cross-tabulations shown in Table 6.8 with a large number of variables indicate that ethnicity is by far the most important socio-demographic characteristic distinguishing the 'low-risk' from 'higher-risk' groups. Young people of Asian origin are least likely to smoke, drink or try drugs; two-thirds of this group are abstainers, compared with just over a third of white and black young people. Social class, whether established by fathers' or mothers' occupation or housing tenure, is not significant, and neither is household composition. Sex is not significant, except among white young people, where young women are most likely to be involved in all three 'risk' activities.

There are no differences between the different risk groups in their desire for more information about stress and depression, nor in their expressed satisfaction with life in general. Significant differences do appear, however, in satisfaction with school achievement, with 65 per cent of those indulging in none of the risky activities expressing satisfaction with their achievement at school compared with only 40 per cent of those who engage in all three activities.[10] These differences are significant for those young people who are intending to continue in education beyond the fifth year, as well as those planning to leave education. While most young people in the highest-risk group view their lifestyles as both healthy and unhealthy, young women, but not young men, are more likely to perceive their lifestyles as unhealthy, and also to fear a great deal the possibility of AIDS.[11]

While normative stereotypes of young people's lifestyles portray smoking, drinking and trying drugs as a significant part of adolescent social life, our figures show that this picture fits only a minority of young people. There is, however, a significant link between these activities and patterns of young people's sociability. Whether measured by going to a party or a pub in the last week, 'walking around' or visiting friends, spending most of one's time with friends rather than family, or spending more than two evenings out a week, smoking, drinking and taking drugs are more likely among the more sociable young people in our sample. This is one reason underlying the link between these activities and ethnicity shown in Table 6.8; young people of Asian origin, especially Asian young women, are particularly likely to be discouraged by their parents from going out at night and, in practice, are highly likely to stay at home (see Chapter 7). A 'sociability score' based on degree of association with friends reveals that 56 per cent of low sociability scorers abstain from smoking, drinking alcohol (in the previous week) and have never tried drugs, compared to 22 per cent of those with high scores. Conversely, only 5 per cent of low scorers are involved in all three activities, compared with just under a third of those with high sociability scores. Table 6.9 shows the relevant figures. Young women are slightly more likely than young men to have high sociability scores and to be indulging in all three 'risk' activities (not shown in table).

Sociability among young people is also associated with availability of

Table 6.8   *Percentages engaged in 'risk' activities (smoking, drinking alcohol, in the previous week, and trying drugs) by ethnicity*

Number of 'risk' activities	Asian % (n)	White % (n)	Black % (n)	Other % (n)	All % (n)
None	69 (99)	35 (183)	42 (36)	50 (30)	43 (348)
One	19 (28)	31 (164)	32 (27)	33 (20)	29 (239)
Two	9 (13)	18 (96)	18 (15)	8 (5)	16 (129)
Three	3 (4)	15 (79)	8 (7)	8 (5)	12 (95)
Base	144	522	85	60	811

$p \ll 0.0001$

Table 6.9   *Engagement in 'risk' activities, by degree of sociability with friends*

	Sociability			
	Low	Medium	High	All
Number of 'risk' activities	% (n)	% (n)	% (n)	% (n)
None	56 (205)	35 (111)	22 (27)	43 (343)
One	29 (104)	32 (100)	24 (30)	29 (234)
Two	10 (38)	19 (59)	24 (30)	16 (127)
Three	5 (17)	14 (43)	29 (36)	12 (96)
Base	364	313	123	800

$p \ll 0.0001$

money. Those who are given, or who earn, more than £20 a week are significantly more likely to report two or more 'risky activities'.

Conclusion

Most of the findings reported on in this chapter come from the schools questionnaire survey which shows that a significant proportion of young people engage in one or more of those risk-taking behaviours identified in health education campaigns targeted at young people. For example, a third of the young women and somewhat less than one in four of the young men say they are regular smokers. About half of both sexes said they had drunk some alcohol in the previous week; the young men who drink do so more heavily than the young women. One in four young men and women report using drugs. However, half this drug use is confined to cannabis. Being offered drugs is twice as common as using them. Only 2 per cent of our sample reported having used hard drugs such as heroin and cocaine. In relation to dietary practices, skipping one or another meal every day is relatively common, especially among young women. The majority of both sexes admit to consuming unhealthy snacks regularly. Almost half of the young women, but only about one in six of the young men, have tried to lose weight recently; nearly half of young women, but less than a third of young men, say they are unhappy with their body size. Dividing our sample of young people into four groups according to the amount of healthy and unhealthy foods reported in their diets, the largest group (33 per cent of the total) is healthy. Only 25 per cent have high unhealthy food and low healthy food scores. The rest fall in between. Two-fifths of our interview sample of 15–16-year-olds report having had sexual intercourse, and over half of these had not used contraception when they first had sex.

We only collected a small amount of data on physical activity. In the questionnaire, we asked about the frequency of taking vigorous exercise, engaging in 'keep fit' exercises or swimming in the preceding week. Over 63 per cent of young women and 46 per cent of young men said they had not engaged in sporting activities, or had done so only once during the week. However, these responses reflect differences between the practices of the different schools, including within the group of state schools. Moreover, with the exception of two state schools in which physical activity was low, young men were significantly more likely than girls to engage in sports.

Since our questionnaire drew upon a health behaviour questionnaire widely used in schools in the UK (Balding, 1989), it is possible to compare our results with these data. Many of our findings are broadly in line with Balding's, and with those of other researchers. Overall, when compared with Balding's surveys, the smoking rates of young people in our study (30 per cent of young women and 17 per cent of young men) are very similar so far as the young men are concerned, but are significantly higher for young women. If we compare the white-only sample of state school pupils with Balding's results, we get an even bigger discrepancy between the two, with 19 per cent of young men and 38 per cent of young women having smoked the previous day as compared with Balding's 15 per cent for young men and 21 per cent for young women. The national figures for England and Wales in 1988 among 11–15-year-olds are 12 per cent for young men and 14 per cent for young women (Central Statistical Office, 1991). Lader and Matheson (1990) found that 25 per cent of both young men and young women in the fifth year were regular smokers and a further 10 per cent were occasional smokers. A survey of six inner London comprehensives reports a higher figure, with 31 per cent of 16-year-olds currently smoking (Swadi, 1988).

With respect to alcohol consumption, Balding's rates are somewhat higher than those found in our study; 76 per cent of young men and 68 per cent of young women took alcohol 'in the previous week' in Balding's sample schools, compared with 47 per cent and 48 per cent, respectively, in our survey. The rates from the national study by Lader and Matheson (1990) are nearer to our own, however, with 42 per cent of young men and 39 per cent of young women in the fifth year having drunk alcohol in a similar period.

Comparing the rates of illegal drug use in our survey with those reported by Balding, we found a higher proportion of young people being offered, as well as trying, drugs (24 per cent). The take-up rate, i.e. the ratio of drugs ever having been used to drugs ever having been offered, is also higher for our survey than for Balding's surveys. Again, our results are closer to those found in Swadi's inner London study, which reports 26 per cent of 15–16-year-olds having ever used drugs. Moreover, 8 per cent have used hard drugs and 21 per cent cannabis, compared with 7 per cent and 18 per cent, respectively, in our study (Swadi, 1988).

As to sexual activity, two-fifths of the relatively small interview sample of young people reported having experienced sexual intercourse, a somewhat lower proportion than that found by other researchers (see, for example, Bowie and Ford, 1989; Holland *et al.*, 1992). A nationally representative survey of 16–19-year-olds conducted in 1990 reports that 31 per cent of both sexes had experienced sexual intercourse by this age (Health Education Authority, 1992).

Our findings concerning diet suggest that our young people have healthier diets than do those surveyed by Balding, with lower consumption of unhealthy items and higher percentages claiming to eat healthier foods on 'most days'. It is arguable that vegetarianism can be considered a measure of a healthy diet since it presupposes a high consumption of fresh fruit and vegetables. In our survey, 7 per cent of young people described themselves as vegetarians, and a further 16 per cent as semi-vegetarians. The best estimate of vegetarianism for the UK population aged 16 and over is 4 per cent rising to 10 per cent if semi-vegetarians are included (Beardsworth and Keil, 1992), while a survey for the Vegetarian Society (1991) cites 8 per cent for the 11–18 age group. Higher rates are reported by the HEA (1992) survey, with 12 per cent of young women aged 16–19 vegetarian or vegan compared with only 4 per cent of young men, an even higher ratio of young women to young men than we found in our survey (11 per cent as against 5 per cent).

In comparing our findings with those of other researchers, three factors in particular need to be borne in mind. First of all, our survey was conducted in London; this would be expected to raise the rates of risk-taking behaviour. Second, a significant proportion of our sample was made up of relatively healthy young people from ethnic minorities: this would be expected to have the opposite effect, that is, to lower estimates of risk. Third, with the exception of data concerning sexual intercourse, the data drawn on in this chapter come from a questionnaire survey, not from face-to-face interviews. Systematic comparison of the two methods of data collection shows that generally higher estimates of risk-taking behaviour are likely to be derived from questionnaire than from interview data (see Oakley *et al.*, 1990).

Comparison between the two sources of data in our study is complicated by the time gap (which varied from six to 15 months) between the survey and the household interviews. Two of the young people who described themselves as never having smoked in the interview claimed to be past smokers on the questionnaire. Four 'new' smokers at the time of the interview were previously reported as past smokers. Cigarette consumption can be compared for weekly use in only 11 cases; in seven, weekly consumption had increased between the questionnaire and the interview, for three it had decreased, and in one case it remained the same. Of 49 interviewees who answered questions on alcohol consumption in both the survey and the interview, ten classified themselves as non-drinkers and 25 as drinkers in both the interviews and the questionnaires. No one previously drinking came out as non-drinking at the interview. Fourteen young people classified as non-drinkers on the questionnaire had become drinkers by the interview. The number claiming to know people taking drugs increased from 30 to 41 between the questionnaire and the interview, with four who had previously claimed acquaintance with drug users denying this at the interview. The number admitting to ever using drugs is also higher at interview – a rise from 13 to 15. Since the data show that exposure to drugs increases over time, these are almost certainly cases in which 'real' drug use is denied in the interview situation.

These differences between questionnaire and interview data are chiefly of methodological interest to those carrying out research in this field. But they are important if the aim is to obtain the most reliable estimates possible of young people's health-related behaviours. Of more substantive interest are our findings concerning the link between various cultural factors and the extent to which young people take risks with their health. We found a consistent tendency for risk-taking to be more highly concentrated among white young people and least so among Asian young people.

Material factors are also significant, though the relationship here is more complex. To some extent, smoking functions, as it does for adults, as a marker of both low social class and high life stress; this is particularly so for young women. Poverty and poor diet are more directly linked. Eating healthy foods is more likely to be found among middle-class young people, an association which may relate to household income and, since young people also eat independently of their households, to personal income. Lack of resources is likely to reduce young people's 'choice' over more expensive food items such as fresh fruit. However, cultural and gender preferences also emerge as significant, with young women more likely than young men to eat a healthy diet. Moreover, Asian and 'other' young men are in the healthiest group compared with white young men and black young men; no differences were found with respect to young women here.

Participation in 'risk' activities – smoking, alcohol and drugs – is structured by cultural factors, with Asian young people considerably less likely to engage in smoking, alcohol consumption and drugs and white young people most likely to engage. Material resources are also relevant, with young people from private schools and those with higher personal disposable income more likely to participate. For example, smoking rates among the young people in our study clearly reflect levels of disposable income and are higher in private schools. Drug-taking is the outstanding example of an income-dependent habit: over half of the private school pupils say they have been offered drugs, compared to a third of the state school pupils; and nearly a third in private schools, but less than a quarter in state schools, report having tried them.

The relationship between engaging in risk activities and personal income is, moreover, complicated by cultural factors. Among Asian young people, low engagement in risk activities is not necessarily associated with low personal income though the pattern is rather different for young Asian women than it is for young Asian males. By contrast, among white young people, high disposable income is associated with engagement in several risk activities.

Notes

1 The following table shows frequency of meals by parental employment patterns:

	Frequency of meals			
Parental employment	Few taken %	Some taken %	Most taken %	Base
None/one part-time	19	36	45	96
One full-time	19	37	43	216
One full-time and one part-time	10	30	60	229
Two full-time	12	42	46	249

$p < 0.005$

2 The following table shows type of lunch by sex and type of school:

	Females		Males	
Type of lunch	State %	Private %	State %	Private %
School lunch	42	33	37	54
Packed lunch	40	54	32	44
Out to shop	10	–	24	1
At home	4	–	5	–
No lunch	3	12	2	1
Base	289	72	347	131

$p < 0.0001$ $p < 0.0001$

3 The following table gives a breakdown of the extent of vegetarianism by sex and ethnicity:

	Females				Males			
	Veg. %	Semi-veg. %	Meat %	Base	Veg. %	Semi-veg. %	Meat %	Base
Asian	25	35	40	57	9	26	65	89
White	7	21	72	228	4	8	88	302
Black	2	17	81	42	6	12	81	48
Other	22	22	56	32	–	10	90	31
	$p \ll 0.0001$				$p < 0.0001$			

4 For food items high in fibre and vitamins (wholemeal bread, fresh fruit and vegetables) a score of 1 was allocated, giving a range of 0–3. A score in the range 0–5 was given for unhealthy food items consumed 'every day' – that is, those items high in fat or sugar (chips, crisps, cakes/biscuits, confectionery and fizzy drinks). Young people scoring 2 or more are thus considered to have a diet high in fat and sugar and those scoring 0 or 1 a diet comparatively low in fat and sugar content.

5 The following table gives the number of unhealthy items eaten most days by sex, household type and father's occupation:

	Number of 'unhealthy' foods eaten most days						
	0 %	1 %	2 %	3 %	4 %	5 %	Base
Sex[a]							
Females	36	26	16	13	7	1	352
Males	21	29	20	17	9	4	461
Household type[b]							
Two parents resident	26	28	19	16	8	3	661
One parent resident	34	26	17	13	9	1	151
Father's occupation[c]							
non-manual	31	32	16	12	8	2	299
manual	22	26	22	20	6	4	310
not employed	23	23	20	13	18	3	39

[a]$p \ll 0.0001$; [b]ns; [c]$p < 0.005$

6 The following table gives the number of healthy food items eaten most days by
sex, household type, and father's occupation:

| | Number of 'healthy' foods eaten most days | | | | |
	0 %	1 %	2 %	3 %	Base
Sex[a]					
Females	14	22	36	27	346
Males	25	29	29	17	469
Household type[b]					
Two parents resident	18	26	33	23	665
One parent resident	29	29	26	15	149
Father's occupation[c]					
non-manual	14	23	35	28	303
manual	24	29	29	18	307
not employed	27	27	32	12	40

[a]$p \ll 0.0001$; [b]$p < 0.001$; [c]$p < 0.001$

7 The following table gives diet scores according to healthy and unhealthy items
eaten most days by sex and father's occupation:

| | Middle class | | Working class | | Non-employed | | All | |
	Females %	Males %	Females %	Males %	Females %	Males %	Females %	Males %
Group 1	58	32	35	21	46	13	44	25
Group 2	16	21	20	20	38	17	19	20
Group 3	17	21	20	23	8	33	19	25
Group 4	9	26	25	36	8	37	18	30
Base	132	164	127	176	13	24	340	457

$p < 0.0001$ · · · · · $p < 0.05$ · · · · · $p < 0.05$ · · · · · $p \ll 0.0001$

8 For more information about smoking in this study see Oakley *et al.* (1992).
9 The list of drugs we asked about was as follows:

amphetamines (speed/stimulants/uppers);
barbiturates (downers/barbies/sleepers);
cannabis leaf, oil or resin (grass/hash/pot/leb/ black/moroccan);
cocaine (coke/crack/snow);
hallucinogens, natural and synthetic (magic mushrooms, acid/angel dust/LSD);
heroin (H/junk/skag/smack);
opiates (morphine/pethidine/diconal);
solvents (glue/gas/cleansing fluid);
tranquillizers (librium/valium).

10 The following table gives percentages of young people satisfied with their achievement at school, by involvement in 'risk' activities*

Number of 'risk' activities	Dissatisfied with achievement %	Not sure %	Satisfied with achievement %	Base
None	19	16	65	350
One	22	16	62	239
Two	36	18	46	130
Three	39	22	40	96

*$p \ll 0.0001$

11 The following table gives an assessment of healthiness of lifestyle and fear of catching AIDS, by involvement in risk activities by sex:

	Number of risk activities				
	0 %	1 %	2 %	3 %	
Assessment of lifestyle					
Females					$p < 0.005$
healthy	31	30	23	8	
mixed	67	67	71	81	
unhealthy	2	3	6	12	
Males					ns
healthy	36	35	33	20	
mixed	60	60	57	72	
unhealthy	4	5	10	8	
Fear of catching AIDS					
Females					$p \ll 0.0001$
little	47	56	58	36	
a lot	23	35	20	55	
not sure	30	9	22	9	
Males					ns
little	57	62	55	57	
a lot	20	17	31	21	
not sure	23	21	15	21	
Base					
Females	146	94	52	52	
Males	200	141	72	40	

7 Families, rules and young people

Parents' attempts to regulate their young people may have significant implications for young people's health and health-related behaviour. Drawing upon the questionnaire data, we explore in this chapter whether young people perceive themselves to be governed by parental rules and if so, in respect of which kinds of issues. We discuss whether young people believe that the delineation of rules and boundaries is 'a good idea' or not. We go on to examine how far parental rules are associated with what young people do in practice. Moving then to the interview accounts of young people and parents, we look at the different cultural values underpinning expectations concerning young people's health-related behaviour and their acquisition of greater autonomy in the transition to adulthood.

On rules and their meaning

We use the term 'household rule' to indicate parents' control over their children's behaviour (see Cunningham-Burley, 1985). The term has both a 'lay' and a technical sociological meaning. As we will go on to show, some young people limit their own behaviour whether or not they say their parents restrict them. Here young people's actions are governed by cultural expectations which are not necessarily articulated. From a sociological perspective, these expectations are conceptualized as 'normative' rather than classified as rules on the basis of actors' own accounts. It is problematic to infer in this way the existence of normative guidelines from actors' reported behaviour, as Finch (1989) points out. Here and in the following chapters we have tried to respect Finch's admonition concerning the role of rules as an *explanation*, namely that researchers should separate what people say they *believe*, from the way these beliefs may be considered to operate in particular situations.

Areas subject to parental rules

In an attempt to find whether young people see themselves as regulated by their parents, we included specific questions in the questionnaire about

Table 7.1 *Young people reporting strict parents on a number of behaviours, by sex of the young person*

Parents strict about:	Females %	Males %	
When you come in at night	44	21	$p < 0.001$
How often you go out	32	13	$p < 0.001$
How much homework you do	22	29	$p < 0.03$
Drinking alcohol	46	40	ns
Smoking	56	63	ns
Base	358	461	

whether parents operate 'strict', 'flexible' or 'no' rules concerning a number of specific issues: keeping bedrooms tidy, going out and coming in at night, homework, money, friends, noise, bedtime, staying in bed, smoking, drinking alcohol, exercise and food.

Parents emerge in young people's answers as most likely to be restrictive about smoking, alcohol use, homework, coming in and going out at night. The percentages of significant numbers of young people (a quarter or more) who report that their parents operate 'strict rules' in respect of these four areas are as follows: smoking (60 per cent); drinking alcohol outside home (43 per cent); coming in at night (31 per cent); amount of homework done (26 per cent). The range of rule-governed activities is extended when those said to be subject to 'flexible rules' are added. Activities reported as subject to either strict or flexible parental rules by more than half of respondents include: when they come in at night (92 per cent); drinking alcohol at home (77 per cent); smoking (77 per cent); room tidiness (77 per cent); how much homework they do (74 per cent); the kind of food they eat (58 per cent); the sound level of music (74 per cent); how often they go out (74 per cent). Areas of activity less likely to be governed by parental rules include: going to religious meetings (25 per cent); taking exercise (31 per cent); which friends young people can visit (40 per cent); how they spend their money (42 per cent); having friends home (45 per cent); time spent in bed (48 per cent); watching videos (48 per cent).

A number of variables differentiate parents reported as strict from those reported as more lenient. Both gender and ethnic origin are important, while parents' occupational class and the household composition show much less association with rule patterns.

Parents of daughters are said to be significantly stricter than parents of sons about coming in at night, the frequency of going out, and the drinking of alcohol outside the home. By contrast, parents of sons are reported to be stricter about homework and smoking (see Table 7.1).

Asian-origin parents employ significantly stricter rules on smoking, alcohol use, going out and times of coming in at night, especially compared

Table 7.2   *Young people reporting strict parents on a number of behaviours, by ethnic origin of the young person*

Parents strict about:	Asian %	White %	Black %	Other %	
When you come in at night	44	26	31	42	p < 0.001
How often you go out	41	14	24	33	p < 0.001
How much homework you do	35	20	32	40	p < 0.001
Drinking alcohol	74	33	41	55	p < 0.001
Smoking	85	52	62	69	p < 0.07
Base	144	528	87	61	

with white parents and black parents. The 'other' ethnic group is closest to the Asian group. Conversely, parents who employ no rules are more likely to be white (see Table 7.2). Asian-origin parents are more likely than parents of other ethnic groups to be described as strict by both young men and young women. Comparing parental restrictiveness *vis-à-vis* young men and young women within the Asian group, young women report their parents as more strict about going out than do the young men (56 per cent as against 32 per cent). Parents are equally strict with both sexes about drinking alcohol and smoking (Table 7.2).

With the exception of rules about smoking and frequency of going out, household composition does not differentiate between strict and lenient parents. Two- (biological) parent households and households headed by single mothers are significantly more likely than other households, those headed by single fathers, to operate strict rules about smoking (see Oakley *et al.*, 1992). An association with housing tenure as an index of social class suggests that there are significant differences with respect to parental rules about how often young people go out and how much homework they do: parents living in mortgaged or privately owned accommodation are more likely to operate strict rules on these issues than parents in rented housing (how often they go out, 23 per cent as against 18 per cent; how much homework they do, 28 per cent as against 21 per cent). Whether or not the mothers of the 16-year-olds are employed full-time, part-time or not at all makes no difference to parental strictness on these issues.

Do young people think parental rules are a good idea?

How far do young people agree that parental rules are a good idea? Just as parents are said to have rules in respect of some, rather than other, issues, so the majority of young people favour parental rules in the same specific areas. Most notably, these are when they come in at night (65 per cent), healthy eating (65 per cent), smoking (53 per cent), alcohol consumption at parties (48 per cent) and homework (39 per cent).

Young women are significantly more likely than young men to say that they think it a good idea for parents to have rules about coming in at night (76 per cent compared to 57 per cent), and drinking alcohol at parties (51 per cent compared to 46 per cent). Young men are significantly more likely than young women to favour parental rules about smoking (56 per cent compared to 49 per cent). This finding also reflects their reports of parental practice.

Just as ethnic background appears to be a significant discriminator of parents' reported practices, so young people's normative beliefs about parental rules vary by ethnic background. Most in favour of parental rules are young people of Asian origin; least in favour are those of white British parentage.[1] We found no differences in young people's normative beliefs about parental rules with respect to household composition. Using housing tenure as an index of class, differences are not consistent across all issues, but those living in privately owned accommodation are more likely to think it a good idea for parents to have rules about smoking, homework and healthy eating. On the other hand, more in this group, compared with those in rented accommodation, think it a bad idea to have rules about smoking. Young men in private schools are particularly likely to think parental rules a bad idea in respect of coming in at night. Similarly, young women at private schools consider rules about homework a bad idea.

Not surprisingly, there is a significant degree of correspondence between whether young people think parental rules a good idea and whether parents are said to operate rules in practice. The degree of association is statistically significant for going out, homework, smoking and alcohol use.

The relationship between parental rules and young people's practices

Do parental rules influence young people's behaviour? Drawing again upon young people's reports of their behaviour in the questionnaires, strict parental rules are statistically associated with a lower incidence of certain behaviours in young people. Young people whose parents are said to be strict about going out at night go out infrequently compared with those whose parents are lenient. (They are no less likely, however, to have part-time jobs while still at school.) On the other hand, there is an association between restrictive parents and the amount of leisure time young people spend with their family rather than in the company of friends.

There is a link, in all ethnic groups, between parental restrictiveness and not smoking or drinking alcohol. However, parental restrictiveness appears to make least difference to behaviour in the Asian-origin group, especially when gender is taken into account. Regardless of their parents, Asian-origin young women are less likely to go out in the evening. As we shall show, this finding is confirmed by the qualitative interview data. Some Asian young women say they have no desire to go out alone at night, although it is clear that if they attempt to go out their parents try to restrict them. Such findings suggest that norms are highly internalized among some groups, notably young women in traditional families.

Similarly, parental strictness about smoking is not statistically related in Asian-origin families to whether the young women smoke. (Only six of the Asian young women in our survey were smokers.) By contrast, for white young women, 38 per cent of whom smoke, parental restrictiveness is statistically associated with not smoking. With alcohol use, Asian-origin parents are reported as the most restrictive, and Asian young people are again the least likely to indulge. Parental restrictiveness is statistically associated with not drinking.

These findings within the Asian-origin group suggest that strong norms endorsed by religion and/or culture are not necessarily articulated. Rather they are internalized so that the self rather than external agents constitute constraints upon action. Moreover, in these cases individuals may describe themselves as free from normative constraints. Conversely, where there is greater normative ambiguity, behaviour may be justified by reference to external sources of enforcement. Thus, while Asian young people, especially young women, appear to conform to parental wishes more than their white peers, this conformity is not necessarily articulated as such. By contrast, the health behaviour of white UK-born young people is linked more closely according to whether or not they say that their parents are strict.

Norms are likely to have a greater or weaker impact depending on how dominant they are within the group or community. While we can only touch on the issue here, a between-school analysis of the questionnaire data produces some interesting findings. These suggest that different ethnic mixes in schools, which may reflect community differences, are associated with different degrees of parental restrictiveness. Minority-group parents of children in schools which are predominantly white are significantly less likely than those whose children are in schools with sizeable ethnic populations to be reported as strict about allowing their children to go out and to drink alcohol. It is notable, however, that young people's actual behaviour does not appear to be linked to the school inter-ethnic mix.

The household interviews

In the interviews, we asked parents and young people an open-ended question about whether there are any rules and routines to which household members are expected to conform. While most (85 per cent) parents mentioned something, only about a half of young people did so. While using the term 'rule', we tried to suggest a variety of meanings, since we were conscious that a great deal of the regulation of young people's behaviour is not seen as such. As one father said: 'There are no rules; it's just not done.'

The absence of articulated rules may be real, or it may mean, as we noted above, that rules are internalized, and hence taken for granted. On the other hand, and as Finch (1989) observes, norms may consist in 'informal guidelines' rather than absolute laws, guiding behaviour and allowing for negotiation. If guidelines are transgressed, sanctions are weak. As one mother says: 'We disapprove if she goes out once a week in school time.'

We were interested to discover whether the issues reported in the questionnaire as governed by parental rules also recurred in the interviews. Three of the main issues – rules to do with smoking, drinking alcohol and homework – were not mentioned in the interviews by either parents or young people. Certainly, our questioning of parents and young people on smoking and alcohol suggests that few parents explicitly forbid or sanction young people engaging in these activities. If parents strongly disapprove, young people are likely to conceal these activities from them, and, if these parents suspect that their teenage children are smoking or drinking, they may turn a blind eye to avoid confronting the fact. Homework is likely to be bound up with the issue of going out, constituting one of the taken-for-granted (and hence unspoken) reasons why parents impose restrictions.

Going out is the issue most frequently mentioned in both the interview (by one-third of interviewees) and the questionnaire as being most subject to rules. Other rule-governed issues mentioned relate almost entirely to intra-household matters: tidying bedrooms, doing household duties, being on time for meals. Many parents complain about teenagers' untidy bedrooms, and the little help they give in the home. Being on time for meals did not appear to be much of an issue in practice.

Rules which curtail young people's freedom to come and go prove to be particularly controversial; these serve as a touchstone in the interviews for the expression of parents' anxieties at this moment in young people's lives. Some fear that young people will be exposed to peer-group pressures, especially the 'bad influence' of those who smoke, drink alcohol and use drugs. Many parents also fear that young people may become sexually active and further that going out will put young people at risk of violence (as victims and perpetrators) on the street, particularly since the study teenagers live in a large, multi-ethnic conurbation.

The teenage years are a peak age for intensive relationships of dyads and groups, and there is often a weakening of family bonds. Young people at 16 seek the company of their peers away from the supervision of their parents. They may want the same curfew times as their friends or try to extend these. Their desire to be responsible for themselves in this respect is also in part a response to the demands of the wider society, which requires young people to earn money and to become consumers. Moreover, a change of school at 16 to a sixth-form college, for example, may necessitate greater geographical movement away from their home territory, with the making of new friends who are unknown to their parents.

Going out is an issue which not only transcends the inside–outside dichotomy, but also raises the general question of young people's progress towards individuation and taking responsibility for themselves. Parents want their young people to manage well in the outside world; allowing them the freedom to go out helps foster initiative and self-reliance, but parents are also fearful of the consequences.

The ways in which parents and their young justify parental rules and guidelines in respect of going out vary. These justifications suggest that parents' beliefs differ both in what they consider to be age-appropriate behaviour and in the meaning of young people's connectedness to their families. In contrast to the UK-born parents, parents brought up in other societies with strong moral values concerning family and kinship are generally less disposed towards ideas of individuation and autonomy for young people. Rather, they emphasize the continuing connectedness of young people to their families. While the beliefs of these parents are modified by the society in which they currently live, family and kinship values are likely to change at a slower pace than those pertaining to behaviour in the wider society.

A content analysis of the interview accounts of parents and their young suggests a variety of discourses around this issue of letting young people out without supervision. The discourse is also articulated with respect to issues in the future, such as young people leaving home. These discourses can be broadly categorized in terms of two ideal types: on the one hand, there is the discourse which emphasizes the connectedness of the young person to the family of origin; at the opposite extreme, the second discourse stresses the individuality and independence of the young person within the family group.

The discourse of connectedness

This discourse is found chiefly among the parents born outside the UK, and is located in a set of cultural beliefs which are sustained by religious mores. It stresses the importance of deference to those hierarchically superior or, in the language of some members of the group, the requirement to have 'respect for elders' in the family. It emphasizes solidaristic relations, rather than the individual autonomy of family members. While this discourse is located within the dominant culture of UK society, these parents, like all parents, distinguish between what they expect of their children in two different contexts – namely that, in the household and kin group, they should adhere to parents' values and that, outside the home, they should behave in accordance with the dominant norms pertaining to those contexts. An Asian-origin mother makes this distinction, adding that she is fearful of the outside world which she regards as a dangerous place:

> [Our children] can't live the European culture, they can't live our own. But if she [Neena] can go to the schools, then it's all right. But when she should go to our place – the religion – she should do like us . . . Children have a double burden. She should allow for both ways. In the family she should do

like us but outside different . . . I don't like my child should go out and come late at night. (Neena Ghosh's mother)

The discourse of connectedness is also gender-specific. Staying connected to family protects young women's moral character from dangerous unsupervised contact with the opposite sex, and from other prohibited practices. A young woman with parents from the Middle East describes a model of growing up which differs from Western notions. For her, adolescence is not marked by separation from the family. Parents continue to be responsible for their daughters until marriage; it is their duty to protect daughters' virginity, and to ensure their behaviour does not jeopardize their marriage chances. The young women are not allowed out with their friends unless chaperoned by their relatives:

My parents are on the other side of the world . . . certain morals and certain views . . . People here have been conditioned to think in another way and I'm caught in between. I have teachers, friends . . . totally opposite of my parents . . . My parents would feel that they should be responsible for me. I should do everything they say for the rest of my life, till I'm 18. Eighteen is just a birthday party. It means nothing. They should be responsible for me till I marry. English people say I should be responsible for myself from a certain age. (Nasreen Mohammed)

In her account, Nasreen mentions the different categories of persons who form her social circle and the very different values among them. In accordance with her parents' values, she sees her parents as being responsible for her for the rest of her life, rather than for the finite periods of childhood and adolescence. But then she implies that parental responsibility continues only 'till I'm 18', positioning herself within Western definitions of adulthood. Quickly she corrects herself, and explains somewhat regretfully that, within the values of her kin group, this age point does not symbolize a transition to adulthood – 'Eighteen is just a birthday', like many others. Finally, she sums up the meaning attributed by British society to the idea of `coming of age': 'I should be responsible for myself.'

Her father's comments, which challenge Western ideas of adolescent development and are delivered in a crisp, succinct fashion, support Nasreen's account:

We don't see the age milestones in such stark terms in our culture. We say a girl remains a girl until she is married. Here, when she is 16, it is a totally different game. Persons in reality don't suddenly change.

Questions about age-appropriate behaviour for young people on the matter of 'leaving home' frequently acted as a prompt in the interviews, leading parents born outside the UK to talk about the nature of young people's relationships with their families and 'the outside'. Rather than seeing leaving home as part of the 'natural' developmental process of growing up, these parents see themselves as responsible for their children's entire lives. The notion of 'leaving home' calls this responsibility into question. For these parents, children never leave home in the sense that kin obligations are not modified by the transition to adult status. In the case of Asian-origin daughters, these obligations are transferred to the families into which they marry. An Asian-origin mother distinguishes between leaving home and getting married:

> We people don't leave home. (*But you did?*) I married – that's something separate, different. We people don't leave home. We're still members of the family. (Mannick Govinda's mother)

An Asian-origin father does not see his son leaving home, though he can envisage the possibility of his living in a separate household (nearby) when he gets married:

> [Leaving home] is something new to us. It's not like what happens here – don't take me wrong – but most of the white families in Western society, when the boy is 18 he will probably settle somewhere else or when a girl is 16 or 17. It doesn't happen in our communities. (*So they will stay at home?*) Hopefully, yes, they will stay at home till they get married . . . Personally I would prefer [my son] to stay near. (Sandeep Kumar's father)

Several parents born outside the UK link the notion of leaving home to the phenomenon of homelessness among British young people. They thereby see homelessness, something which they find very shocking, as a direct consequence of encouraging young people to become independent.

The value placed upon continuing connectedness to family contrasts with alternative models of bringing up young people. Parents may be highly restrictive, or they may assert their cultural values, but turn a blind eye to situations in which young people explore Western freedoms to act more autonomously. Many parents born outside the UK are fearful of the physical dangers of the outside world associated with racism, but justify their fears in moral terms. Thus smoking and drinking are constructed as 'bad' behaviours, and not as dangers to their children's health:

> I think it is better that we are Asian because there are so many rules and regulations that in a way we haven't got so much freedom. Whatever we have got, we are happy with it. (*It protects you?*) Yes, it has protected us from so many things, you know, like kids going out. I have seen kids going out, drinking and smoking and drugs and things like that. I'm not going to say that Asian people don't do it. They do – behind their parents' backs. (Maya Gupte's mother)

The discourse of connectedness emphasizes the benefits of staying in as well as the moral dangers of going out: 'It's good to spend time with family.' However, young people in these households are not deprived of opportunities for sociability with their peers. Rather, they are expected to attend family parties with a broad spectrum of age groups and to mix with their peers as long as they are related to them through kinship:

We are always together at home, we didn't go out, the children. And always I tell them to be at home with their relatives ... and we go to special [ethnic] club. When we go we take them altogether. They enjoy together there, or through the church ... But they don't go out with their friends too much ... Sometimes, but very few, not too much. (Abrahim Samuel's mother)

Another positive image of home is its importance as a place for studying, an activity which parents born outside the UK see as something to be encouraged. They frequently exempt their young people on this account from household duties, although Asian young people, especially young women, report in the questionnaire a higher performance of housework tasks than the other ethnic groups. These first-generation immigrant parents place a high value upon education and studying for the long-term rewards these activities may bring in raising the economic status of the second generation, and also as intrinsically 'good' activities reflecting the high regard for educated people in their own societies of origin. Study is not, therefore, simply valued instrumentally as a means by which young people are contained in the home. Moreover, the act of going away to study, for example to university, does not imply that the young person has left home. By contrast, UK-born parents, especially middle-class ones, do not speak about study in such a reverential way. Rather, they stress that their children should do their homework because of the importance of examination success for its central role in terms of opening up occupational opportunities.

As we have suggested, parents born outside the UK share the values of the societies in which they now live, though they are unhappy when these threaten their own values relating to family relations. One way of dealing with the contradiction is to turn a blind eye when young people transgress household norms. However, these parents frequently distance themselves from the methods of raising children adopted by their own parents. For example, Maya Gupte's mother, who is of Asian origin, says that, compared with her relationship with her own mother, she has a qualitatively different relationship with her daughter: 'We are just like a friend to each other.' Although she does not see herself as imposing a great many rules on her children, the children are very restricted compared with many of their peers, especially in respect of going out. The mother's strategy of control is to be her children's constant companion. Not only does she go everywhere with them, she participates in her daughter's leisure activities and also in her studies:

I'm less strict. My brother is a bit strict, just like my father. They don't let their kids look at the telly after eight. If they are going to watch a film I always sit with them. (*Always?*) Always. I don't let them sit by themselves. And when they study, my daughter, she studies up to eleven o'clock, I always give her company.

The discourse of individuation

The dominant Western discourse concerning adolescence emphasizes the process of separation on the part of young people in their relationships with their families. This discourse of individuation is found in our study among UK-born parents. It draws upon prescriptions concerning the 'normal' ways in which young people are supposed to achieve the transition to adulthood through the process of individuation. As Walkerdine and Lucey (1989) argue so graphically, this discourse presumes that the process of individuation begins in childhood. The child is free to discover individuality and autonomy; he or she is free to learn self-regulation – 'the only luggage needed in the conflict-free path to democracy' (Walkerdine and Lucey, 1989: 29). Accordingly, the path of democracy begins in the kitchen of the sensitive mother. It depends on the removal from consciousness of any sense of oppression, powerlessness, or exploitation. Parents', or rather mothers', role is to guide and to be seen to guide rather than to control children; they should regard it as 'good' to let go of their teenage children, and to give them space in which to create adult identities and take up their individual rights of citizenship. By contrast, there are no exit rituals for parents as they leave behind their more onerous responsibilities as parents.

This discourse of individuation and individual rights is based upon not only a Western cultural perspective, but also on a male model (Gilligan, 1982). The discourse underplays the notion of responsibility, a concept which is more significant for women and young women. As Gilligan argues, and a wealth of research on women demonstrates, women characteristically attach more importance than men to the responsibilities they have towards others, and frequently underplay the notion of their own rights as individuals. Thus, during adolescence, the model of individuation is closer to the experience of young men, while young women retain their connectedness, or seek to make new connections, with their families (Apter, 1990).

In this study also, the public discourse of adolescence remains largely ungendered. It is, however, clear that the material forms of individuation vary in different social classes. An upper middle-class father, reflecting upon his own youth, spent largely in a private single-sex boarding school, recounts how his education taught him to 'learn to stand on [his] own feet and develop a sense of self-reliance'.

Among working-class parents, the discourse is articulated in the expectation that the entry to paid employment is 'the symbol and stepping stone to independence and adulthood' (Allatt and Yeandle, 1992). In our study, the working-class UK-born parents of the young people who left school at 16 exerted less control over them once they joined the labour market or youth training schemes. Only two young people with parents born outside the UK had left full-time education by the time of their interview – the one parent who was interviewed continues to be restrictive.

A mother whose youngest child had recently left school fought battles with her daughter about coming home at a reasonable hour. Now she has a job, she sees no justification for trying to restrict her going out:

> She definitely has a lot more freedom than our other children. Before she left school bedtime during school days should be 10.30. Not necessarily to go to bed, but she should be in. She abused that on one or two occasions . . .
> We don't say anything about it now. She's over 16 and we trust, well, she's at work now. (Stella Wheeler's mother)

When young people enter waged work, the idea of individuation is also apparent in working-class parents' expectation that young people should contribute financially to the household. The notion of paying board or self-provisioning supports the individual rights model – the idea of being responsible for yourself as a working member of the household in return for which you acquire certain rights and status. However, there is evidence to suggest that parents often save the money earned by their working sons and daughters and repay it when they get married (Allatt and Yeandle, 1992). In our study, most UK-born parents claim not to expect payment until their young are earning 'a proper wage'.

By contrast, parents born outside the UK are opposed in principle to the idea of young people paying board. Given that they continue to see their young as part of the family collectivity – both in terms of their contribution to the household and what they receive from it, this is not surprising. However, responsibility for paying 'poll tax' stretches collectivist values too far; parents are of the same mind as UK-born parents. They do not expect to pay the tax on behalf of their young people, although they do not necessarily think that young people should pay either.

For young people, the desire for greater independence at 16 focuses on having more freedom to go out, either to have contact with their peers, or to earn and spend money. UK-born parents are more sympathetic to these goals than are parents not born in the UK. Indeed, some UK-born middle-class parents with sons at the single-sex private school are especially concerned that, because of academic pressures, their sons do not socialize enough, and may not develop essential social skills. By contrast, among parents born overseas, sociability is part of the discourse of connectedness. Young people are expected to be sociable, but within the context of their kinship networks; their socialization in this respect extends to the ability to mix with all age groups, not only peers, and to learn how to entertain guests.

UK-born parents are faced with a dilemma: on the one hand, to protect their children from the dangers of the outside world and, on the other, to allow them the greater freedom which they have brought them up to expect. As we shall describe in Chapter 10, parents in this group, notably mothers, seek to renegotiate relationships with young people by laying emphasis on the importance of communication. Young people are expected to inform parents of their whereabouts and to 'talk' to their parents, thereby establishing closeness through communication. Parents reconnect with their children drawing on discourses of individual rights and equality. At the same time, communication provides a vehicle of control. In allowing their young people the right to go out, parents seek to know where young people are going, with whom, and when they are likely to return home. Young people are granted greater freedoms and, in return, parents acquire knowledge of their whereabouts. This knowledge enables parents to feel that they are not evading their parental responsibilities, while also legitimizing the fact that young people are taking responsibility for themselves. The requirement upon young people to communicate information concerning their whereabouts is suggestive of what Bernstein (1971) has called 'personalized' modes of control. These forms of legitimation contrast with 'institutional' modes of control employed by parents born overseas. A young woman says:

> When you get to be my age you want to be like an adult, don't you? . . . My mum lets me have a certain amount of freedom, but she is quite strict with me. As long as she *knows* where I am and what time I'm going to be in . . . (Sally Rimmer; emphasis added)

The grounds on which parents justify their demand that young people communicate their whereabouts to them are various and are suggestive of weak rather than strong rule enforcement. In the following example, a UK-born father claims that communication is a matter of 'common politeness' as well as a rule:

> Letting everyone know what the hell is happening which is a rule . . . and having friends in, the rule is 'you tell us'. Again, it's a rule of what-you-call-it – common sense, politeness, manners rather than a rule. (Colin Clark's father)

Some parents simply say that they like to know, rather than require to know, when their children are coming home. This language, too, is suggestive of weak rather than strong rules:

> No hard and fast rules. I just *like* to be told when they are coming in, where they are going and they all know they can ring if they need a lift. (David Monk's mother)

In this last remark, the mother suggests that the way is also open for the young person to make demands upon the parents for their help and protection – namely the invitation to ring up for a lift. Knowledge is represented as reciprocal: just as the parent knows the whereabouts of the young person, so too does the young person know about the availability of the parent to help out.

In addition to preference and common politeness, some parents – notably mothers – give a further justification for knowing about their children's whereabouts, namely that knowledge alleviates worry.[2] While we might expect more parents born outside the UK to express worry about their young people because of racism in the society, worry emerged more commonly among the UK-born mothers. Thus, a mother says that she worries if her children do not notify her in advance when they are staying out in the evening after school or after work. Moreover, she presents her tendency to worry as an individual failing rather than a consequence of real external dangers:

> I always like them to phone up if they're not coming straight home from work because I have a dinner waiting . . . I would worry if they didn't . . .
> Worry is one of my downfalls. I do see dangers. (William Lovelock's mother)

In accordance with her failure to see her own feelings as legitimate, she remarks that it is her son's dinner which is the main reason for his coming home on time.

Mothers are aware that worry has markedly less legitimacy than other reasons for trying to restrict young people; worry is seen as a female weakness to which only mothers are 'prone'. The fact that worry is a likely consequence of bearing a life-long responsibility for children from their birth onwards is insufficient. Worry is also a product of the contradiction of continuing to be responsible for young people but at a distance.

We end this chapter with two cases which portray the different discourses of connectedness and individuation. They exemplify parents' and young people's perspectives concerning the amount of freedom young people should have with respect to going out and what young people do in practice. In the first case, a young woman is given considerable freedom by her UK-born parents. In the second, a young Asian-origin woman is much more restricted, but breaks the rules unbeknown to her mother.

Emma Kerr

Emma is 17, the second of two daughters of UK-born parents. Her father is a lecturer in youth work and her mother works part-time as a secretary. She has just started an A-level course at a further education college. Her relationship with her mother is said to be 'good', while her relationship with her father, whom we were unable to interview, is described as 'poor'. Her mother takes it for granted that she has boyfriends (the father is said to be less happy), and that she goes out a lot at night with her friends: 'But I like her to be in by 11 or 11.30 in the week.' At weekends, she is prepared for her daughter to stay out later. However, she worries about this a great deal and often gives her daughter the money to get a taxi home. Her mother's reason for worrying is the fear that her daughter will fall into 'the wrong company'. She also notes that her daughter smokes, but does not try to stop her, although she does not approve. She also believes she 'is sensible enough in her attitude to drugs'. In order to protect her, she says that she gives her daughter 'the third degree' before she goes out. 'But I just want to know roughly where she is and what time she is coming in.' She comments that, in contrast to her older daughter,

Emma 'gets a lot more independence than her sister at the same age'.

Emma's account tallies with her mother's. In the questionnaire, she portrays her parents as fairly lenient. In addition, she indicates both in the questionnaire and the interview that she would like to stay out later than she is allowed. She says of her parents:

> [They are] not really strict. It depends. If they don't know exactly where I'm going or if my mum has got an idea about a club, if she thinks it might be dangerous . . . I think it's fine. Now and again there's a bit of tension . . . Sometimes I say I'm going out and I don't know if I'll be staying at someone's house or coming back. She likes to know that. There isn't a set time. She'll say: 'Oh, don't be too late.' But our definitions of late are very different. She's worried about the men that might be around, in case any strange man tries to pick me up.

Soraya Khan

Despite some similarities, the contrast between Emma and Soraya is striking. Soraya is also 17; she is the daughter of an East African Asian businessman who is no longer living with his wife and children. She lives with her mother, who is a full-time mother, and her younger brother and sister. Like Emma, she doesn't get on with her father and has a good relationship with her mother. Also like Emma, Soraya has just gone to a further education college to do her A levels.

Soraya's mother says that her daughter never goes out at night, nor does she have friends home, because her friends are not allowed out either. However, she stresses that she does not try to stop her daughter going out, although it is clear that mother and daughter have had tussles over this issue in the past. Rather, the mother says that her daughter is constrained by the culture, especially the demands of 'family and study'. In practice, Soraya is expected to help look after her siblings, and also to provide companionship for her mother. Her mother wants her daughter to study hard in order 'to make something of herself'. Soraya is keen to study and prefers to do her A levels at a college rather than follow her mother's advice and stay on at school. In addition to studying, her mother wants her to get married, though she does not necessarily want an arranged marriage, especially since her own has been unsuccessful:

> She can't go out because of the way she was brought up. She says she is under pressure. (*But she would like to?*) Well, I don't stop her really. She is brought up like that. She feels she should go out with her friends, but she doesn't want to go out with them because she has to look after her mum . . . There are loads and loads of other pressures as well. I mean studies and family – I think Asian kids have a lot more pressure. (*What about being a girl?*) Yeah, being an Asian girl.

According to her mother, the household rule is to be home on time after college, a practice which prevents Soraya from getting into 'bad ways'. Because Soraya's father is absent, her mother feels especially responsible for her. However, she makes no attempt to enforce this particular rule because:

> I trust her so much . . . Even if she comes home I never ask her where she has come from. . . I trust her. That is why she come back to me . . . I have seen young women just hang around and hardly go to school. I have seen them do stupid things – drinking and smoking . . . I don't want Soraya to do anything behind my back. That is why I have done everything in my power [to keep a good relationship] . . . I don't want [my husband] coming home and people saying: 'You can't look after her.'

Soraya's mother is afraid that if she puts her foot down, she will alienate her daughter, who may then try to leave home:

> But we don't leave home . . . I have seen young women leaving home, running away and not coming back. I don't want that to happen . . . When I was a teenager I never heard of anyone leaving home and sleeping it off on the street, and drinking alcohol and drugs. They just need more attention. That is what it is. You can't lock them in the house.

Soraya's account corresponds with her mother's. She portrays a very restricted lifestyle, especially for Asian-origin young women: 'They are only supposed to see kitchen and bed'; 'Boyfriends are forbidden unless you're engaged to them.' Soraya was interviewed some months before her mother, a period when they were having a lot of disagreements. By the time the mother is interviewed relations have improved, highlighting a major characteristic of these discourses and negotiations, that there can be rapid change over short periods of time. In the interview, Soraya talks about the misdemeanours which she has kept from her mother, notably a secret relationship she has had with an older man who is a family friend; the relationship has just ended at the time of the interview, and Soraya is very hurt by this. In order to go out with the man during the afternoon, thereby not infringing the rule about going out at night, Soraya 'bunked off school'. The disappointment concerning her relationship precipitates Soraya into a bout of religiosity; she turns to religion for comfort and, significantly, starts wearing traditional Indian dress.

Before the start of this illicit relationship, Soraya also says that she had a period of spending the afternoons going around shopping centres 'raving' with a group of white and Asian friends. Soraya is torn by a desire to 'just go out and enjoy yourself – go out, rave, go mad' and a wish not to hurt her mother by such behaviour. She regards Asian-origin young women as 'narrow-minded – don't go out, don't smoke, don't talk to white people, don't go out with them – they're bad', but she also feels relieved to be restricted. The chief reason for this is because she fears 'going overboard':

> I think it's good I'm restricted, cos if I wasn't I don't know what I'd get up to. I'd spend nights away from home. The other day I went out and got home at ten o'clock. I felt really guilty because I didn't tell the truth. [My mother] has given up her life for us and I'm still being horrible.

Conclusion

Within the limitations of a self-completion questionnaire, we attempted to investigate young people's reports and views of parental restrictiveness. Young people report considerable restrictiveness by their parents on a number of issues, especially concerning the freedom to go out at night without parental supervision. They also mention rules about homework, smoking and alcohol use. A greater proportion of parents of young women are said to be strict about their going out and drinking alcohol, while more parents of young men are strict about smoking.

The most consistent factors in differentiating parental strictness are the ethnic origin and the gender of the young people. These are more important than household composition and social class. Asian-origin parents are strict on all these issues compared with other groups of parents. White British parents are least strict, closely followed by black parents, while the 'other' group are closest to the Asian parents. However, according to the questionnaire data, an imperfect fit exists between parental rules and young people's practices. One critical issue here concerns the locus of control of norms and rules – how far they are internalized, and how far they are (described as) externally imposed. We find that, for example, Asian-origin young women are unlikely to engage in forbidden activities even when, as some of them say in their interviews (though not the questionnaires), that their parents do not restrict them, and that they are acting of their own free will.

Parents and young people draw upon a variety of discourses in talking about parental restrictiveness and young people's freedom to go out. These vary according to the cultural mores of the parents and are discussed in terms of two ideal types – the discourse of connectedness to family and the discourse of individuation. These two discourses reflect very different ideas concerning the nature of adolescence and young people's relationships with their parents.

Notes

1 The differences are only statistically significant with respect to healthy eating, alcohol at parties and smoking, and not with respect to coming in at night and homework.
2 As we saw in Chapter 3, worrying is a strongly gendered aspect of parenthood.

8 Household negotiations and food

In this chapter, we consider how far young people's diet is within their own control, and how far it remains the responsibility of parents. We saw in Chapter 4 that parents and young people are roughly equally divided on the issue of who should be responsible for young people's health. This ambiguity arises in part because health covers a wide variety of issues, though most parents and young people talked about bodily health. Food is also central to the way young people view their changing bodies and the self-esteem related to this. However, the consumption of food is not solely a health and body-image issue. Food has a social and symbolic signifi- cance, particularly in so far as it involves the relationships of those who partake in the ritual of sharing meals (Douglas, 1984). Through their participation in family meals, what young people eat is partially visible to their parents. This marks dietary practices as different from other health- risk behaviours such as smoking.

For official purposes, sharing a common table constitutes an important part of the definition of a 'household' (OPCS, 1990). Anthropologists have suggested that the sharing of meals is a ritual process which sets bound- aries of inclusion and exclusion, and thus expresses the identity of the group which eats together. But family meals represent inequalities as well as expressing group solidarity (see Charles and Kerr, 1988; Mennell *et al.*, 1992). Studies show that male heads of households generally receive more of the higher-status foods such as red meat than do women and children. Moreover, the transformation of food into meals falls inequitably on the shoulders of women (Delphy, 1979; Murcott, 1983).

A main focus of this chapter is on the position of young people in relation to their participation in family meals. Sociological examinations of patterns of meal-taking suggest that the cooked meal is dominant (Murcott, 1983); at least, this has been shown to be the case for white families with at least one child under five in the North of England (Charles and Kerr, 1988). The multi-ethnic population from which the households in our own study are drawn, together with their later stage of family development and with most mothers in paid employment, suggest a priori a greater variation in meal patterns.

Eating meals together

The idea of eating together appeals less to young people than to their parents. Just under half of all parents said in the interview that it is 'very important' to eat together – while only a quarter of all young people concurred. This view is also more widely subscribed to by those parents born outside the UK and their families than by those born in the UK and their families. Despite differences in attitude to this practice, however, similar proportions of parents and young people (just over two-fifths) report actually eating together most of the time.[1] The pattern of meal-taking is also highly variable over time, depending on the day of the week and the commitments of parents and young people. A quarter of parents and their children eat together 'sometimes'. One-third rarely eat together. Young people were asked if they cooked or bought their own meals, and over three-quarters do so on a regular basis.

In terms of the diet scores of the interviewees who took part in the questionnaire survey, those who often eat meals with their families are rather more likely than those who eat together only sometimes or rarely, to be in the healthiest diet group described in Chapter 6, but differences are small.[2]

Who decides what young people eat at home?

In the interview, all household members agree that the most likely person to determine the diet of young people in the household is the mother (around two-fifths of young people and one-half of parents say this). Next most likely (accounting for over a third of cases) is that responsibility is taken by the mother and/or father in conjunction with the teenager. It is less common that young people themselves take responsibility – under a tenth of cases, though here fathers' estimations are higher. Those with parents born outside the UK are rather more likely to report that mothers make decisions concerning what young people eat. As with household meal patterns, those young people whose diets are said to be controlled by their mothers are slightly more likely to be in the healthiest diet group according to the questionnaire scores.[3]

When the extent of parental responsibility for young people's diet is examined in relation to whether meals are eaten together, a range of patterns emerges. Table 8.1 presents information on 64 households. The most common pattern is the traditional 'mother-centred' model in which the mother is responsible for the young person's diet and meals are eaten together mostly or sometimes. In the middle are those more egalitarian households in which responsibility is shared between young people and parents, and meals are eaten together to a variable degree. At the extreme is the small minority of households in which young people take most

Table 8.1   *Parental responsibility for young people's diet, by regularity of eating together as a household**

Who takes responsibility for what young person eats	Eat together mostly % (n)	Eat together sometimes % (n)	Eat together rarely % (n)	All % (n)
Mother	25 (16)	16 (10)	11 (7)	52 (33)
Parents and young person share	16 (10)	6 (4)	17 (11)	39 (25)
Young person	2 (1)	3 (2)	5 (3)	9 (6)
All	42 (27)	25 (16)	33 (21)	Base = 64

*These responses are based on mothers' accounts supplemented by those of the young people where the mothers were not interviewed. The converse strategy (young people's accounts supplemented by mothers' accounts) gives a similar picture.

Figure 8.1   *Amount of maternal influence, by degree of young people's autonomy*

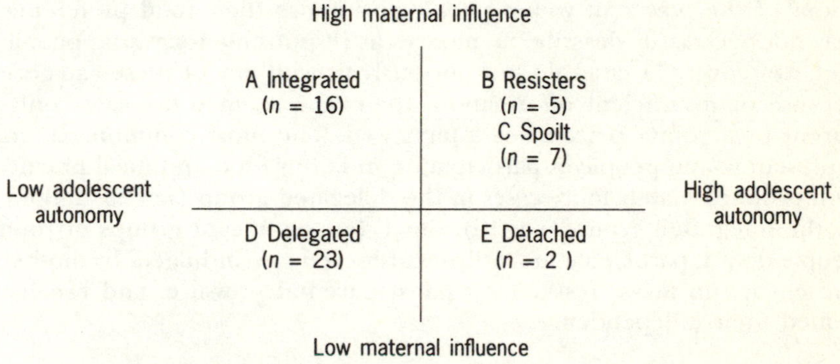

responsibility for what they eat, and rarely participate in family meals. To add to the complexity, households operate different patterns through the week, depending on, for example, shift work and outside commitments such as sports and evening classes.

The rest of the chapter draws on and discusses all the qualitative inter-view data concerning food and meals, not only the responses to the direct questions on which the information in Table 8.1 is based. The households are located in relation to two axes concerning the degree of maternal[4] influence over food and meal matters and the degree of young people's autonomy in this area. The matrix produces five clusters of cases, which are identified in Figure 8.1. In the top left quadrant (A), are those young people who conform to the normative pattern, whereby mothers take responsibility for food in the household, and young people generally participate in family meals. In the top right quadrant (B and C), there are two small groups of mothers who take a similarly high degree of responsibility but with young people trying to exert independence. In the case of what we call the 'resisters', young people resist maternal influence by opting for a different diet such as vegetarianism, or refusing the food provided. In the case of what we call the 'spoilt', mothers collaborate in young people's resistance by 'spoiling' young people through the provision of different foods or separate meals. In the bottom left quadrant (D), parents share responsibility with the young people for dietary matters, and, although they give them some autonomy in the preparation of food and meal-taking, responsibility is only partially delegated to the young people. Moreover, in these households, dietary responsibility and meal patterns vary considerably over the course of the week. In the bottom right quadrant (E), parental responsibility for young people's diet is entirely given over to the young people, and young people act quite autonomously in food matters.

It is important to note that these clusters or ideal types do not exactly replicate the patterns presented in Table 8.1. For example, mothers of the 'spoilt' group who score high on maternal influence, and who are conscious of the power of young people to impose their food preferences, may not necessarily describe themselves as responsible for young people's diet. Moreover, 11 cases do not obviously fit with any of these categories because of insufficient information; for example, in some cases only a parent or a young person was interviewed. The most common patterns represent young people as participating in family food and meal practices with proportionately more cases in the delegated group ($n = 23$) followed by the integrated group ($n = 16$). Small but significant groups of young people do not participate in family meals: seven are 'indulged' by mothers, five engage in active resistance against parental pressure, and two have gained their independence.

The 'integrated'

We describe young people in this group as 'integrated' since they both eat meals as a family and conform to a traditional model in which mothers manage the family diet. Most cases in this group are middle-class households, with parents born both in and outside the UK. In the latter, the family meal is typically a social occasion, and the idea of eating together is taken for granted. One young man of Chinese origin, Chenglie Wang, the son of an architect, describes mealtimes thus:

(*So you eat with your parents every night?*) Yeh . . . We're not the sort of household, someone comes in, just takes something and goes out. We always try to get the whole family down eating.

Chenglie more or less accepts the obligations placed on him by his parents. He believes that his parents' general expectations of him – to study hard and go to university – are in his own interests. Appearing at family meals is one of many such obligations. Despite parental control over his diet, he achieved a 'poor' diet score on the answers he gave in the questionnaire: he does not eat wholemeal bread, only eats fruit occasionally and eats an excessive amount of sweet snacks. Chenglie mentions his 'skinny' build as the reason for his high calorie diet:

> I'm trying to put on weight, but I can't get anywhere . . . It doesn't matter how much I eat, I always somehow lose it. (*Why is that?*) I'm active probably . . . (*Why do you want to put on weight?*) I'm too skinny. I don't want to be muscle-bound, I just wanna be – I just want to get a bit more meat on me. So I don't have to be embarrassed.

A young woman of Asian origin, Sai Kumar, belongs to a similar household. She appears to have an eating disorder. Her mother, who works full-time, does all the cooking, though her daughter helps 'to cut the salad and stuff'. Dishes are decided upon collectively:

> We vote on something. We pick something and say 'Shall we have curry tonight?', and we sort of have a vote.

The whole family cannot get round their small table so they divide into two groups, the three teenagers on one table, and their parents on a smaller table at the side. It is significant that the young woman keeps her relationship with her boyfriend secret from her strict father. She also keeps her eating disorder from him, though her mother is aware of her 'bingeing' and fasting:

> On Sunday I just pig myself. I eat loads, cakes and stuff, and feel sick. I had an argument with my boyfriend on Saturday and I didn't eat for 24 hours, and I told my mum and she had a go at me because my sister used to do that as well. (Sai Kumar)

The elder sister was thrown out of the house by her father for 'smoking and having boyfriends', and thus brought disrepute on the family. Sai is frightened the same will happen to her. The ritual of the family meal, though apparently consolidating family relationships, masks a considerable degree of tension in the household. The daughter's eating problem may be related to this.

Family meals, eaten together and prepared by a parent, can serve the purpose of incorporating newcomers, such as step-parents, into families. Susan Peacock's father, a company executive, who is bringing up two teenagers with his second wife, lays particular emphasis on their eating together. He has gained custody of his children from his first wife, who was deemed to have neglected their basic care. He describes sharing domestic chores with his second wife in terms of shopping, making meals and eating together. However, although the family eats the same meal – they eat on their laps in front of the TV – he disapproves of the arrangement because of the reduced opportunity for social contact and because it suggests a lack of parental respect:

> I would rather eat around the table without the television so it becomes a social event . . . if it's one thing that I get irritated about, it's after I've done

the cooking and somebody isn't ready to sit down at the table. Therefore they haven't treated it as an important event. I get upset! (Susan Peacock's father)

In a second stepfamily, a working-class stepmother describes taking responsibility for cooking the family meals, even though her new husband has cared as a lone parent for his two sons for many years. She works part-time and ensures that her hours fit round her stepsons' return from school. For the father, food and mealtimes are now important in terms of asserting his new-found authority as a husband and patriarch:

I will not have the same meal twice. Say we had, er, egg and chips yesterday . . . I wouldn't want egg and chips today. I never have done that. So I always try to vary it. (*Do you eat meals together every day?*) Yeah. (*Do you feel that's important?*) Er, yeah. I think it gives you a chance to put your point of view, that sort of thing, you know, and all that happened in school, what happened in work, what happens here. (*So do you make sure that your sons are both here?*) Yeah. I demand it. Mind you I don't get it, but I demand it . . . But meal times I say, 'Your dinner's going to be at six o'clock', I say, 'I want you home here at six, cos your dinner's gonna be on the table' . . . I demand that they be there. (Andrew Brown's father)

Andrew Brown's stepmother talks mainly about improving her own, rather than the family, diet by eating products low in fat; she has recently been diagnosed as having a high level of cholesterol. Consequently, the diet of the whole family benefits:

I have to look for non-animal fats in some of the products, because I can't eat it. They don't seem to mind, I mean, I buy low fat sausages, they don't mind them. In fact I think they like them better.

Neither father nor son appear to have noticed the changes, except for the substitution of vegetable oil for lard, and they are uninterested in the idea of having a healthy diet. The son's favourites are 'fast food, McDonald's, fish and chips, things like that', while his father says foods like bacon and eggs 'have never done me any harm', and sees no reason to change his eating habits.

Another working-class father, who is retired and thus considerably older than most of the men interviewed, also demands set mealtimes and punctuality. He does not justify the practice of eating together in terms of the opportunity for communication mentioned by many families, but talks instead about keeping an eye on the manners of his son, Alec. Alec's mother also confirms the pattern of regularity: 'We do stick to those rules you know. There's no "Come and help yourself."' But in contrast to her husband, Alec's mother thinks meals are an opportunity for her rather quiet and reclusive son (he rarely goes out in the evenings and seems to have few friends) to sit and talk: 'I think it gives them an anchor line if they've got problems.'

The creation of a sense of family connectedness through joint meal-taking also extends to middle-class families, even though some of these young people lead very active social lives and have a high degree of personal independence. The parents of one such young woman, Andrea, who is the eldest of four children, are very keen that she is present at the evening meal which, since both parents work full-time, requires a great deal of forethought and organization. Andrea is half in awe of the order and routine and half irritated by it:

> Everything in the house is a routine. There's a routine for absolutely everything . . . There's things like dinner at seven and if I'm not in for dinner I have to phone. And there's – everything falls into a pattern. It's just easier. Like mum goes shopping on a Wednesday, and my dad gets the frozen stuff on Thursday. And this kind of stuff. Rarely a change in that kind of routine . . . The basic rule of my house, I have to be home for Sunday dinner – I don't have to eat dinner with my family on any other day of the week, but I have to be there at Sunday dinner cos I have to speak to my family at least one hour every week. (*And what do you feel about rules like that?*) I think they're all quite reasonable. I get a bit annoyed when I'm actually wanting to do something on Sunday, and I have to rush home at six o'clock to eat some roast dinner, that I don't really want to eat or whatever. (Andrea Dewar)

Andrea's parents both value eating together as a family:

> *Father*: I suppose there is an element of – we're a family and we ought to spend time together and we ought to be able to converse, relate to each other, rely on each other maybe. It's a bit of the old Victorian family.
> *Mother*: I think that's incredibly important. (*Why?*) Exchange of views, I mean she wouldn't see the little young men very much at all if she didn't eat with them sometimes. Ummm, I don't know, I think it's quite a good place to discuss things, you learn about each other then.

Here again, the father explicitly acknowledges traditional values attached to eating as a family, perhaps suggesting the lack of an arena to express this in any other way. The mother, on the other hand, suggests the importance of family togetherness with her comment that mealtimes provide opportunities for family members to make, as well as sustain, relationships, especially when an older child develops outside interests.

Another comparatively large middle-class family goes to even greater lengths to maintain meals as an important family occasion. The mother constantly changes the times of the evening meal in order to accommodate outside commitments. She thinks it 'very important to sit down as a family' in order to relax and enjoy one another's company. Again, this mother emphasizes the importance of communication:

> I think there's so much stress and rushing around during the day, that it's very pleasant for us all – we have a glass of wine sometimes and the children will have a shandy, or whatever – to sit down and relax, to chat about what has and hasn't happened during the day, and their hopes and plans, and talk about what they've read in the press and things like that. (Graham Williams's mother)

The formality of the meal – 'We behave almost as if it was a dinner party' – expresses her sense of domestic order, the home as a haven in the storm, and leads her to insist that the television and music (they are a very musical family) are turned off while they eat:

> We used to have music in the background until we realized that the ears were on that and not on the conversation.

In two households, professional middle-class fathers do most of the cooking and food shopping. They articulate beliefs about sharing the workload and co-operating in family life:

> My wife works hard . . . – in the home and in her job – so it's really trying to take some of the load off her shoulders . . . (*Have you always been as involved?*) Yeah, since the children came anyway. For the last 12, 15 years.

Both wives work full-time (one also works in the evening), also in professional occupations. The fathers see family life as coming before work:

> I've never been able to classify myself as a company man . . . putting work first, being prepared to travel and devote a lot of unsocial hours to the company.

Unusually for men, these two fathers value mealtimes as an opportunity for communication:

> (*Do you eat together?*) Almost inevitably yes. (*Is that important?*) . . . it's a good opportunity to discuss the events of the day and talk about what the children have been doing. Are there any – do we see any sort of worried looks on their faces . . . it's a good opportunity to get things out in the open, I think. We tend to do a lot of talking at the dinner table . . . By instinct you can sense if one of the children, or even my wife, has had a bad day, and you try to probe gently to see if they want to talk about it . . . by the end of the meal, it's the proportion, the proportions of the problem are much less. (Sandra Purcell's father)

At the instigation of the daughter, Sandra, this family has drastically reduced their consumption of red meat. Sandra's father approves of young people's attitudes, regarding them as generally environmentally conscious:

> Young people are much more aware of the environment, and I think they set themselves up as the leaders in this, because they can jolly well see that the older generations have made an unholy mess.

In these households, eating together is part and parcel of everyday life, a pattern which some young people try to frustrate.

The 'resisters'

Young people's resistance may take the form of eating different foods, or having their meals separately from their families. The cases discussed here are those in which mothers are still struggling to maintain some control, in contrast to the cases discussed in the 'detached' group and, to some extent, in the 'delegated' group.

The cases in the 'resister' group are significantly all young women; they also all come from middle-class families. They tend to be high achievers in academic terms. From the viewpoint of the quality of their diets, they are in the healthiest group. Significantly, the young women are concerned about being slim. Two 'resisters' live in Asian-origin households and one in a Muslim family from the Middle East, while two have UK-born, middle-class parents.

Conflicts about eating are associated with these young people's sense of powerlessness in respect of family events and situations which make them unhappy. Refusing to eat the family meal constitutes a form of open rebellion, particularly in households where young people are subject to considerable restriction. One teenager, Aruni Kathiresan, who is from a middle-class, dual-career household of South-East Asian origin, prepares most of her own meals during the week, refusing to wait until her mother returns from work, though at weekends she eats with the family as required. She enjoys this degree of detachment from her family, which she sees as restrictive and over-protective. She often chooses food such as pizza, tuna or fish fingers from the freezer, rather than the Asian dishes her mother cooks. Aruni obviously enjoys having the house to herself before her parents arrive home from work. Her ostensible reason for not participating in the family meal is that the food is 'fatty and full of carbo-hydrates': 'It's not because I want to slim but I don't want to become fat.'

A young woman of Middle East origin, Nasreen Mohammed, avoids eating with her family whenever possible, and gives the excuse that if she did she would be tempted to eat too many calories. However, in addition, she sees herself as having a number of insuperable problems, including not believing in God while having to behave as a 'perfect' Muslim woman. Nasreen is not expected to be friends with non-Muslims, and is frequently chaperoned when she goes out, a practice which she finds oppressive and sometimes farcical. She links these conflicts with bouts of excessive slimming:

> The fact that I don't believe in God or the fact that I don't have anyone to turn to if I have a problem, I think that could have made me take my problems out on my food or my parents, in a sense obsessively.

Nasreen has become obsessed with her weight and describes starving herself for days on end in order to lose weight quickly:

> The way I diet is definitely unhealthy, ridiculous, pathetic. If I want to be healthy, I shouldn't diet that way. I have tried lots of other ways, and they haven't worked at all. (*You are trying to slim at the moment?*) Yes . . . I put on about a stone or something. It's annoying, because I look better when I'm slimmer. I wouldn't say I did it as a reaction to the media or anything. I look more elegant when I'm thinner. (*So how do you lose weight?*) Er, I either

cut down on my food and exercise, that's the hard way, or I don't eat. (*You go for long periods without food?*) Maximum of ten days. (*You eat nothing for ten days?*) A couple of carrots, black coffee. I have only done it for ten days at the most. And that was great, I didn't put weight on afterwards at all.

Nasreen's mother is worried, and believes her daughter is showing symptoms of anorexia. Nasreen also thinks she is a candidate for this illness, about which her comments show considerable insight:

[Mother] didn't like [that I was not eating]. She thought I was going anorexic, so did my brother, because I didn't feel hungry after ten days, so I didn't want to eat. But I thought I had better, because I would get anorexic. (*Are you worried there was an element of that?*) Well, my family thought so, and I didn't really. When I think about it, I suppose I would be a kind of candidate for it. High achiever, father absent, protective mother, that sort of stereotype, which I fit into quite nicely.

Nasreen's mother trusts her daughter's judgement concerning her condition, and feels reassured that she is in control, but she also consults a family friend, who is a GP, about her daughter's condition. Nasreen's father's role is to struggle to maintain parental authority by insisting that his daughter joins family meals at least at weekends:

I try to eat the evening meal with the household. My daughter doesn't comply. It's part of her attitude to food, her attitude to freedom. Generally she likes to please herself, eat what she likes. I've tried to persuade her eating isn't just about eating, it's a social situation . . . Nasreen doesn't comply. It's part of her attitude to food, her attitude to freedom. . . . In the weekend I apply a little pressure. (Nasreen Mohammed's father)

Questions of control – self-control and social control – are the central issue here. Both father and daughter see the struggle over food and meals as a form of resistance to family mores.

Another 'resister' is a thin and depressed young woman of Asian origin, Soraya Khan, whose violent father has recently separated from her mother. It would appear that her feelings of anger and lack of control of the situation are expressed through food refusal. Soraya's mother, greatly concerned, sees her daughter's refusal to eat as a poor reflection on her mothering, and as an additional source of conflict between her and her husband:

She only eats a lot of fruit, which is my responsibility, because if it finishes, then my husband goes berserk . . . She has stopped eating, you know. . . . I have to be after her all the time . . . you wouldn't believe it. I have to go in the kitchen and give food to her in her hand. . . . She says she wants to lose weight. If she doesn't want to eat, then I say to her, 'Well, just have an apple' . . . It's me that has got to feed them . . . (*Are you responsible for keeping her healthy?*) Yes, I think so, because if her dad came back he is going to kill me. (Soraya Khan's mother)

Soraya has not only become very abstemious about food, she has also recently decided to become a strict vegetarian. She describes her decision to stop eating meat as an act of purification in a corrupt world, and as linked to her recent decision to find God through Sikhism. Uncontrolled and predatory male sexuality is counterposed with feminine spirituality:

> My first priority is my spiritual life cos it's been – because I think my spirit has been banged about too much in this life already. I need to be better friends with God, because I don't come to terms with my situation easily . . . The main thing in becoming religious is controlling your senses, controlling your desires . . . The world's coming to an end. There's pornography, little children are being molested, there's rapes going on . . . I saw a documentary on cruelty to animals. It was horrific. I just sat there, and I cried for about an hour afterwards. After that I didn't want meat.
> (Soraya Khan)

As Twigg (1983) argues, food is part of a gendered hierarchy in Western culture. At the top, red meat is a masculine food, because it is seen as increasing potency and physical strength, with more feminine white foods such as chicken and fish lower down the hierarchy. At the bottom are the least masculine, 'weak' foods such as fruit and vegetables. Twigg describes how the food choices of some vegetarians are ideologically linked with the motive of 'desensualizing' and 'feminizing' human nature. The last point is particularly relevant to the case discussed above in the link the young woman makes between food and violence. With some cause, Soraya conceptualizes masculinity as threatening her both outside the home (she has recently been seduced by a much older family friend) and, until recently, inside the home (by her violent father). She finds refuge in spirituality from her vision of male violence, and her eating habits are implicated in this.

Soraya's mother exerts her authority to maintain family togetherness by insisting that the family eat together. To facilitate her daughter's participation at meals, she takes account of her vegetarianism by cutting down on the household's meat consumption. Soraya describes their eating together as 'a bit like the Boswells', the large, Catholic family often shown eating communally around the table, 'prayers an' all', in the TV situation comedy *Bread*.

The other two 'resisters' are middle-class young women with UK-born parents who enjoy a high degree of freedom in their personal lives. Like the latter young woman, they are experiencing anxiety and stress, one because of serious illness in the family, the other arising from a sense of rejection by her mother's new partner. In the latter case, the daughter, Anna, became a vegetarian, which she explains as a response to her anger at cruelty to animals, but which also expresses her sense of personal and moral purity: 'I feel clean inside, it's my conscience basically.' Because of her mother's extremely long working day, she often cooks and eats on her own. But when her mother is at home she eats different foods: 'So there's nothing we eat as a family, cos we're not really a family as far as I'm concerned.' Thus Anna also uses food as a way of expressing her hostility to the household situation:

> I sit there with great boxes of cornflakes and things in front of me, so that I don't have to see everyone else's meat on their plate. I barricade myself in with big pieces of cardboard. That causes massive problems cos my mum says I'm being totally pathetic. (Anna Gibb)

Anna's vegetarianism helps to separate the clean from the unclean, effectively putting a stop to the 'family meal' and rejecting her mother's new partner as part of the 'family'. Anna's mother does not mention her daughter's resistance at table, and instead presents her daughter's food decisions approvingly as part of 'growing up, being independent, being capable and enjoying it'. Her licensing of her daughter's vegetarianism does not, however, mean she cedes all parental control. On the contrary, she prevents her daughter from becoming 'detached' by making her choose from a list of food items which she buys. Even then, she finds it difficult to tolerate her daughter's selection if her diet is not a 'good balance': 'I only start to scream when it's all pasta or bread.' But in general Anna is allowed to express her sense of independence through her particular eating practices.

A similarly libertarian middle-class attitude prevails in another household in which the daughter, Angela, is conscious of her weight. Since early adolescence Angela has prepared her own meals, a practice which her mother describes in terms of a rightful bid for independence. Angela's mother sees it as a necessary and valuable experience of learning to be self-reliant, rather than as a threat to parental authority or family cohesion. However, she still prefers the family to eat together at weekends and, as in the previous case, partly controls the quality of her daughter's diet by buying foods from which Angela makes a choice:

> I mean, Angela is always eating these strange foods and things like that and, you know, I just fill up the fridge and they help themselves, that's part of their independence. (*So you don't cook every night?*) Oh, I cook for my husband and I, but I don't cook for them, no, so they're free to do what they wish, but on Saturdays and Sundays we always eat together. (*Is there anybody on a special diet?*) . . . She's always on some sort of diet. She's conscious of her weight, because she is quite a big girl. (Angela Pearce's mother)

It would seem that four of these five young women express through food and meal practices feelings of powerlessness about household events with which they are unhappy. The intake of food and eating meals are areas of activity over which they have some control. In effect these young women thwart their mothers' efforts by refusing to eat with the household; they fast, or refuse food, or they adopt a vegetarian diet. However, the mothers retain residual power over their daughters' diets by doing the shopping and choosing what goes in the fridge. When their daughters' diets get out of balance, mothers mobilize arguments about the need to eat healthily. In addition, they resist the resisters by insisting that, for example, they partake in family meals on at least some occasions, particularly at weekends.

The 'spoilt'

A third group of young people whose diets mothers continue to regard as being their responsibility we term the 'spoilt'. In these cases, mothers fulfil their sense of responsibility for young people's diet by cooking special foods for them and often providing separate meals. These young people have opted out (either partially or totally) of the family meal but, unlike the 'resisters' and the 'detached' (see below), they do not exercise independence by trying to cook for themselves. Rather, they are serviced by their mothers, who in the process create a great deal more work for themselves. This extra work may be seen as a 'gift' to the young persons in order to keep them attached in the future (Barker, 1972). Most of the young people in this category are the youngest in their families, and are either already in paid employment or are planning to leave school in the near future; they are thus rapidly moving towards a more economically independent existence. Significantly, all but one are young men. With one exception, their parents are working-class and were born in the UK.

Mothers justify catering to the wishes of these teenagers in terms of their 'food personae'. Some see their children as having always been 'faddy'; they are thus only continuing to provide the kinds of food they gave to their children when they were younger.

While faddiness is part of the child's persona, in the teenage years some young people may acquire other types of food character. William Lovelock's mother describes her employed son, her youngest, as a 'snack person', who, by definition, is not 'a fruit, salad or a vegetable person': 'If I gave him a cheese roll for his evening meal he'd be very happy . . . I do try to force him to eat a dinner every night but he's very picky.' She tries introducing 'healthy food' without much success: 'I used to encourage him to have cereals, but now I can't. I do buy yoghurts, and I encourage him to eat that because there's some fruit in them.' The young man in question refused to be interviewed but, from his questionnaire, it appears he eats few of the healthy items and regularly consumes crisps, chips, sweets, cakes and fizzy drinks.

Another mother describes her son as 'a tray person', as if eating separately was a question of taste, rather than a way of ignoring or flouting the household conventions which she had religiously adhered to with her older children.

> My daughter wasn't allowed to leave the table until everybody had finished. With my son . . . he just gets up and walks out. I think he's just worn me down. (Peter Greenway's mother)

In one household, the parents see their son's faddiness and food practices as linked with other aspects of his behaviour. When the relationship between father and son reached a crisis, his parents had him tested for food allergies, convinced that he was hyperactive because of all the additives in junk food. His father describes his son's diet:

> He'll say 'I don't like that!' He won't eat curries, spaghetti bolognese, curries, so it goes on. If he had the opportunity he'd live on turkey burgers, beef burgers and sausages. . . . He likes pizza, which isn't too bad, and I mean we do grill everything. (*Vegetables and salad?*) Doesn't like salad or any sort of vegetable. . . . Baked beans he loves. (Jim Lowe's father)

Jim's mother notes that if she did not cater for him separately, he would refuse to eat. This is a situation which her sense of maternal responsibility does not allow her to contemplate:

> I do tend to cook things for him, otherwise he doesn't get anything. And I reckon sooner or later – I mean they all get better when they go away on school trips. I said 'The only choice you'll get is you starve.' So I'm hoping he'll just eat everything. (Jim Lowe's mother)

Unable to prevent him from eating the sweets and chocolate he consumes at school, she encourages him to buy an apple and a Mars bar. 'Just to keep me quiet sort of thing, he said he did.' As far as the young man himself is concerned, his only incentive to cut down on confectionery is his concern with becoming overweight.

Mothers often blame themselves for their sons' limited food preferences. One mother attributes indulging her son, James, to the fact that James's father works in the evenings and James is the only one she has to cater for:

> Quite often I do something different for James because he won't eat stews or casseroles, so I spoil him like that. (*What does he like?*) Well, the usual, junk, chips, burgers. The things he does like, ooh, he'll eat mountains . . . He usually tells me what he wants and I make it for him . . . He's better now, he still won't eat a lot of vegetables, but he's better than he was. (James Signorelli's mother)

However, concerned about the quality of young people's diet, mothers do not necessarily spoil these young people all the time. One mother responds to the faddiness of her son, again the youngest child in the family, by alternating dishes he likes with those he tolerates:

> Peter likes chips with everything . . . pizzas and pies. (*So you cook him what he likes?*) What I try to do, like on a Sunday we have a roast, and then on Monday I give him something he likes, like pizza. Then Tuesday we'll have casserole, and the next day he can have what he likes . . . He's always had a good appetite. He's now just started eating vegetables. (Peter Greenway's mother)

The young people in this group describe their diets as unhealthy or mixed, while their mothers express only muted censure. As they have discovered over the years of motherhood, it is difficult to force children to eat what they do not like. The only young woman in the 'spoilt' group resists her single mother's healthy eating regime and insists on a different meal. Unlike her mother and sister, Catherine prefers 'chips, pies, beans, pizzas, and McDonald's, of course'. She thinks health messages about diet are 'all hype' and almost proudly declares her diet to be unhealthy. Her mother's efforts to improve her diet, which the mother describes as 'idiosyncratic', meet with no success. With one daughter highly selective in what she eats, and another a vegetarian, Catherine's mother provides three different meals every day. She finds this very difficult, especially as she is on a low income. But, by catering separately, she also feels she is not wasting food: 'I don't believe in giving them anything they don't like, because it's a waste.'

Mostly these mothers seem unwilling to regard these young people's eating habits as intentionally disruptive, believing instead that they are part of their make-up, something to worry about perhaps, but something which as mothers they must accept and deal with. Young men, especially youngest sons, appear to use their food faddiness as a strategy for persuading their mothers to continue to cook for them, and, by catering for them separately, to provide the kinds of food they enjoyed as children. In so far as the mothers comply, they sacrifice their time in the kitchen.

The 'delegated'

The most dominant pattern in the study is one in which parents delegate responsibility for the diet of their young people, especially evening meals, to the young people themselves, or share it with them. Unlike the 'resister' group, young people do not appear to have contested parental influence. Rather, the parents have initiated the handing over of responsibility, or it has been unproblematically negotiated.

Significantly, almost all the mothers in this group of households are in employment. A few are also single parents. In many of these cases, mothers' entry into (usually full-time) employment appears to have precipitated a more equitable redistribution of work within the household, particularly as regards food preparation; in full-time, dual-earner households, young people (young men as well as young women) claim to cook meals for themselves regularly at least once a week. In this group, many young people cook for themselves in the evening because they arrive home, often hungry, before their parents. One young woman, Jane, describes the arrangements in her family:

> During the week we don't usually eat together cos we're all, like, coming in at different times, and going out and doing different activities. And my mum usually eats when she comes in from [her work] which is about eight, nine. And my dad usually eats when he comes in, which is about seven. And, depending on what I'm doing, I eat when I come in from school or after my

activities, so it's all different times. But at weekends, well Saturday evening, we usually all have a meal together, and Sunday lunchtime. (Jane Richards)

The division of labour in terms of food preparation varies enormously within this group and over time, depending upon the commitments of the young people and their parents. In one case, the birth of a child radically altered a young woman's contribution at home. For others, responsibility only extends to cooking snacks for themselves.

Colin Clark's mother works as a catering supervisor in a school kitchen, and describes cooking meals as the last thing she wants to do on arriving home. She takes pride in her son's independence and capacity to be self-sufficient:

> I've brought them both up to be capable of cooking their own meals, so, I mean, if he's hungry before any of us, then it's 'Go and help yourself.'

Her husband has mixed feelings, first glossing over, and then expressing regret about, the passing of the family meal:

> Routine meals in this family is a mis-known thing. (*Is eating together important?*) I have to say no to that. We do eat together more now than we – actually that's just not true, we used to eat together, and it would be at peculiar times because of the work pattern. As they sort of got to 15 and 16 and they were more freelance ... We're almost *à la carte*. 'I fancy this', and 'Oh no, I don't.' 'Well, you have that, and you have this.' The reason it's got *à la carte*, having said that we come in and have a look and say, 'Help yourselves, you know how to cook.' (Colin Clark's father)

Colin comments:

> It's usually us on a week day. Sometimes if my mum's tired, my mum won't cook, so it's get what you want. But if my mum's cooking it'll be, it'll probably be a family meal. (*What kind of food do you make for yourself?*) Well, it depends. Sometimes I'll get carried away and I'll make myself a big meal. (*What do you count as a big meal?*) A sort of spaghetti or something like that ... If I start going out every night, I don't have a square meal every night and then – I've had experience about that and I've, I just get on a low, I just run out of energy quite quickly.

Even though Colin's mother regards delegating meals as a positive development, she thinks her son is not eating properly. His diet score from the questionnaire confirms her fears. Colin's father blames his son's less than healthy diet on his 'freelance' activities, which often lead to his missing meals altogether. Colin, on the other hand, subscribes to the idea of the 'family' meal – a 'square' meal cooked by his mother and the absence of which he connects with his recent bout of glandular fever.

In the case of Ukande's mother, who works shifts and is a single parent, her absence from home at mealtimes leads to quite elaborate rotas and delegated routines. Ukande's mother is from Nigeria and has responsibility for eight children including stepchildren and children of relatives. She requires the older children, all sons, to cook for and look after the younger ones when she is on night duty – at least two evenings a week. She prepares a basic dish at the weekend:

> We have our own way of preparing our soup in Nigeria. When I've prepared the soup, what I do is I keep it in the plastic bags, and put it in the freezer and [my teenage sons] could prepare the rice, and bring the soup from the freezer and warm it up in the microwave . . . I make sure I phone them from work: 'Have you prepared your food? Are you reading your book now? Make sure all the lights are off. Check the gas and all the doors. Goodbye!'
> (Ukande Osunde's mother)

Only one other young person in the study, Billy Johnson, takes on this level of responsibility. Unlike in the case above, this arrangement is carried out on a paid basis. It came about when Billy's mother began working full-time:

> We needed the money and Billy was responsible so we had a discussion about it, and I said, you know, 'You'd have to do different things if I went out to work when you come home from school.' (*What sort of things?*) Well, mainly [Billy] then cos he was the oldest, he was gonna get the meals ready. I'd leave it all prepared and he would just have to cook it, and his sister would have to tidy up and lay the table. (*Did they do that?*) Yes, yes, they still do it now, actually, yeah, it worked out quite well . . . I give them the family allowance, I divide it between the two of them . . . I just tell him what meat we're having, and then, if he's stuck at all, he'll phone me at work: 'Mum, what do I do with this?' But on the whole, no, he's quite a good cook, he's had to be when he was in the Scouts. (Billy Johnson's mother)

Ian's mother, who works irregular shifts, goes to similar lengths to provide 'proper' cooked meals by allocating responsibility to her elder daughters, who are expected to have a meal on the table when Ian, the youngest, returns from work:

> If my mum's working lates, my youngest sister cooks, or whichever one's in, or if they're not in, just make yourself something when you get in. (*How many times does your mum work late?*) She works a week of earlies and a week of lates. So it's alternate weeks . . . (*Right, so how do you work that with your sister, then?*) My mum tells her what to cook and she cooks it. (*Right. So you don't usually cook for yourself?*) Not all the time. It's mainly like ready for when we come in. Like mainly ready for about quarter past to half past six.
> (Ian Winter)

Shift work and long working hours affect all four working members of this household (Ian's father is a long-distance lorry driver). Eating together is rarely possible now in the week. However, Ian's mother is convinced that one 'solid' meal is essential to her family's health, and can counteract any 'bad' food they eat during the day:

> (*Do you think he eats in a healthy way?*) Oh yes, because I only, I cook meat, vegetables, potatoes and that. It's only about once a week, I think, we ever have chips and anything like that, because I don't believe in all that . . .
> If they're getting one solid, good, nourishing meal a day, then whatever

else they eat shouldn't hurt them. As long as they're getting the vitamins and that. (Ian Winter's mother)

The notion of 'good' counteracting 'bad' food is common. Ian, the young man in the last household quoted, eats fast food during the long working day in the garage, paid for by tips from customers. But as long as he is not overweight, he does not worry about his diet.

Several young people in this group say they enjoy cooking. One young man, Michael, comments:

I cook for myself, and I cook for the family occasionally. (*What do you cook?*) Anything really, because my dad's a pretty dab hand in the kitchen, so he's been teaching me since I was pretty young, so's my mum . . . I like a lot of special exotic meals . . . Chinese, Hungarian, Italian, anything . . . If it's something for myself, some pasta or pizza or something. (Michael Hammoud)

The 'detached'

This last group of two young people are the most autonomous. They have taken over responsibility for their diet and cater entirely for themselves, having totally abandoned the idea and practice of participating in family meals. This change took place out of a desire to assert their independence. In one case, Sonia began to eat independently even before she left school and started work. The other case, David, says the decision to abandon the evening meal came about when he and his two elder brothers began refusing their mother's meals, and she reacted by suggesting they take responsibility for their own food:

I was the one that started it, you cook your own food as well, it's only Sundays that you don't. (*Tell me about that.*) Well, I don't know, my mum used to cook, but then everyone used to take the mickey, you know. I don't know, sometimes like if you eat it a bit and then go, 'Oh I don't want that', and she goes 'Cook your own.' (*When did that start?*) About two years now. It's okay. Then, you know, if you can't cook, then you're stuck. (*Right, what do you do for yourselves, you come in from school and you start thinking about your meal?*) Er, yeah, it depends on what mood I'm in. If I feel like standing there for a long time, I'll have, you know, chips and all that, but otherwise I'll just grab a sandwich and go out . . . Er, it's only Sundays that they cook. (*Who cooks the Sunday lunch?*) Takes it in turns. (*You have a rota for that?*) Yeah, Dad one week then Mum the next. Yeah. And if they're out then my brother's girlfriend will do it, so it's okay cos I can't cook roast or anything. (David Monk)

Family meals are seen as the antithesis of personal freedom. David says:

My brother used to start eating upstairs, so I went up, so we just eat anywhere now. (*How did your mum and dad feel about it?*) Well, at the, I don't know, at the beginning, they were moody cos they felt like, you know, it should be, you know, a family thing. But they don't care now. (*How do you feel?*) I like it better cos then, you know, you're on your own, and you can do what you want. (David Monk)

David's mother is half embarrassed, half aghast at the situation; she regards it as her fault and blames her full-time job, working in the family cleaning business with its unsocial hours. Her own memory of the traditional meal eaten at the proper time, in the proper place, makes her sense of inadequacy even more acute:

That's another thing I feel guilty about because they are left to virtually get their own tea . . . (*Do you eat together as a household at all?*) Well it's dreadful to say this, but usually only on a Sunday, that's Sunday lunch . . . My mum would turn in her grave, because we were a family that had three meals, we all sat at the table and you ate your meal. When they were younger we did that, but as they got older and more independent, I must admit we didn't . . . (*Do you think it is important to eat together?*) Yes, I do. (*Because?*) Well, I think it's something you all do, even if it is only once a week, it's a coming together.

As the one woman in an otherwise all-male, rather macho, working-class household – the young men are interested in motorbikes and heavy rock – David's mother regrets the passing of the symbolic 'togetherness' of family meals, which are now only experienced on Sundays and at Christmas.

The effect on the quality of David's diet is significant. According to his own account, and the answers given on the questionnaire, he skips breakfast, and often has quick meals such as sandwiches for lunch and tea. His diet is high in fat and sugar (he consumes chips, sweets and a fizzy drink every day), and low in fibre, especially fruit and vegetables. David reasons that, because he does not eat a lot, no damage is being done to his health. He is aware that his mother wants him to eat more regular meals, but says that she 'can't be there all the time for me'. His mother's account of his diet is more critical: 'The children wouldn't know how to exist without a microwave. Their whole life is convenience.' The word 'convenience' here has a double meaning; its apparently positive connotation of labour-saving is compromised by the overt moral tone of disapproval which suggests her son's lack of effort – taking the easy way out. The same disapproval marks her description of her own diet:

It's no breakfast, no dinner, with maybe a snatched tea, which could be at any time, you know, before I go to work . . . Then I eat all the wrong things, chips. (*Why's that?*) Laziness.

In a second case, even more extreme, the young woman, Sonia, has entered the labour market and is the only member of the household who has detached herself from family meals. The decision is of her own making, and is consistent with other practices such as retiring to her own room where she eats, watches television and entertains her boyfriend whom she expects to marry in the next year: 'as I got older, I wanted to be by myself a lot more'. She tells her mother exactly what food to buy, and pays for it out of her wages. In effect, she constitutes a household within a household. This situation appears to create no animosity or dissatisfaction in the house, with her mother accepting it as part of becoming independent and making her own decisions.

According to her questionnaire, the quality of Sonia's diet is poor; she rarely eats fruit, vegetables or wholewheat bread, and consumes confectionery and fizzy drinks every day. She also reports eating very irregularly, skipping breakfast and evening meals. By the time of her interview some months later, a number of changes have taken place; she describes substituting mashed potatoes for chips several times a week, grilling food instead of frying it, and eating fruit every day. In contrast with her heavy smoking, lack of exercise and having unprotected sex with her boyfriend, she has become very concerned about her diet since starting work.

Changes in diet were not uncommon over the course of the two stages of the study. We asked parents and young people in the interviews if the young people had tried to change their diet over the past year: 14 out of 26 young women and 12 out of 29 young men who responded said that they had made changes, with a higher proportion of mothers (36 out of 53) than fathers (15 out of 28) making mention of this.

Conclusion

The eating practices of households with 16-year-olds vary in many ways. The pattern of eating together as a household on a regular basis is still common, at least with respect to the evening meal. Moreover, in roughly half the households, mothers still make the main decisions concerning what young people eat at home.

When meal practices are considered in relation to the locus of responsibility for diet, it is possible to see new patterns emerging. While the traditional model of mothers as food deciders and providers of the collective family meal is still the most common pattern, variations are also apparent. One group of young people tries to subvert the latter pattern by refusing to eat with the household and/or by changing their diets in significant ways. The 'resisters', as we have termed them, since parents are still locked in a struggle over the initiatives taken by the young people, are all young women, many of whom are concerned about their body shape and size. A third group consists of young people whose mothers allow them to eat separately, or consume special foods which the mothers prepare for them. Most are young men, often youngest children. The indulgent pattern of 'spoiling' adopted by these mothers has roots in the young people's childhood food faddiness, to which they continue to cater. They construct young people's food preferences in terms of food personae which they see as an intrinsic part of young people's make-up. If mothers decided not to service their children's needs in this way, and instead let them 'go hungry', this would be seen by them as a dereliction of maternal responsibility.

A further type of negotiation is visible in the 'delegated' group. Here, decisions about diet and meal preparation are shared between parents and young people, though they do not always eat together. This pattern may be a transitory stage, in which young people begin to take greater responsibility for themselves. However, the process by which this pattern comes into play appears to have less to do with normative developmental transitions of young people, and a good deal more to do with mothers' transitions as they move into full-time employment. Typically a situation arises in which mothers are absent from the house when young people arrive home hungry from school. This is the circumstance which prompts young people to cook for themselves, or to prepare the family meal.

The fifth group, while consisting of very few cases, represents the completion of the transition to adulthood, at least as far as food is concerned. Young people in the 'detached' group constitute separate households within households with respect to food. The reasons for this do not necessarily have to do with mothers' other responsibilities. For example, in one case the mother is at home on a full-time basis and potentially available to prepare the meal for her daughter. Even so the young woman considers herself an independent person and anticipates the transition into employment by becoming an independent food-preparer at an early age. The other case concerns a young man who similarly anticipates his economic independence by making his own meals, no longer meeting resistance in this from his mother.

The evidence concerning the relationship between different patterns of meal practices and healthiness of food intake is not clear-cut. For one thing, our measure of quality of diet relates to the time of the survey (though the interview accounts also provide some pointers) while the meal patterns derive from the interviews. Having said this, those who eat family meals prepared by their parents appear to have the healthiest diets. Similarly, those young people who resist parental pressures to eat with their families do not appear to eat particularly badly; several became vegetarians. By contrast, the tastes of the 'spoilt' group to which their mothers cater are particularly unadventurous, with several young men avoiding vegetables and fresh fruit. Of the two young people who were catering for themselves, one clearly ate poorly while the other (the young woman) had recently sought to improve the quality of her diet.

Notes

1 Exact agreement concerning frequency exists in only half the pairs of mothers and young people.
2 Of those who eat meals together, 55 per cent (12 out of 22) are in the healthiest diet group (group 1, Chapter 6). This compares with 31 per cent (5 out of 16) who eat meals together sometimes, and 22 per cent (4 out of 18) who eat meals together rarely. For consistency with Table 8.1, the mothers' responses concerning meal patterns are used unless they are not available, in which case those of their sons or daughters are taken instead.

3 Of those young people whose mothers decide what they eat, 43 per cent (12 out of 28) are in the healthiest diet group (group 1, Chapter 6). This compares with 32 per cent (7 out of 22) of young people who share the responsibility with one or both parents, and 33 per cent (2 out of 6) who take the responsibility themselves. As with the figures for meal-taking, the mothers' accounts of diet responsibility are taken unless these are not available, in which case those of their sons or daughters are taken instead.

4 In practice, fathers did not play a significant role here.

9 Household negotiations: sex, smoking, alcohol and drugs

In Chapter 7, we suggested that culture is a significant influence on whether families define rules concerning a range of activities, such as smoking and drinking alcohol, which have implications for young people's health. The existence of parental rules on these issues is related to the likelihood of young people engaging in them. Chapter 6 looked at the prevalence of young people's behaviour with respect to smoking, drinking alcohol, drug-taking and sex. In this chapter, we examine the interview accounts given by young people and parents concerning the ways in which rules are negotiated with respect to these health-related activities. We draw on the interview material to present an overview of parents' and young people's attitudes towards teenage participation in these activities, and the views of both groups about the extent to which parents influence these aspects of young people's behaviour.

Parental attitudes

In addition to open-ended questions concerning rules posed in the interview (Chapter 7) parents and young people were asked specifically whether they thought young people *should* smoke, drink alcohol, take drugs and have sex. As Table 9.1 indicates, young people are *less* likely than parents to say they approve of smoking and drinking alcohol, and much less likely than fathers to approve of teenage sex. Drinking alcohol is seen by parents and young people as the most acceptable activity, with fathers most likely to be accepting. This is not surprising when 28 out of 29 fathers (97 per cent) say they drink alcohol, compared with 41 of 55 mothers (75 per cent). Sex is the second most acceptable activity, while only a minority of parents and young people report being in favour of teenage smoking and young people are most likely to say they are against it. Around one-third of the parents admit to smoking themselves, 16 out of 55 mothers and 10 out of 29 fathers. A minority of young people, but

Table 9.1 *Positive and accepting attitudes* expressed by parents and young people towards young people engaging in smoking, alcohol, drugs and sex (interview data)*

| | Approve of | | | | |
	Smoking % (n)	Alcohol % (n)	Drugs % (n)	Sex % (n)	Base
Mothers	17 (9)	59 (32)	2 (1)	26 (14)	54
Fathers	29 (8)	82 (23)	4 (1)	43 (12)	28
Young people	10 (5)	51 (28)	16 (9)	25 (14)	55

*'Positive' means accepting, positive or positive 'with reservations'.

almost no parents, favour drug-taking, although 10 parents admit to having tried drugs in the past.

Other data from the interviews suggest almost universal acceptance on the part of parents and young people concerning parental provision of contraceptive information. It is perhaps striking, in view of this, that only half the parents said they had actually broached the subject with their own teenage sons and daughters (see Chapter 10). We asked both parents and their young people whether in principle they approved of those who are under-age being given contraception by their GPs without parental consent: overall, more parents and young people are in favour than are against, with 32 out of 45 mothers and 15 out of 27 fathers being either positive or accepting in their attitudes compared with 17 out of 25 young women and 16 out of 29 young men. Only nine mothers and eight fathers were against advice being given, together with two young women and seven young men.

Parental influence

Asking parents and their young people how far the former have influenced whether or not the latter have engaged in these activities is problematic. Influence often occurs by example, a means which may not be acknowledged in responses to direct questions. Similar proportions of parents and young people report in the interviews that parents have had some influence in the direction of non-engagement. Around two-fifths of young people report parents discouraging smoking, and a quarter say their parents effectively discourage the consumption of alcohol. Just over half the young people said that parental attitudes had some effect on whether or not they took drugs. Similar proportions of parents reported having some influence in dissuading young people from taking part in these activities. The exception is drug-taking, for which parents' estimates of their impact greatly exceed those of young people.

As we will see later (in Chapter 10), discussion between parents and their young people about sex and sexuality is patchy. Of those parents who know their teenagers have boyfriends or girlfriends, two-thirds say they have never given any advice or emotional support. The young people's estimates of their parents' support on these matters are even lower.

Parental knowledge

In the interviews young people admit that they do not generally conceal from their parents the fact that they drink alcohol. However, the small group of young people of Asian and Middle Eastern origin constitutes an exception here. Smoking is more likely to be covert, with seven of the 19 smokers keeping their smoking secret from their parents. Drug-taking is most likely to be subject to secrecy, but six parents of the 17 young people who had ever used drugs were aware that their child had used drugs. Moreover, as mentioned in Chapter 6, though estimates of drug use increased between the two stages of the study, in four cases questionnaire responses are not confirmed at interview by young people who chose not to give this information in a face-to-face interview. With respect to sexuality, of the 22 young people with some sexual experience, only four young women (including one who became pregnant) and one young man said that both parents knew they had had intercourse. Another seven confided in their mothers only, leaving half who had kept their sexual activities secret from their parents.

Household negotiations

Parents' and young people's accounts of their negotiations concerning these health-related activities focus not only on the discourse of 'health risks', but on more general moral discourses concerning 'right' and 'wrong'.

Parents and young people describe a number of ways in which young people's initiation or lack of initiation into smoking, alcohol, drugs and sexual relations is 'negotiated'. In using the term 'negotiation', we do not mean to imply that parents or young people necessarily consider these activities negotiable. In so far as they are regarded as *non-negotiable*, young people may decide to conform to parental wishes not to participate in the activity, or they may ignore the prohibition, either by openly carrying out the activity, or by doing so in secret. In so far as these activities are seen as *negotiable*, albeit regarded by parents as undesirable, young people may initiate themselves into the activity, while their parents may adopt the passive position of acceptance. Alternatively, parents may take pre-emptive action by, for example, helping their young people obtain contraception when they become sexually active. Styles of negotiation vary in relation to the degree of negotiability and the nature of the particular activity. We identified four broad types of negotiation in the household interviews in our study:

1 'Consensual' negotiations: these take place where parents proscribe potentially deviant activities and young people do not engage in them.

2 'Conflict avoidance': this occurs where parents forbid young people from engaging in these activities and young people carry them out in secret.
3 'Conflictual' negotiations: these arise where young people openly flout parental prohibition with respect to a particular activity.
4 Parental acceptance/active response: when young people become initiated into an activity, parents may adopt a passive position of acceptance or, more actively, they may take pre-emptive action to protect young people when they do engage in the activity.

Some households fall into more than one category, depending upon the activity under discussion. Negotiations can be 'consensual' with respect to smoking and drinking alcohol, but a sexual relationship may be kept secret. The situation may differ according to whether the activity is engaged in regularly or infrequently. In addition, one parent may license a young person to participate, while the other parent may not, or may be kept in the dark. The fourfold typology outlined above should be seen as dynamic, as circumstances change and parents and young people shift their positions and resolve their differences.

Non-negotiable activities – 'consensual' negotiations

Households in which young people conform to parental expectations in terms of not engaging in any negatively constructed health behaviours divide along cultural and structural lines. They tend to be found in middle-class households (14 out of 18 cases, or 78 per cent), disproportionately headed by parents born outside the UK (9 out of 18, or 50 per cent) and, in addition, the young people expect to go on to higher education. The four working-class young people also expect to stay in education, with the exception of a young man who, because of his dyslexia, decided to leave school to train as a carpenter. In these families, high value is placed upon deferred gratification – parents urge young people to work hard at their academic studies and to forgo any activities which will 'distract' them. Going out, with the associated 'risk' of succumbing to negative peer-group pressures, is thus discouraged (see Chapter 7). One mother of African origin describes her hopes for her son in terms of career and family:

> Their careers are very, very, important to them, which I believe is the most important thing for them to feel . . . If they didn't face up to their studies, then I'd be worried. But they don't waste their time . . . I want him to be a professional man, not financially, but morally. To be like a father and be responsible . . . And make sure he stays fast to the church. (Ukande Osunde's mother)

Among parents born outside the UK, parental prohibition is also justified on religious or moral grounds. Many of the young people appear to accept this. One young man, whose parents are of Chinese origin, articulates a highly critical moral attitude to smoking:

> (*What do you think about smoking?*) I always try to persuade them not to do it. (*Why?*) Because they're my friends . . . they're killing themselves, basically. They're only doing it because they think they look cool. I think it's totally stupid. (*Have they ever offered you a cigarette?*) They know the sort of person I am! So they know that if they ever said that to me, they'd be in big trouble . . . (*Have your parents ever said anything to you about smoking?*) No, well, basically we're grown up, and we know what's right and wrong. (Chenglie Wang)

Similarly, a young man, whose parents are evangelical Christians, speaks about sex:

> I think it [sex] should be with your wife. (*What do your friends think?*) I always let them know how I feel, and so if you're not ashamed – if you're ashamed, then they've got a reason to tease you. If you stand firm on what you believe in, they usually respect you for it. (Philip Stevens)

While young people in this group are not currently seeking a great deal of freedom and independence from their families, they are not treated as dependants at home. Their parents appear to have high expectations of their contribution to the household, and many see them as responsible for their own health. Several young people have quite onerous domestic responsibilities, including one young man who regularly cares for his younger brothers and sisters while their single-parent mother works night shifts. Others act as hosts or hostesses to family visitors, or they work unpaid in the family business.

Most of these young people say they have never tried smoking, alcohol or drugs. Most have never had a regular boyfriend or girlfriend. Their free time is usually spent with family or other kin. A young Sikh woman is an extreme case. Currently studying for three A levels at school, she plans to become a pharmacist or a dentist. She rarely goes out without her mother, and says she prefers to be at home. Her social life consists of visiting relatives who live in the area, or entertaining them at home. According to the mores of the household and their religion, sexual activity before marriage is morally taboo. Not smoking has a similar symbolic significance. Even talking about smoking is seen as distasteful:

> No one, not even my husband smokes . . . This kind of subject we never had to talk about at all. It doesn't belong to a Sikh family I think. (Maya Gupte's mother)

When asked if she thinks her daughter is old enough to have a boyfriend, the mother says not; talk of any possible sexual activity is cut short by a curt 'It's very bad.' As she has absolute trust that her daughter will be a virgin when she marries, sex is not seen as a threat. By contrast drugs are:

> I'm always telling them . . . never take anything. I tell them drugs is bad –
> they know that by themselves – drugs are bad. They are bad for health,
> they ruin your life.

Morality only gives way on the question of alcohol when, rather shame-
fully, she explains that she is not a strict Sikh, and so allows alcohol in the
house, as her husband likes to drink. The daughter has, however, never
tasted alcohol nor tried a cigarette. Significantly, she regards abstinence
as a question of 'will power' and strength of character.

Non-negotiable activities – 'conflict avoidance'

Some young people try to avoid conflict with parents who prohibit smoking,
drinking alcohol, trying drugs or having sex by engaging in these activities
without their knowledge. Conflict arises when a parent discovers the
activity and tries to stop it in the face of the son or daughter's resistance
(see 'Conflictual negotiations'). Under half the young people (12 out of
29) engage in secret activities only occasionally; 17 do so on a regular
basis. Half the young people are engaged in secret risk-taking with respect
to only one activity. Slightly more young people in this group have working-
class rather than middle-class origins. There are more young men than
young women.

Some young people from non-UK backgrounds no longer share their
parents' religious, moral or health views concerning smoking, drugs and
sexual relationships. They are thus rebels from previously consensual
households. In these households, drinking alcohol, smoking and having
relationships with the opposite sex are forbidden. Sex before marriage is
unthinkable. Thus, young people who wish to take part in these activities
have to observe total secrecy from their families and from their communities
if they do not wish to challenge their authority.

Young Asians find secret sexual relationships particularly difficult to
organize. They describe travelling outside their area of residence to meet
their partners. An elder sister in the family of the Muslim young woman
in the study was 'beaten' and turned out of the household for having a
boyfriend. A young woman regularly 'bunked off' school, and others met
after school on the pretext of studying, or they snatched time at weekends.
Two of the male partners had cars and their own flats, which helped.

Two Asian-origin young men were opportunistic about obtaining their
sexual partners, and casual to the point of brutality in their attitudes to
Asian women willing to have sex with them:

> It's up to the girl. If she gives it to them, that's her problem. If she doesn't
> that's fine – she isn't one of the slags.

These young men are the only members of the sample to report a large
number of sexual partners. Both say they now use condoms, though they
have not always done so. Involved in local gangs and possibly in criminal

activity, they have a considerable investment in secrecy in general, and not only with respect to smoking, drinking alcohol, and drug-taking:

> I drink at nights when my mum's at work ... I don't smoke in the house. That's restricted definitely ... [My mother] doesn't know ... she thinks I'm safe, so I want to keep it that way. I only smoke in the park, right at the back. If anybody down there grasses on me I'm going to do their windows in with bricks. For doing that. (Amin Choudry)

An extreme case concerns a young Asian woman who covertly rebels against the mores of her cultural group:

> You don't go out. You don't smoke. You don't talk to white people. You don't go out with them because they're bad. It's really stereotyped. You keep thinking white people are bad because they go out, smoke, they drink – they're bad ... I got sick of them and started hanging round with the people that were doing that. (*How did your parents react?*) I didn't tell them. I never used to tell them anything. (Soraya Khan)

However, despite her protestations, this young woman retains many of her strongly held religious principles, and is ambivalent about having had sex. She also disapproves of her boyfriend's use of condoms; she had wanted to be pregnant so that he would marry her:

> You should have sex if you're going to have children, not because you've got to have some pleasure for five minutes ... The main thing in becoming religious is controlling your senses, controlling your desires.

As to smoking, drinking or taking drugs, she is adamantly hostile:

> They're doping themselves. They should face life ... They're just cracking up, most of them.

When parents suspect that young people are breaking the rules, they often turn a blind eye, rather than provoke a confrontation. One father, an ex-smoker who is vociferously anti-smoking, is suspicious of his son's 'odd' night-time walks. Although he has 'been meaning' to talk to his son for some time, he has not yet done so. The son himself says that, although he has been a smoker for about a year, smoking 80 cigarettes a week, he never smokes at home, because he knows his parents will disapprove. He thinks his parents have recently become suspicious but, as nothing has been said, he does not intend to raise the matter and has no intention of stopping.

The mother of a now secret drinker describes how she actively banned her son from drinking in the house:

> I would be really happy if he never ever took a drink ... I've got this thing that he would never drink, so he has never drunk. (Peter Greenway's mother)

She tells a cautionary story about how she was culpable in not stepping in to prevent her elder son from being led astray by 'drinking people'.

As most parents in this group readily concede, even if they strongly disapprove of certain activities, they are not in a position to make young people desist. As Sandeep Kumar's father asks: 'How are you going to stop them?' Given their powerlessness, maintaining the appearance of parental authority becomes paramount. Denial and 'turning a blind eye' are both ways of achieving this. Moreover, from the young people's perspective, keeping their activities secret from their parents may be interpreted as a sign of respect for them.

If parents do exercise authority by stopping young people from engaging in these activities, they risk alienating young people. A formerly disciplinarian father, of British working-class origins, now adopts gentler tactics:

> You don't push them, and you don't pull them, you just hope you're
> nudging them in the right direction. You're easing them away from the bad
> elements . . . you're steering them on whatever course they're on . . . It's our
> responsibility to see that hopefully, we steer him away from smoking, see he
> doesn't drink, hopefully we never see him take drugs. If there's an illness
> developing we're astute enough to stop it earlier. (Peter Greenway's father)

Mr Greenway's active vocabulary of 'nudging', 'easing' and 'steering' is echoed by other parents who talk of 'discouraging', 'nagging' and 'advising' their teenage sons and daughters in the 'right' direction, and away from the 'bad elements'. The delicacy of these negotiations means that direct confrontation or coercion is avoided, and thus the parent's authority is not challenged:

> As they get a bit older, a bit wiser and a bit more independent, so you
> would be less inclined to tell them 'You mustn't do this', or they'll be telling
> you to mind your own business. Disrespect!

Non-negotiable activities – conflictual negotiations

In only a minority of households (four in total) did parents and their young admit to current conflict; in two the issue is smoking, and in two others both smoking and sex. The overall lack of conflict in our sample is perhaps not surprising, as by the time teenagers reach the age of 16, physical coercion is rarely an option for most parents. In addition, others may have already passed through and resolved a stage of active conflict with their parents. Eleven cases of past conflict, mostly concerning smoking, are reported. In some of these cases, parents see themselves as having successfully intervened, or describe young people as having 'learned a lesson'. A mother describes what happened when her daughter once got drunk:

> She came back a bit the worse for wear. She didn't know where she was.
> After cleaning up all down here I went upstairs and found her in my bed.
> She was absolutely disgusting . . . I blew my top the next day. She didn't do it
> intentionally, but she's never touched a drop since. (Catherine Sheppard's
> mother)

Robert Muir describes how his father 'battered' him after his brother told his father he was smoking. However, he resumed smoking after his father separated from his mother. Andrew Brown's father describes how he'd caught his son smoking a few years ago, and categorically insisted that he would only be allowed to smoke when he was 18 or when he left home: 'I don't believe in kids smoking.' The stepmother in this household, who gave up smoking on the recommendation of her doctor, describes a strategy of creating revulsion and instilling fear in Andrew: when she found his younger brother smoking, she threatened to make him smoke fifty cigarettes one after the other, as a matter of 'kill or cure'. She also uses her health problems to frighten him: 'If you want a chest like I've got, you carry on smoking.' Andrew confirms that he gave up partly out of fear.

In the four households in which parents currently express strong disapproval of teenagers' smoking or sexual activities, parents are not prepared either to ignore or to license these activities. One strategy is to make young people feel guilty by directly appealing to them to stop. Emma Kerr says:

> My mum asked me to give up smoking, and I felt really guilty. She just said 'Can you give up smoking?' And it made me feel so bad, because she's worried about me. (*Do you want to stop?*) I'm not sure. I do enjoy smoking.

In only one case is there evidence of serious current conflict leading to possible rupture of family relationships. The case is deviant in structural terms; unlike other young people in the study, this young woman, Rachel Pemberton, negotiated a double transition as a new single mother and a member of the workforce. Her anti-smoking mother says she stops everyone smoking in the house, but is unsuccessful with Rachel. Rachel's mother was pleased when her daughter gave up during her pregnancy. But when she resumed smoking after she finished breast feeding, her mother used a strategy of trying to induce guilt by appealing to Rachel's sense of responsibility for her child, arguing that passive smoking will hurt the baby. Rachel complains about her mother:

> (*What do you think about smoking?*) I don't think it's that much of a big thing. I mean, my mum made a big deal about it. (*How?*) She went on about cancer, and I just said to her: 'Mum, give it a rest.' And she said: 'What about the baby?' I said: 'I don't smoke near him' ... But, you know, she said: 'You'll give him cancer'. ... But if I'm round my boyfriend's house then he will hold the baby while I have a cigarette and vice versa and we do it like that. (*So you don't feel he's at risk?*) No, definitely not. (*And you?*) I don't think about it.

Despite the moral pressure, Rachel is determined to continue smoking since it helps her to cope.

> (*When do you most feel like a smoke?*) If I'm upset, like when the baby starts crying and he won't – like yesterday, I ended up going for a walk because he was crying and I was getting upset ... I get very tired when, because he cries

and I get upset. I mean a couple of times I've had a cigarette in the bathroom and she's found out. She comes up and says 'Did you have a cigarette?' and I've said 'Yes', and she says 'Don't do it again!'

Despite Rachel's new adult status as both worker and mother, her mother tries to control her sexuality, prohibiting her from going to her boyfriend's house, because she is fearful that she may get pregnant again. Her mother no longer 'trusts' her, which she sees as a problem as much for herself as for her daughter:

It isn't just her, it's me. I said, 'I've got to learn to trust people with you.' I say, 'No, I don't want you going round a fella's house now at all, I'd rather you were round here.' 'But mum, I'm not going to do anything.' I say, 'I'm sorry, love, but I still won't forget certain things.' I've got to build up in myself. It's not, I don't think, that I don't trust her.

Rachel is thinking of leaving home on account of her mother's restrictiveness, and despite the very considerable practical and financial support which her parents provide for her and the baby. Having reached adulthood in two respects – as worker and mother – she sees herself as having 'the right' to resist her mother's control.

Negotiable activities – parental acceptance and pre-emptive action

The small number of cases (six only) in this group all concern sexuality. Four of these young people are female; all are sexually experienced. Four are smokers, and all but one are regular drinkers; two have tried drugs and four are regular users, mainly of cannabis. Four young people are of mainly working-class backgrounds, and have left school; two middle-class young people are doing their A levels, and intending to go on to higher education.

Parental acceptance of young people's autonomy is likely to be greater when young people move into the labour market, and achieve some financial independence. Since working-class young people are likely to start work earlier than middle-class young people, it is not surprising to find greater parental acceptance of risk behaviour in these households.

When young people resist their parents' attempts to control their activities, some parents adopt a passive position, and give way, accepting that they are powerless to influence young people. Other parents appear to have taken a lenient line for a long time. Parents may accept that young people engage in some activities, but not in others. As noted earlier, parents are most accepting of young people drinking alcohol (in moderation). In one household, smoking cigarettes is contested, while the mother is reported by her son to accept his using cannabis, provided this is on an occasional basis.

Parents in some households clearly state that young people at 16 should take moral responsibility for their own actions; they have legitimate rights which parents should not infringe. Such parents do not necessarily approve of young people's behaviour. Rather, they agree to respect their decisions, provided that certain conditions are met. A working-class single parent justifies her accepting stance on the basis of the increasing difficulty of making young people follow a particular path, and the need to balance parental responsibility with young people's 'individual rights':

> You can't program a person's brain to think like yours. You can't insist on them wanting to do something – they've got the right to choose. You've got to give them guidelines – too much freedom is as bad as being too cooped up and not being allowed to open your mouth. I don't believe in that, you've got to find the happy medium, definitely . . . You've got to say, 'Whatever you do is OK by me, as long as you know best what you want.' But the hardest thing is trying to encourage them to find what they want. That's the hardest thing. (Catherine Sheppard's mother)

According to Western democratic ideals, young people in adolescence are expected to achieve 'individual rights' and to be free from interference. Thus, even though in one household a mother of Afro-Caribbean origin[1] is herself strongly opposed to smoking and sex before marriage, her general attitude is to encourage her recently employed daughter to make her own decisions with respect to having sex with her boyfriend. The young person, Margaret Nelson, has left school despite her parents' desire for her to continue with her education, and is working full-time after a period of unemployment.

> It's their decision what they do . . . They're individuals. They have ideas of their own and thoughts of their own . . . They should be helped to develop their thoughts, but they can't live their parents' lives . . . I am no longer responsible for their development, though I'll be supportive at all levels. (Margaret Nelson's mother)

Margaret's stepfather (of UK origin) is even more explicit about their acceptance of their daughter's decision to have sex, as long as she uses contraceptives. In this household, contraception is openly discussed and condoms made available: 'The whole thing is very open and free.'

With respect to sex, such parents tend to respond in a proactive way. (On the other hand, if sex is not regarded as negotiable, parents may prefer not to know that young people are sexually active.) In one household with three young people all in the workforce, parents take for granted the right of young people to have sexual relationships, and condone this as long as they take 'precautions'. The mother prides herself in being open about sexuality, and is pleased when her sons and daughters are accepting of a lesbian friend who comes to stay. Her only stipulation, mainly at the father's behest, is that her children, especially her daughters, must not have sex with their partners on the premises, at least while the parents are at home.

In the interview situation, working-class mothers are more reticent than middle-class mothers concerning their daughters' emergent sexuality. For example, one mother omits mentioning the fact that she accompanied her daughter, then aged 15, to the GP for a prescription for the contraceptive pill. The daughter has no such inhibitions, and talks openly about the incident. She justifies her demand for the pill in terms of having 'grown up quick', and wanting to enjoy herself – 'as you're only young once'. Her mother's only reference is to a discussion concerning the 'right' time to have sex, maintaining that you can only 'guide' them:

> It's down to them in the end. You can't watch them 24 hours a day.
> (Sally Rimmer's mother)

Action to obtain the contraceptive pill was taken by three other young women with the active participation or support of their mothers. According to one young woman, again in full-time work, the decision to take the pill after having unprotected sex with her much older partner was entirely her own:

> I'd been going out with my boyfriend for two years, and I just decided that I didn't want to get pregnant. So I went to the doctor's and he just prescribed it for me. (*Did you talk to your parents before you went?*) No . . . I came home after and told my mum. (*What did she say?*) Nothing really. I think she was pleased I made the decision . . . It was from then that we started getting on a bit better . . . She started saying, 'Oh you can take responsibility.' (Alison James)

This young woman was rather contemptuous about 'silly' 16-year-olds who were always wanting to 'experience' life, rather than 'live it'. But here, again, the working-class mother declines to discuss her daughter's sexual life in the interview, though she says that young women ought to be able to have contraceptives before the age of 16 on the grounds that they will engage in sex whatever their parents' views: 'A lot of them are active before that age.'

Less inhibition is shown in the interviews of two middle-class mothers whose daughters are still in full-time education. They freely discuss their daughters' quests for contraceptive advice from their GPs. One mother focuses on the GP, rather than her daughter:

> She went to our GP, which I have to say I was slightly appalled about, because she didn't examine her beforehand . . . What actually happened was that [the GP] gave her, I think it was a three-month course, and she only took it for a month . . . She wasn't having a very good time on it . . . she felt sick. I would have insisted that she went back for a check-up, and at least they could have changed it or found out about it . . . We did talk about it and I said, 'The next time, if you decide to go on the pill, you must insist on [an examination]'. (Anna Gibb's mother)

In this account, going on the pill meets with no moral criticism. Rather, the mother expresses, as part of her parental responsibility, concern about the health risks. She also talks about her desire that her daughter should have a 'loving and giving relationship'. This 'person-centred approach' has been interpreted as characteristic of the 'new' progressive middle class.

According to Aggleton (1987), 'good' heterosexual teenage sex should be 'diligent', 'industrious', 'committed' and not concealed. True to type, this middle-class mother wants her daughter to value long-term loving monogamy: 'Casual sex I think of as one of today's tragedies.' But contrary to her mother's exhortations, the young woman herself does not want to be confined to 'committed' relationships, and does not think it essential to love the person in order to have sex with them:

> That's where me and my mum are different, very severely . . . The first person I slept with was someone who was a lot older than me, a lot more experienced. I was totally inexperienced. My mum said it was awful that it happened with someone like that, because I don't like him at all now. I think of it as experience . . . She's very sad that the first time I slept with someone, it wasn't someone that I'd been going out with for longer. It wasn't someone I loved, or someone I could entirely trust. (Anna Gibb)

Two different views of self-development are expressed here. While the mother values person-centred relationships, and sees her daughter as 'stupid', the young woman emphasizes the importance of individual 'experience' and constructs her mother's view as 'stupid'. She does, however, agree with her mother that she was 'stupid' on one occasion, and tells a shamefaced story about having once had unprotected sex and needing to take the 'morning after' pill. Her mother gave her 'the third degree, literally interrogated me . . . I was so embarrassed at being such a total idiot.'

A second middle-class mother with a progressive approach describes parental responsibility at this age as shared: 'a movable feast – she takes responsibility and I watch'. She is more proactive in her approach to her daughter's sexuality and arranged for her daughter to get the contraceptive pill:

> With the two eldest, they said, 'Mum I want to go on the pill', so we went down to the doctors and got put on the pill . . . I knew Angela has had sexual experience with her boyfriend, but she wasn't protected. (Angela Pearce's mother)

Angela takes up the story:

> My mum discussed with me about going on the pill, and she said, 'We'll go along and get it.' She insisted on coming with me, and I just knew they're going to ask me, 'Have you had sex before?' Anyway, so she came along, only I didn't want to talk to her about it, because it's a bit personal. When the doctor asked me, I did actually say 'No'. But then when we went outside, my mum said, 'Why did you say that, when you have had?' I said, 'I knew you knew' (laughs).

This young woman expresses some ambivalence about having her mother so closely involved in her sexual life: 'It's funny, it's too sort of incestuous, too close to home sort of thing.'

Conclusion

We have suggested that, of the four risk-taking activities looked at in this chapter with the exception of drinking alcohol, most parents and young people disapprove of 16-year-olds engaging in smoking, drug-taking and sex. They disapprove of these activities on grounds of morality as well as the risk to health. Where young people conform to parental views or rules, this process appears to be achieved through reward rather than sanction – encouragement to study and the deferred rewards of educational achievement – especially among those parents not born in the UK. Where young people decide to engage in activities in the face of proscriptive moral norms, they frequently resort to secrecy. This enables the public face of parental authority to be preserved; parents remain in ignorance or turn a 'blind eye'. In only a small minority of households in our study are young people in the process of openly flouting parental prohibition. On the other side of the fence, some parents accept young people's initiation into risk-taking activities. For working-class UK-born parents, leniency is structurally prescribed when young people achieve independence by joining the labour market. Some parents, however, justify adolescent independence in terms of a personality characteristic, rather than the new status of worker: 'She's got a head on her shoulders and knows what she wants.' This parallels some parental constructions of young people's food choices, described in Chapter 7, where these are seen in terms of some consistent personality trait rather than as a feature of adolescence as such. A particularly interesting case in our sample is that of the young woman who has achieved adulthood in two different respects: she has both started work and become a mother. Her account of risk-taking behaviour, particularly smoking, exhibits features of the way in which adult women with caring responsibilities talk about smoking; smoking is a way of coping with stress, and a way of 'doing something for oneself' (see Graham, 1987). However, as she is still living in her parents' household, smoking and other forms of risk-taking behaviour have at the same time features of adolescent rebellion. This double phenomenon is reflected in her mother's comments.

Some middle-class UK-born parents accept young people's participation in risk-taking activities. Significantly, they justify their acceptance in terms of an 'individual rights' morality, respecting young people's right to make their own decisions. In these cases, they see their parental role as guiding (often covertly) young people without trying to exercise authority.

We have identified four types of negotiations which take place between young people and their parents around the risk-taking activities of smoking, drinking alcohol, trying drugs and having sex. When parents consider these activities to be non-negotiable, their actual negotiations with young people are 'consensual', 'conflict-avoiding' or 'conflictual'. Where activities are considered by parents to be negotiable, parents come to accept, if not to approve of, young people's initiation into one or other of these activities. Young people's initiation into sexual relations appears to be something of a special case here, and parents who accept this tend to adopt a proactive position, for example by helping their daughters to obtain contraception.

Note

1 We placed this household with the UK-born parents' group because one parent (the stepfather) was of UK origin and the other of Afro-Caribbean origin. The young woman had had no contact with her biological father since early childhood.

10 Relations between parents and young people

Parents are expected to provide a 'good' upbringing for their children. As we saw in Chapter 3, key ingredients are the provision of material support, protecting the young from abuse and danger, being caring and concerned, and instilling norms and values which guide children's behaviour and prevent them from breaking societal rules. Societies and social groups differ in how they interpret parental obligations – both the nature of the goals and the means by which the goals are to be achieved. This is so throughout the ages and stages of childrearing, but is particularly marked in the teenage years. In this chapter, we examine the ways in which parents of different gender, class and ethnic origins interpret the twin aspects of parental responsibility – care and control – in the face of their sons' and daughters' transitions from childhood to adulthood. The renegotiation of relationships that takes place is examined from the perspectives of both young people and their parents; what a parent considers to be love and concern, the young person may perceive as interference.

In the first part of the chapter, we give a brief overview of the quantitative data from the survey and the interviews concerning parents' and teenagers' relationships in terms of quality and closeness. Next, we outline how far parents and young people communicate about particular matters. In a case analysis from the interview study, we turn to the qualitative material and examine the different patterns of relationships in terms of a conceptual model which relates parents' modes of control to young people's autonomy. We also examine the way in which gender makes a difference to these patterns, and their relationship to different cultural values and class positions.

Models and discourses: the role of communication

With respect to the management of transitions to adulthood, one model is for parents and young people to subscribe to an 'individual rights' perspective; young people are ideally freed from parental interference in their move to *achieve* independent adult status. An alternative model emphasizes the parental role in prescribing characteristics of young people's new adult status; it is parents who confer upon young people new responsibilities, especially towards others. In this second model young people's new status is *ascribed* rather than achieved.

Individual scheduling of young people's transitions to adulthood needs to be located in relation to a range of contemporary social discourses. One critical discourse is that of parental responsibility for young people; the role of parents is asserted in contradistinction to the idea that the state should be responsible for young people, for example, in providing an income for those who leave school and are unable to find jobs, or in providing housing for those who choose, or are forced, to leave the parental home. Rising levels of youth unemployment in the UK and other countries have given this discourse of parental responsibility a new significance. Its implications are to tie young people more closely to their parents (and vice versa) at a time when many young people might prefer greater independence.

A discourse which has the opposite consequences for young people's relationships with their parents – signifying their independence, rather than their dependence – is the movement which may be described as personal development or 'person-centredness'. This has been particularly influential among the 'new' middle classes. Its underlying philosophy constructs relationships as voluntaristic, not only at their inception but also in their continuation. Relationships are seen as constantly renegotiated, as people consider whether they wish to continue to stay together.

Giddens (1991) articulates the idea in terms of the 'pure relationship' in which the individual is afforded opportunities for 'intensified intimacy'. In his view, the 'pure relationship' is tied to the individual's need to engage in what he describes as 'the reflexive project of the self''; this project is underpinned by the idea of commitment made on the basis of choice. The implication is that relationships persist only as long as both parties are in receipt of reflexive rewards from them.

Giddens suggests that the pure relationship may be applicable to relationships between parents and young people. The central idea is that, in the transition to adulthood, parents and young people renegotiate their relationships on the basis of voluntarism. Given that the onus is on the young person to push for independence, it is beholden upon the parent to create the conditions under which the relationship can continue. Norms concerning family obligations are relegated to the status of 'guideline', rather than strict rule (Finch, 1989). If parents want 'close relations' with their children to continue into adulthood, they must, as part of their reflexive endeavours, re-create ties on the basis of equality and reciprocal liking, trust and understanding.

Another way to conceptualize this process is in terms of parents keeping young people 'close', but with a view to long-term material reciprocity (Barker, 1972). Keeping young people close is the mother's role, in line with the principal defining feature of modern motherhood, which is emotional attachment to children. As we have already seen in this book, the lived experience of adolescence is a gendered and cultural phenomenon, by contrast to theoretical ideas of adolescent development which take little account of gender and other axes of cultural difference. As Apter (1990) suggests, in practice, young women and mothers are less concerned with the individuation and separation from parents which is presumed to be a central and 'normal' feature of adolescence according to the model. Mothers and daughters are more concerned with the creation of ways of reconnection. For fathers, the problem is different. Since fatherhood with respect to young people is felt to be not clearly defined, it is less obvious to many fathers what their new role should look like.

Just as the discourse of pure relationships in marriage-like partnerships de-emphasizes or, as some would argue (for example, Brannen and Moss, 1991), obscures power, so parents' renegotiation of ties with their children tends to play down the hierarchical relations between them. Parents try to be 'like friends' and to be confidants to their children. These changes are described in terms of communication patterns – for example, the requirement upon young people to provide information concerning their whereabouts in return for which parents allow them to go out. This means that parents have to 'trust' that young people are telling them the truth, and that they will conduct themselves in a way which befits their new adult status.

The concept of the pure relationship draws attention to the ideological aspects of the renegotiation of relationships – the meanings with which relationships are inscribed. While these meanings relate to practices, they do not uniformly shape them. The problems of power and control remain. For, as we shall show, parents do not in practice give up being responsible or trying to influence their children as they become adult. Rather, control mechanisms undergo change. As Bernstein (1971; 1975) argues and demonstrates, language is a vehicle of social control and constructs, or reconstructs, the social relationships between parties to it.

In the re-creation of relationships between parents and young people, communicative strategies may constitute a key means of control – what Bernstein (1971) refers to as 'personal modes of control'. As we have argued, some parents view the transition to adolescence from an individual rights perspective and place emphasis upon the individual young person's achievement of independent adult status. For these parents, the form of communication is the form of control. Other parents, by contrast, see the transition to adulthood as ascribed rather than achieved and confer new responsibilities upon young people. In these cases, the form of control issues from the rights and duties of parental status rather than from the form of communication *per se*.

The use of communicative forms of control enables parents to monitor young people outside face-to-face relationships by requiring to be informed of their activities outside the home. This surveillance involves a shift from visible to invisible forms of control (Bernstein, 1975). Its effectiveness depends, however, upon the ways in which young people perceive and respond to it. If young people perceive parental communication as too intrusive, they may develop counter strategies to fend off parents and to create boundaries around their presumed 'autonomy'. A crucial strategy available to the young people is to withhold information about their activities outside the home. Alternatively, they may *threaten* to do so, thereby testing parents and exposing the invisible power upon which the relationship rests. In combination, the various strategies of parents and young people result in processes of negotiation, renegotiation and bargaining, as we have seen in Chapters 8 and 9.

Whether or not the parents in our study rely upon communicative strategies, the leitmotiv of their accounts concerning their relations with young people is communication. Asked to describe their relationship, a mother refers to 'talk', 'discussion' and 'understanding'. However, the asymmetrical aspect of the relationship is appended in the following:

> Just a typical mother–son relationship. You know, we understand each other, we talk to each other which I think is quite important, discuss things. He listens on the whole, I think. (Jo Saunders' mother)

In one sense, the mother's account suggests that talk acts as a leveller in social relations. This suggestion is apparently supported by her son's comment: 'She treats me like an adult – the way she talks to me.' But talk also serves another purpose for the mother, that of maintaining a hold over her son. Thus, while seeming to emphasize the equality of the parties and to recognize her son's right to independence, communication also constitutes a strategy of covert control.

In contrast, and as we saw in Chapter 8, many of the accounts of young people are about *not* talking to parents, especially when parents demand information about their activities which they are unwilling to give. In the following, a young man explains why he does not feel close to his father. While his remarks suggest a lack of enthusiasm for communication, at the same time he regards talk as indicative of the achievement of adult status:

> Cos I'm a bit quieter. I'm not the sort of person who'd go around talking to everyone – explaining problems and that sort of thing ... [My elder sister] is now treated as a sort of friend because she's an adult, and they're sort of *talking* on a level. They don't treat her as like, 'You're my daughter. You've got to do as I say.' (Christopher Spence)

The main concern for many young people at this time is with doing what they want without parental interference. In seeking greater independence, the potential loss of parental approval is less of an issue; young people are caught up with the present and with their own lives, and are not particularly interested in the future and their parents' dilemmas. This means that maintaining channels of communication has a different kind of significance for them. Rather, it is the control aspects of the Janus-headed

Table 10.1   *Young people's questionnaire reports of quality of relationship with parents by household composition*

| | | | Household composition | | | | | |
| | All | | Two biological parents | | Parent + other* | | Single parent | |
Quality of relationship	Females %	Males %	Females %	Males %	Females %	Males %	Females %	Males %
With mother								
excellent/good	82	86	82	86	82	79	79	88
fair	11	10	12	10	7	9	6	8
poor/very poor	7	4	5	4	11	12	15	4
Base	339	450	259	341	27	33	53	76
With father								
excellent/good	67	82	68	82	[2]	[4]	[3]	[9]
fair	21	13	22	12	[2]	[2]	–	[2]
poor/very poor	11	5	10	6	[3]	–	[3]	–
Base	272	358	259	341	7	6	6	11

*'Parent + other' includes all households where one parent lives in a couple relationship with a parent-type person.

character of communication in parent–child relationships which concerns them more. While young people may interpret gentle enquiry from parents as signs of love and concern, more persistent demands for information may be perceived as unwarranted and unwelcome prying and interference.

On the other hand, communication with parents is not unimportant to young people. In shaking off the shackles of childhood, they may spurn what they see as 'too much' affection. In this sense, talk may act as a substitute for the expression of physical warmth, especially among young men, whose masculinity is defined in terms of *not* showing affection. Moreover, in so far as discussion is part of being adult, being asked for one's opinion by parents may constitute an important source of self-esteem for young people.

Quality of relations between parents and young people

In the questionnaire, young people were asked to rate their relationships with their parents on a five-point scale from 'excellent' to 'very poor'. Over four-fifths report 'good' or 'excellent' relationships with their mothers. Roughly similar proportions of young men but rather fewer young women report 'good' or 'excellent' relations with biological fathers living with them in the same household. At the other end of the scale, more young women than young men report 'poor' or 'very poor' relations with their fathers. Seven per cent of young women and 4 per cent of young men report 'poor' or 'very poor' relations with their mothers. Table 10.1 shows the relevant figures.

Young people reporting good relations with mothers are more frequently found among only children, the white UK-born group and the 'other' ethnic group. Rather more young people in single-parent and step-parent households report poor or very poor relationships with parents, compared with those in households with two biological parents. Young men living in mother-headed households report more positive relations with their mothers, and young women report less good relations when compared with those in two-parent households. More young women in mother-headed households report poor relations with mothers, when compared with all other groups. Since most young people living with only one bio-logical parent live with their mothers, numbers living with resident fathers are too small to analyse.

The figures in Table 10.1 only relate to those relationships where parent and young person live in the same household. We carried out a separate analysis for young people and non-resident biological parents. This sug-gests that both young men and young women with non-resident parents report considerably fewer good and more poor relationships.[1]

Our questionnaire survey also provided data on relationships with step-parents. With the exception of young men's relations with stepfathers, far fewer young people, compared with those reporting on 'natural' resident parents, report good relations with resident step-parents. Indeed, relations with step-parents may be said to be on a par with those with non-resident parents.[2]

At both ends of the quality-of-relationship spectrum, differences by sex are more marked with respect to fathers. Young women in nuclear and non-nuclear households are significantly less likely to report good rela-tionships with fathers, including stepfathers and non-resident fathers, and are more likely to report poor relationships than are young men. Other questionnaire evidence supports this. Asked in the questionnaire with which adult young people got on best, only 9 per cent of young women and 14 per cent of young men mention fathers, while 52 per cent cite mothers.

The interview material from young people generally supports the survey findings on quality of relationships with parents, though the questions asked were not quite the same. In the interviews, we questioned parents as well as young people about relationships, and then went on in the analysis to create 'ratings' of both 'positive' and 'negative' dimensions of relationships which took account of all the comments made. Overall, we found relationships to be most positive and least negative among mothers and daughters, closely followed by mothers and sons. Fathers and sons come next, followed lastly by fathers and daughters.

Nearly three-quarters of young people are rated as having positive, and no negative, affect towards their mothers. This included rather higher proportions of young women (19 out of 25) than young men (19 out of 29). With respect to fathers, only a third of young people, and more young men (14 out of 28) than young women (6 out of 24) have predom-inantly positive ratings. Eight young people are rated predominantly negative; in all cases (four of each sex) negative feelings were concerned with the fathers.[3]

Compared with young people, parents' ratings of relationships are rather more positive and less negative, though the trends are in the same direction as for the young people's ratings. An exception concerns fathers who, in contrast with the young people, give more optimistic reports of negative aspects of their relationships. Comparing the reports of individual young people and their respective parents, there is less agreement concerning negative aspects of the relationships, but high agreement on the positive aspects.

We can also compare parents' and young people's views of each other's perception of the quality of the relationship. Here parents are, again, more optimistic than young people. The majority of both mothers (33 out of 45) and fathers (19 out of 27) say they think their sons or daughters would say that they get on well together. With the exception of sons' reports of mothers' views of the relationship, proportionately fewer young people, compared with parents, gave positive accounts; the majority, however, were favourable. Young people's reports of fathers' views were significantly less likely to be favourable, compared with their perceptions of mothers' views.[4]

'Closeness'

'Closeness' is a term which we allowed participants to define. Asked in the interview which parent the young person was 'closest to', mothers have a lead over fathers. Out of 25 young women, 15 said they were closest to their mothers, one closest to her father, five to both parents, and four to neither parent or to no one. In the case of young men, 13 out of 30 said they were closest to their mothers, three closest to their fathers, ten to both parents, and four to neither or no one. Young people of Asian origin are less likely than other groups to report being close to their mothers; there is no difference with respect to fathers.

Parents' reports of closeness generally support those of young people. Ten of the 23 mother–daughter pairs and eight of the 21 mother–son pairs cite the mother as the parent they are closest to. Likewise, two of the 11 father–daughter pairs and five of the 14 father–son pairs agree that the mother is the closest parent. These findings contrast with reports concerning closeness to fathers: none of the mother–daughter pairs, one of the mother–son pairs, none of the father–daughter pairs and two of the father–son pairs cite the young person as being closest to the father.

Communication patterns

Communicating personal matters usually involves talking about feelings and may signal a need for emotional support. As many studies have shown with respect to crisis situations (see, for example, Brannen and Collard, 1982), the provision of emotional support is largely the province of women.

Table 10.2   *Young people's interview responses as to whether they would turn to mothers and fathers, if worried or unhappy by sex of young person*

| | Mothers | | Fathers | |
	Females % (n)	Males % (n)	Females % (n)	Males % (n)
Yes, without reservations	28 (7)	14 (4)	4 (1)	7 (2)
Yes, with reservations	44 (11)	32 (9)	26 (6)	19 (5)
No	28 (7)	54 (15)	70 (16)	74 (20)
Base	25	28	23	27

Men are also less likely to describe themselves as needing such support. Young people's reports of their propensity to speak about personal matters are gendered. According to the interview data, young women (13 out of 25 or 52 per cent) are significantly more likely than young men (5 out of 30, 17 per cent) to say that they disclose their feelings when they are worried or upset about something. According to the questionnaire data, substantially more young men (17 per cent) than young women (7 per cent) report that they have 'no need to talk' to their parents. In the interviews, mothers (27 out of 53, 51 per cent) are more likely than fathers (6 out of 29, 21 per cent) to report that their young people disclose to parents. Two interview comments, the first from a young woman and the second from a young man, indicate the polarity of responses concerning attitudes to and competence in disclosure:

I always need to relate to people. I'm not one of these people that stays quiet. If there's something on my mind, I'll just come straight out with it.

Generally I keep it to myself, sort it out that way, decide what's best.

Disclosure also varies according to cultural origins. Young people with two parents of non-indigenous origins are more likely than those with UK-born parents to say that they keep their feelings to themselves – 7 out of 18 (39 per cent) as against 11 out of 37 (30 per cent). Similarly, those young people from working-class households who have joined the labour market are more likely than those staying on in full-time education to see themselves as non-disclosers.

Most young people view disclosure to parents as problematic. Asked to whom they would 'turn' if they are worried or unhappy, only a minority of both sexes say that they would talk to parents unreservedly; young women are more likely to say they would turn to someone. The proportion of young men as well as young women who say that they turn to their fathers is particularly small; the figures are given in Table 10.2.

Parents' interview accounts reflect the patterns shown in Table 10.2, with similar proportions of individual pairs of parents and young people saying that the young people would turn to parents.[5] Significantly, mothers comment that they often have to 'drag' information out of young people.

Young people's comments about turning to others suggest that young women turn to friends, while young men would prefer to avoid disclosing to anyone. Young women prefer to talk to same-sex friends or to their boyfriends about personal matters, rather than to their parents. As one young woman puts it:

> It's like I trust my mum. But there are some things you can't really tell your mum, do you know what I mean? ... I'm glad my friends are there. (Judith Gabriel)

Though some young men also mention talking to friends, many also dwell on the constraints against disclosure, rather than the conditions under which disclosure takes place: 'I will turn to someone if I have to. But if it's not sort of over-important, I'll keep it to myself.'

Answers to questions aimed at discovering whether young people do disclose to their parents suggest that patterns vary according to the issue. We asked in the questionnaire whether young people talked to their parents about health. Young women emerge as significantly more likely than young men to have talked to a parent (84 per cent as against 70 per cent), and also more likely both to have talked to someone else (80 per cent against 60 per cent) and to more persons.

Young people's disclosure attitudes and practices may have implications for consulting health professionals. The questionnaire data suggest that talking to a parent is associated with talking to health professionals: 53 per cent of young women who have spoken to a parent about health have also spoken to a health professional, while only 24 per cent of those who have had no discussion with parents about their health have talked to a professional. Similarly for young men, 43 per cent of those who have talked to parents have also talked to health professionals, compared with only 15 per cent of those who have not talked to their parents. These findings are borne out by other questionnaire data. For example, significantly more young men who report difficulty talking to their parents, or who say that their parents have no time to talk to them, want more information about dealing with stress (66 per cent) than do those young men who report no such difficulty (59 per cent). Significantly more young women who report difficulty talking to parents want more information about coping with depression (73 per cent) than do those young women who report no such difficulty (59 per cent).

Talking to parents about plans at the end of the fifth year – whether to stay on in education after 16 – is a matter of some considerable importance to young people. Nearly two-thirds of all young people mention discussing this with their mothers, and over half with their fathers. In general, agreement between parents and young people concerning whether discussion took place is high on this issue (around 60 per cent), with slightly more young people than parents mentioning it. It is, however, important to distinguish between discussing the matter and making decisions. Parents are careful to emphasize that they have not made young people's decisions for them. Moreover, in some, notably working-class, households, young people set the context of the discussion, explaining to their parents the educational system and the options available.

Compared with education, the evidence concerning communication over sexual matters suggests significantly less discussion. Moreover, patterns of communication on these issues are markedly gendered. Asked in the interviews whether young people have talked to their parents in the past about puberty, the great majority of mothers (17 out of 19) say they have discussed the matter with their daughters, with 5 out of 20 having discussions with their sons, compared with only 2 fathers who talked to sons and none to daughters. According to young people's accounts, 14 out of 23 young women and 4 out of 26 young men report talking to their mothers, and 3 with both parents.[6]

As we saw in Chapter 9, while most parents and young people agree that young people ought to receive sex education from their parents, in practice relatively few parents appear to have discussed these matters in any great depth. According to the questionnaire data, 40 per cent of young women and 29 per cent of young men say that parents ought to be the main source of information about sex, while only 27 per cent of young women and 14 per cent of young men say this is so in practice. In the young people's interviews, nearly half (13 out of 25 young women and 12 out of 28 young men) say that parents, in conjunction usually with teachers, ought to be the main providers of sex education. In practice, young people say that parents are the main channels of such information for only a minority (7 out of 25 young women and 3 out of 29 young men). Parents' accounts, by contrast, are more optimistic in respect of their normative role and their actual practice of providing such information.

Difficulties experienced in discussing sex are mentioned by both parties. In the interviews, three-quarters of the young people (12 out of 19 young women and 21 out of 26 young men) say that both they and their parents find it difficult. Many parents agree. Most non-indigenous parents do not expect to give such information to young people, since sex is forbidden outside marriage and cannot even be mentioned.

Parents were asked whether they discussed with young people a list of items, including sexual behaviour, reproduction, contraception, AIDS and sexual orientation. The proportions saying they have discussed these issues range from under a third to under two-thirds, depending on the issue and the sex of the parent; the relevant figures are shown in Table 10.3.

Mothers are most likely to say that they have discussed these matters, especially with their daughters, and fathers least likely, again with daughters. On closer questioning, many parents appear to have spoken about these matters either in passing or in very general terms. Notably, TV programmes are cited as triggering general, open discussions.

We also asked about reciprocal support, namely the extent to which

Table 10.3   *Percentages of parents in interviews saying they have discussed sexual issues with young people, by sex of parent*

Discussed:	Mothers %	Fathers %
Puberty	57	12
Sexual behaviour	41	39
Reproduction	46	35
Contraception	53	50
AIDS	62	52
Homosexuality	48	32
Base	53	26

parents turned to young people. Again sex differences are evident, with significantly more mothers (47 out of 51) than fathers (9 out of 24) saying that young people have been supportive to them, usually in emotional terms. Similarly, more young women (13 out of 22) than young men (9 out of 24) say this.

The household material

Analysis of the study data in terms of individual households shows the ways in which communication varies according to not only the sex of parent and young person, but also the ethnic and social class origins of the households.

In making sense of these data below, we attempt to distinguish conceptually two types of household according to the dichotomy discussed at the beginning of this chapter. The substantive issue is parental expectations concerning young people's status transitions. On the one hand, there are those parents for whom the young person's status is *achieved* as s/he moves into adulthood, and who draw upon the individual developmental or individual rights model of adolescence. On the other hand, there are those parents for whom the young person's status transition is *ascribed*. As we shall suggest, these latter expectations define young people's status changes in relation to the prescribed age of entry to the labour market. Such expectations are class-based; they derive historically from the time when there were plenty of low-status jobs available for 16-year-olds. Parental expectations are also culturally based, that is, structured by norms which prescribe young people's continuing attachment to their ethnic or kinship groups. As with many other issues, these different types of parental expectation are also shaped by the sex of the parent and the young person.

The conceptual distinction between parents in terms of their expectations of young people's status transitions translates into different approaches to the regulation or control of young people. Our earlier argument that communication may itself constitute a (covert) control strategy is a crucial

Figure 10.1   *A model of parental control strategies and outcomes for young people's autonomy*

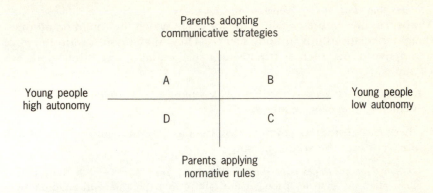

dimension for distinguishing between parents, who may be considered to lie along a continuum (vertical axis in Figure 10.1) between two ideal types:

1 Parents who hold an individual developmental view of adolescence, for whom young people's status transitions are individually achieved, and who exercise control by indirect or covert means, and principally through enforcement of communicative strategies.
2 Parents who do *not* hold an individual developmental model of adolescence, who see young people's status changes as normatively ascribed on the grounds of their belonging to a collectivity, whether of ethnicity or social class, and who exercise control overtly through enforcement of normatively prescribed rules.

The consequences of parental strategies for young people are represented on the horizontal axis in Figure 10.1 in terms of autonomy. In the case of the parents who regulate young people overtly through prescribed norms, communication is not demanded from young people concerning their activities and whereabouts, since, by definition, there are no boundaries between public and private spheres; whatever the context, it is assumed that young people are bound by one set of salient, normative rules which apply to the collectivity of class, culture or kin.

Parental communicative strategies – young people high on autonomy

In the top left quadrant, young people are relatively autonomous outside the home but parents characteristically try to control them through communicative strategies. Communication sets up an arena in which bargaining can take place between parents and young people. This pattern is most commonly found among mothers and daughters and mothers and sons; the mothers are mainly from middle-class, professional households, and the young still in full-time education.

Mothers and daughters – closeness and openness
Mothers in this group see talk as the means by which they build on mother–daughter relationships in adolescence. They draw upon a wide range of descriptive terms, such as friendship, trust, equality, and sisterhood. For example:

> It's very open. It's a very trusting relationship . . . It's a friendship.
> (Catherine Sheppard's mother)

In these cases, mothers connect closeness to communication; lack of it is said to 'cut off' the young person:

> (*Do you think she thinks it's a good relationship?*) Yes I do. We both think that. She'll often say that her friends can't talk to their parents, and a couple of her friends have had quite tough times and felt quite cut off. Yes, she thinks we get on very well. (Anna Gibb's mother)

By contrast, while these daughters may describe their mother as 'my best mate', they do not disclose everything:

> My mum, I got closer to her when I grew up. I started telling my mum things and just talking to her about anything, well not everything, not everything, though. Some things you've got to keep away from your parents. (Judith Gabriel)

Sandra Purcell comes from a comfortable white British middle-class family with liberal values. Her father is a manager in a public relations company, and her mother is a teacher. They have struggled financially to send Sandra and her siblings to private schools. Sandra is not restricted by her parents, her relationship with whom she describes as both 'close', in affect terms, and 'open', meaning that she tells her parents about her whereabouts. Her mother's portrayal is one of parental licence in response to her daughter's bid for greater freedom:

> We don't clamp down rigidly. We gradually got to that stage without too many major upsets . . . It's letting them do these things they want to . . . I still get worried, but you've got to allow them to do certain things. You just can't say 'no' all the time.

Sandra describes herself as a discloser: 'I can speak to people, the people I'm closest to – friends, my mum, my cousin.' Her mother says: 'She'd certainly talk to me about it. I wouldn't say everything, but she certainly talks to me about most things.' Both mother and daughter appear to have discussed a number of key issues; for example, they discussed the start of Sandra's periods, and a number of other matters relating to sex and sex education. Sandra's mother says Sandra talks to her about her boyfriend, though somewhat superficially. According to Sandra, her parents know that she has had sex, though information was relayed through the discovery of her diary. Quite how this happened was not revealed, but Sandra did not make any complaint in the interview about 'prying parents': 'It was through a diary. It was very stupid. It caused quite a lot of tension . . . But they got over it.' Were such a discovery to be made by parents who adopt more overt ('normative') strategies of control, they would probably have responded much more severely, and young people in those households would almost certainly have gone to greater lengths to keep their 'illicit' activities secret (Chapter 9).

In accordance with the communicative strategy of control adopted by her mother, Sandra is expected to say where she is going, with whom and for how long. As Sandra says, her parents are fairly free and easy about her going out, but:

> My mum likes to *know* where I am and er what time I'll be back . . . They do try to let me be as independent as possible. (Emphasis added)

In return for being open about her activities, Sandra has a higher degree of autonomy. Through the acquisition of information from her daughter, Sandra's mother alleviates her own anxiety about her welfare, and her sense of maternal responsibility is discharged. Thus, though she lacks the power to constrain her daughter, at least she feels she knows where she is.

Mothers and sons
Mothers who adopt communicative strategies with respect to sons tend to meet with resistance. It would seem that young men's autonomy is less constrained by this form of regulation. While most mothers and sons appear to have good relationships, and to be close to one another, mothers regard their sons as generally poor communicators, in contrast with daughters, who are seen to withhold only particular categories and kinds of information. When we compare sons' and daughters' accounts of relationships, young men emerge as rather less articulate in the interviews on this topic, especially. In part this may be because there is less overt conflict between mothers and sons than between mothers and daughters.

Mothers in this group try to engineer communication. They speak about 'talking him out of something', or creating the conditions under which sons may eventually 'come out' with a problem:

> Normally I know if there's something wrong, and if he doesn't want to talk about it, then I don't push it. But gradually then he will come round. He'll drop hints.

However, mothers seem to accept their sons' reticence as part of their make-up, although some like to believe, contrary to the evidence, that their sons 'would' turn to them. Moreover, sons' non-communicativeness does not necessarily deter mothers from talking to them:

> Actually, I can confide in him, and have done on many occasions.
> (David Monk's mother)

The son describes how his mother talks to him about her recent illness (cancer):

> I mean, when she does talk about it, you know, you don't actually know what to say. You don't know how to comfort her, so I just try.

Jeremy Talbot's mother puts her son's lack of communicativeness down to immaturity. Her lack of success in getting him to communicate leaves her at a loss. While in the past she was able to express her concern through physical affection, she feels this is no longer quite appropriate:

> The only thing is when there's anything wrong you could just pick them up and cuddle them and get it out. It's not that easy at this age.

Even so, when asked to describe the relationship, both mother and son define it in terms of communication:

> *Son*: She understands me more than my dad. That's basically it. I just can't talk to him that easily.
> *Mother*: I think he'll discuss anything with me.

In practice, communication is limited. Although Jeremy Talbot's mother sees herself as liberal on sexual matters – with respect to sexual maturation, for example, she speaks about having 'an open bathroom' – there is little evidence of communication. Despite saying that her son told her that he had a girlfriend, and discussed his disappointing exam results with her, the depth of the communication is unclear, especially when the son's account is considered. For example, the parents have no idea about his sexual relationship. Similarly, although the son says that his mother knows that he smokes and disapproves, the matter is not discussed at home.

Parental communicative strategies – young people low on autonomy

No cases were found in the top right quadrant. Theoretically, this is not surprising, since parental communicative strategies relate to their beliefs about the desirability of young people acting autonomously and come about in response to young people's bids for independence.

Parents as normative regulators – young people low on autonomy

In the bottom right quadrant, parents do not control young people through communication. Instead, regulation is embedded in cultural norms. Parents assume that young people will comply with the rules of their ethnic or kin group outside the home; in any event, young people's autonomy outside the home is heavily constrained. There ought not, therefore, to be private practices for the young person to disclose or confess to. If young people contravene cultural norms outside the home, they withhold this information from parents. Cases in this group include mother–daughter relationships, father–daughter relationships and father–son relationships.

In all cases, both parents were born and brought up outside the UK, mostly in Asia, East Africa or the Middle East.

Mothers and daughters

Ruth Graham is a particularly reticent young woman from an orthodox Jewish background who has not so far infringed her parents' cultural mores. Ruth is the eldest child; she lives with her mother, a director of a small company, her stepfather, her younger sister and new half-brother. Like Sandra above, she goes to a private girls' school. Unlike her, she is not expected to have a boyfriend or to go out without adult supervision. Her mother says they have a 'good' relationship and defines them as 'close'. She describes her daughter as a non-discloser, but later says: 'If there's anything, she'd talk to me rather than anybody else.' Ruth's view of their relationship corroborates her mother's description in terms of not confiding in her: 'I'm closest to my mum but not really close.' Ruth is significantly vague about whether her mother has ever talked to her about sexual matters. The issue of boyfriends does not come up, because 'She doesn't think girls of my age should go out with boys.'

In practice, Ruth's mother exerts considerable control over her daughter. Notably, she says that she 'tells' her daughter what to do when she observes that she is unwell, and when the issue of staying on at school at the end of the fifth year comes up. Ruth accepts her mother's restrictiveness. For example, noting that her mother prefers her to have Jewish friends and disapproves of her best friend, she remarks 'I mean, I don't really pursue it.'

Fathers and daughters

Fathers' strategies of regulation differ from those of mothers. They are often portrayed as 'strict', and as demanding 'respect' from young people.

Aznive's parents are from a country bordering the Persian Gulf, and are Christians. She has a younger brother and sister and is still at school. They live over her father's shop (a chain grocer's) in which mother and daughter work unpaid. She says her father is 'very strict'. Her father's account makes it clear that he is very concerned who his daughter mixes with, fearing that, in associating with young men, she may lose her (sexual) 'respectability': 'I'm very strict on that. If I lose my temper, they know it.' Paternal authority appears to have become especially marked in Aznive's adolescence. Aznive says that she and her father were closer during her childhood: 'We've grown apart just a bit.' Asked how she thinks her father feels about her, she says that 'He tends to hide his feelings, and doesn't like to express himself too much. But I know he cares about me.' Caring is thus expressed not through affect but through paternal strictness. In his interview, her father does not put into words what he feels for his daughter, and says he does not know his daughter's view of their relationship. One reason for the father's silence may be that he felt uncomfortable with a female interviewer, though the alternative argument is persuasive – that his failure to articulate care may suggest that it cannot be divorced from his paternal role.

According to Aznive, her teenage years have brought increasing domestic responsibility. She is expected to help her father unpaid in the family business, and to do a large amount of the housework. She shouldered most of the housework, including taking care of her younger siblings during the period of her GCSE examinations, because her mother had to go away to recover from a severe attack of rheumatoid arthritis. Aznive largely conforms to parental expectations, but also displays some resistance to the restrictive regime. Thus, despite acknowledging that her upbringing has made her more responsible – in accordance with her parents' view of what her new status should be – she also suggests some increase in autonomy. A 'freer' side to her character is beginning to emerge, a public identity which she conceals within a grumpy exterior in the private space of her family:

> I went through a stage where I was rude to my parents. I don't know why. I just snapped at them all the time ... I went through a stage when I wanted to be myself – to have my own space type of thing ... They say girls mature quicker than boys. I must have had it hard in my early teens ... [My parents] were very strict ... cos at home I have quite a lot of responsibilities, and, like, I've taken these responsibilities seriously ... Like when I go out with my parents – cos there's a lot of social activities ... I know how to handle myself. I'm a very kind of mature person. But when I'm with my own friends I'm totally different. I can relax and be myself ... slightly doubled.

Unsurprisingly, Aznive does not discuss sexual matters with her father, and does not expect to: 'With my dad, I can only tell him certain things that he needs to know.' Nor have they talked about educational decisions at the end of the fifth year. Her mother's recent serious illness was also not discussed. With her mother she is 'more open'. Her father also states that 'She can talk to her mother.' Asked about discussing boyfriends and sex education, he replies curtly: '[My children] know my opinion very well.'

Fathers and sons

Chenglie Wang's father is a mild-mannered man whose son describes him as 'easygoing' and 'unselfish': 'Whatever he does, he does for us, like. When he works so hard he's working for us.' His manner and style belie his rather authoritarian orientation to parenting. Of Chinese origin, he grew up in Malaysia. From peasant roots, he moved continents twice in order to pursue his studies, finally completing his architectural training in the UK. His main aim is that his children should 'do well at school', and he is no less strict with his youngest child, his only son, Chenglie. He restricts his son's activities and vets his friends, wanting to know 'what type of family ... how they study'.

Chenglie is generally in agreement with his father's educational

aspirations, and is aiming to go to university. He accepts and conforms to
the house rules:

> I wouldn't say there are strict rules. But all the children [his sisters are
> grown up but live at home] know what they should be doing, what's
> expected of them. No one says . . . It's like a mental compromise between all
> of us. We all know where we can go and where we can't. (*How do you feel?*) I
> think it's good. I mean we can learn about rules that are always there.
> (*Like?*) Like you always have to study . . . You can't always go out every day –
> stay out to a really late time. There are set rules. Everyone knows them.

While Chenglie abides by the rules, describing himself as a 'young adult
. . . still under the guidance of parents', he is slightly resentful that his
parents see no place for 'fun'. Moreover, as already indicated, he respects
his father for his 'provider role'.

Neither party describes the relationship as 'close'. Significantly, Chenglie
mentions a connection which belongs to the past rather than the present
– the way his father used to help him with his maths homework. He
excuses his father now on the grounds that 'He's so busy', and also makes
some interesting comments concerning the expression of parental caring
in which he contrasts his two parents. While his mother is said to express
her concern through worry, the ascribed nature of the father–son relationship is sufficient justification although he is initially somewhat hesitant
in reply to the question whether he thinks his father cares for him:

> I think so . . . My dad's not a worrier. If you know someone's worrying a lot,
> then they obviously care for you. If he does, he doesn't show it that much.
> (*You mean physical affection?*) Not that much . . . But I think he does care, cos
> I'm the only boy in the family and fathers always like to have sons. So if I do
> well, he's happy.

Worry is seen as a form of weakness and thereby the antithesis of fatherhood.

Communication between father and son is limited; neither sees it as an
important issue. Indeed, since Chenglie conforms to the rules, there is
nothing to tell that his parents do not already know about. Chenglie
describes his attitude to disclosure as 'mainly keeping things to myself',
while his father's only reference to and concern about communication
with his son is to do with studying. On educational decisions, his father
assumes that his son is staying on at school. Discussion of sexual matters
is taboo, and both Chenglie and his father consider that he is too young
to have a girlfriend.

In this household, normative rules governing fatherhood and age
relations preclude father and son being close in an affective sense. The
son's progress through the education system is their main point of connection. Thus caring is embodied in the shared activity rather than the
expression of concern. Since the son largely abides by the household
rules, he has little personal autonomy, and has no need to confide or
confess private matters. For the same reason, there is no conflict in the

father–son relationship. As another son of Asian parents puts it, respect demands distance in a relationship:

> (*What do you mean by respect?*) They're older than you. You can't treat them as if they're your age. I can't treat my dad like my best mate, or I'm in trouble. Some things I can say to my friends. I can mess around, joke around. I can't say that to my dad. (Sandeep Kumar)

While Chenglie is closer to his mother, there is not a great deal of communication between them either. In this respect, Chenglie's remarks about the importance of having a girlfriend (he does not have one) are significant. Asked whether he approves of young men of his age having girlfriends, he comments: 'It's good to have someone to talk to openly.' Paradoxically, the notion of openness serves to underline the desired boundedness between the public and private spheres of his life.

Parents as normative regulators – young people high on autonomy

In the bottom left quadrant, parents adhere to prescribed rules concerning the transition to adulthood. Notable here are working-class parents born in the UK who assume that, once their young people have reached the age of economic independence, they no longer have the right to expect young people to conform to norms expected of dependants. They do not, therefore, require that their young people provide them with information concerning their private practices and activities outside the home. Instead, they must put their 'trust' in them.

Mothers and daughters

Sally Rimmer has recently left school and found a job with an optician. She lives with her mother, a single parent who has two (low-status) part-time jobs, and her elder sister who is also at work. Both mother and daughter describe a 'close' relationship, which, they say, is based on 'trust' and 'friendship'. Her mother says, somewhat hopefully: 'Deep down, she thinks we can sit and talk about anything.' Even before Sally left school, her mother allowed her considerable freedom, although she did expect to be informed of her daughter's whereabouts: 'I think you do worry, but, basically, you've got to put your trust in them to a certain extent. You can only guide them.' Since leaving school, Sally has a new boyfriend who is much older than she. However, despite being close to her mother, Sally is not forthcoming about her relationship, which annoys her mother:

> She didn't tell me. He's five years older than her . . . I think she's been out with him a few times before she told me. I was a bit annoyed . . . I said I'd sooner know than not know.

Like the mothers who deploy communicative strategies, Sally's mother wishes to be informed about her daughter's new relationship, but since her daughter's new status as a worker gives her autonomy, she finds it impossible and unjustifiable to insist on this.

Fathers and daughters

Many UK-born fathers want to be different from their own fathers, whom they describe as hierarchical and distant. Unlike mothers, notably UK-born middle-class mothers, fathers rarely describe their role in terms of communication. Rather, they strive to be 'friends' with their sons and daughters. Andrea Dewar's father is a middle manager in a large company. He has four children. His eldest daughter, the one included in our study, has just done very well in her GCSE examinations and plans to go to university. He believes he allows her considerable autonomy. He contrasts his relationship with his daughter favourably with his own upbringing:

> I think Andrea is much better off, one hopes, and perhaps I'm trying to form a relationship with her. I think we do have a reasonable relationship ... I've listened to her and tried to understand, and given her that bedrock that I felt I didn't have of a dad you could talk to and *maybe* confide in. (Emphasis added)

The suggestion that he confides in his daughter is put forward tentatively and fits with his mention of his backstage role ('bedrock') in his daughter's upbringing. In practice, both father and daughter give little indication of any intimate exchanges. Describing her relationship with her parents as being 'more of an equal now' (Andrea is the eldest child), she tries to explain the decline in closeness with her father:

> I don't know, I have a different relationship with my dad. I couldn't put my finger on it. It's all a bit of a joke, it's all a bit of a laugh ... I think my dad doesn't like the fact that he only ever knows what I think through my mum ... probably feels a bit shut out ... I think it's because he's not around that much – always away and stuff.

Within this household, the mother employs a communicative strategy and relays information divulged by the daughter to her husband. The father's relationship with his daughter takes the form of joking. Joking in this relationship involves ambiguity: it is suggestive of equality and friendship but is also indicative of hierarchical relations. That Andrea is less happy with her father's approach reveals the underlying generational differences and their resource consequences. According to Radcliffe-Brown (1962: 57): 'The joking relationship is clearly only appropriate between persons who in the general social structure can treat each other as equals, and this generally means persons of the same generation.' Thus, joking represents the father's attempt to override or test hierarchical differences in the father–daughter relationship, while for the daughter it underlines the continuing difference in their statuses. When joking occurs among unequals, it is experienced as teasing, since the subordinate person is put at a disadvantage.

According to both the survey and interview data, fathers emerge as less emotionally close to their daughters than do mothers. Their main route to closeness is through physical proximity and shared interests. But fathers are generally around less than mothers through working longer hours away from home, and/or they lack hobbies or interests in common with their daughters. Relations based on proximity or shared interests are likely to weaken when daughters start to absent themselves from family activities and to go out more with their friends. Adolescence is the peak age of friendships. One father clearly regrets the decline of family bonds:

> The last couple of years we haven't had so much in common as we once had. . . . Something I need to work on . . . She probably hasn't got enough time for the old man these days . . . She tends not to come on family picnics or family walks – the sort of activity where you can talk and enjoy things together . . . I've got regrets about that, yeah. (Sandra Purcell's father)

Fathers do not allude to matters of personal significance to the young women which may have something to do with the fact that they do not easily disclose themselves. Even with respect to crises which are a stringent test of the ability to confide and express feeling – in two instances the mothers had recently developed cancer – fathers appear to have kept the matter to themselves. In one case, the father did not even mention the matter in his own interview. In the other case, the daughter said:

> When it actually happened, I couldn't talk about it to Dad. We were both sort of worried about Mum, and I would say something to him and he would snap back. And it just got to the point, you know, where we were just causing friction . . . I used to think he is not really bothered how I feel and that, you know, if I care, or if I don't care, about my mum. But now he's OK, you know, he worries about me. (Sara Mitchell)

The father's view of this situation is that his daughter did not want to disclose her feelings. He is significantly silent in the interview about his own feelings.

Fathers and daughters, especially those in middle-class households, appear to communicate more over 'public' issues such as education and employment matters. Young people discuss these matters equally with their mothers, most of whom are themselves in the labour market. The fathers are anxious to stress (and the young people's accounts support this) that their daughters made up their own minds about whether to stay at school, or go to college, and which courses to take.

In accordance with the culture of masculinity, fathers appear to lack skills to talk about personal things both in the interviews and in their reported actions. Their failure to acquire such skills is reflected in their regretted inability to connect with their own fathers. Understandably, fathers have a problem in viewing their daughters' transformation into sexual beings which makes them reluctant to talk about such matters. While childhood is assumed to be an age of sexual innocence, parents are forced to confront the biological implications of adolescence. The change is likely to be felt most acutely by fathers about their daughters.

Thus, in so far as UK-born fathers do not aspire to the status of authority figure, and do not take on the role of 'keeping their children close' (Barker, 1972) by whatever means, their role in their daughters' lives lacks clarity. Historically stripped of their traditional patriarchal authority, they are confronted both with the increased independence of young people in modern society, and with daughters' relatively greater closeness to mothers, as expressed through communication but also through shared interests through their common gender. As we discuss elsewhere, fathers exert less responsibility than mothers in respect of teenage children. The changing norms concerning what young people should, or should not, do at 16 lead to parental demands upon young people to communicate their where-abouts, but there is little evidence of such communication in father–daughter relationships. Creating lines of communication is chiefly a maternal strategy, especially adopted in middle-class families; it functions as a way of exercising (often covert) control, and at the same time as a way of maintaining loving relationships as children move towards independence.

Mothers and sons

Relationships in normatively regulated households based on strict cultural mores concerning what young people should not do ought to result in low adolescent autonomy. However, sons have notably greater autonomy than daughters within the same household, and mothers are more indulgent with them than fathers.

Sandeep Kumar is still at school and hopes to do A levels; he lives with his siblings in a Punjabi family which is part of a Punjabi community. The father works from home, using his house for jewellery production and drawing on his wife and sons as unpaid labour. It is significant that the father, rather than the mother, offered himself for interview. In order to interview the mother, we telephoned several times before a time convenient for the wife could be arranged.

In this household, rules restricting young people's behaviour about friends, and especially opposite-sex relationships, as well as going out at night and other 'risky' activities such as smoking, are clearly understood, but Sandeep does not always follow them. In the past Sandeep had a (sexual) relationship with a girl which he kept secret; he also smokes and drinks on occasion outside the house and enjoys 'dossing around', by which he means 'walking around and relaxing, basically. Going round, anywhere, town, look around, see what's going on.' Neither father nor mother openly admit that they know that their son is breaking the rules. The son is quite frank in his interview, admitting to ignoring family rules while trying to appear not to flout them. He describes making 'a com-promise', namely not going to parties or staying out particularly late. As to communicating his whereabouts to his parents, the son says that he does not discuss his activities inside the family or with his kin. His mother comments: 'Everything I try to ask but he never tells me.'

The mother's role in this household is to try 'to keep young people close' to her. As in other Asian households, the parental strategy is not to come down hard on sons when they break the household's rules. To acknowledge that a young person is breaking rules means having to chastise them, and so put at risk the positive aspects of the relationship. However, not to chastise means undermining the system of values and the father's authority. Thus, many mothers (and fathers) in these households turn a blind eye in respect of children's 'illicit' activities, especially those of sons.

In the above case, the fact that Sandeep disobeyed his parents and sometimes went out at night was less important than if it had been a daughter acting in this way. Indeed, all three family members interviewed confirm that the daughter of the household is much more restricted than the sons. Asked why this is so, the mother says:

> Because she's a girl if men try to – I'm worried about that. Girls are something ... (*They have to be protected?*) Yes.

Sandeep himself comments:

> If my sister went out with a boy her reputation would be ruined ... If she gets married it makes it difficult ... Our community's like that – lots of gossips. One thing goes wrong and everybody knows about it.

The daughter's value to the household is measured primarily in terms of her ascribed status as a marriageable woman; moreover, she is expected to remain a virgin until marriage. Sons, on the other hand, are expected to provide material support for their parents' old age while daughters-in-law carry out the actual caring work.

Since Asian households are also part of the wider British culture, parents cannot necessarily count upon the strength of traditional kinship norms which define that sons should stay close and support them in old age. Ideas which emphasize the value of young people becoming independent compete with cultural mores and interests concerning the household as a collectivity and strong family obligations. Parents must rely upon other means, that is, they must indulge sons in order to keep them close. The communicative strategy adopted by UK-born, middle-class parents is not open to them, since they cannot require young people to provide information about activities which are heavily sanctioned.

As head of the household, Sandeep's father is the symbolic representative of familial values. The mother is better positioned to be indulgent to her son. One option is to turn a blind eye when her son breaks the rules. Indeed, according to her own account, the mother acts as the peacemaker in the family, repairing relationships when her husband and son argue about their son's public activities: 'I never argue, not personally. I have to keep the peace.' The main resources enabling her to carry out this difficult balancing act of keeping her resistant son within the family group are love and affection. Yet the requirement upon Sandeep to keep his activities secret from his mother in itself creates a barrier to closeness.

Thus, although he says that he feels close to his mother because 'If there's something wrong – things like that – she'll notice it straightaway. She'll pick it up', in practice when his relationship with his girlfriend (unbeknown to his mother) broke up, he was unable to turn to her. In this respect, his view of the importance of having a girlfriend as 'someone to talk to' is significant.

Another Asian household in the study has not been so successful in keeping a renegade son close to the family. A father tells with obvious reluctance and distaste how his elder son (the brother of the young person in our study) fell into bad company, and was said to be on drugs. The father banished him from the house, and has not seen him since. It is, however, clear from the younger son's account that from time to time his brother slips back to visit his mother. Again, it is the mother who maintains the ties. Unfortunately, in this, as in some other Asian households, we were unable to interview the mother.

Fathers and sons
Explicit rules of transition apply also in working-class families. On the whole, working-class fathers confer autonomy upon their sons and cease to be strict at the point when their sons join the labour market. They justify this change in attitude in a variety of ways. In two cases, the fathers say they vacated the authoritarian role with their youngest children. One of these fathers, whose prowess as a sportsman is failing, says that, at 55, he feels generally 'past it', and he can no longer compete with his golfer son. Also, he believes that the disciplinarian role he once played with respect to his older children is 'rather passé'. In a third case, the father attributes the change in his uncompromising position – 'My philosophy is if a kid's done wrong, beat him' – to his son starting work:

> Once they've left school, you can only take so much responsibility. Once they are over 18 or they're out earning money, they've got to be responsible for their own actions. They are expected to be semi-adult. When they're kids at school, yes, parents should be responsible. They should expect to know where their kids are. (Ian Winter's father)

A fourth father says he has simply given up, since his son completely ignores him, leading his own life, and only coming home for the odd meal and change of clothes.

Like other fathers, these UK-born, working-class fathers do not describe themselves as particularly close to their sons; the sons are closer to their mothers. Only two share interests with their sons (sport and going to the pub). Communication over personal matters is rare. In so far as sons 'let on' concerning their feelings (not a manly thing to do), they do so via their mothers, who are the main channels of information. It is interesting to note that the son in this group who has the best relationship with his father describes it in terms of being able to talk and joke, and have an equal relationship. But he also refers to their former hierarchical relationship and the difficulty men have in displaying affection towards one other:

> Yeah, we have [a good relationship]. Like we talk more now. We sort of understand each other. We joke now and that ... We go bowling [and drinking] and have a good laugh ... I care for my dad, as well as mum, but it's harder for a bloke to say it's – like that ... It's mainly my dad's more in charge cos he's like ... He's the man of the house ... But we're mainly sort of equal now, like since we've all left school. (Ian Winter, now at work)

Conclusion

When young people make bids for independence, parents steer a course between care and control. All parents are concerned about the quality of their relationships with young people but also seek to continue to guide them as they move towards adulthood. While most parents want to keep close in affect terms, closeness contains other meanings where it refers to the work of caring for and regulating young people.

For some parents, notably UK-born mothers of middle-class status, closeness with teenagers translates into 'openness'. Control is exerted through communicative strategies whereby the separation of the public and private spaces in which young people operate is acknowledged, together with young people's right to traverse the boundaries. At the same time these parents seek to regulate young people's activities across these boundaries by covert means. In practice this means requiring young people to communicate openly concerning their whereabouts as a trade-off for their freedom. However, the mode of control is to deny its regulatory function, from the perspective of parent if not from that of the young person.

By contrast, other parents, notably parents born outside the UK and working-class UK-born parents, tend to regulate the status transitions of their young people in terms of prescribed norms which govern the ascription of status rather than its individual achievement. In the case of the parents born outside the UK., since their cultural values do not recognize a demand for greater independence as an intrinsic part of adolescence, there is less need for the renegotiation of relationships at this point. Since young people are not supposed to go out with friends or to have opposite-sex relationships, their parents do not require to be told where they are going, and they do not need to create distanced strategies of covert surveillance. In this context, for young people to talk about personal matters may be tantamount to a confession of breaking the house rules. Closeness does not, therefore, depend upon openness.

Similarly, many working-class parents regulate young people through norm enforcement. Age-related rules govern young people's transitions to adulthood, and norms governing how much autonomy young people should acquire are related to young people's acquisition of independent economic status. When young people enter the labour market, parents accept that they no longer have the right to regulate their external behaviour.

In addition to culture and social class, the gender of both parent and young person is relevant to the conduct of these relationships. Just as mothers take the main burden of responsibility for the physical care of both young and older children, so, too, the parent as communicator is a gendered role. It is mothers who see it as their task to create a 'talking relationship' with their children, and are generally more successful in this with daughters than with sons.

Although young people may resist giving information, there are also incentives and trade-offs for them to do so. The incentives relate to communication as a form of love: the sharing of experiences which is possible in these renegotiations. The trade-offs are parental impotence – parents' promises not to act upon the knowledge given to them by young people.

Mothers' rewards are similar to those of the young people – the main-tenance or re-creation of close ties. The strategy by which these are achieved is also an insurance policy in terms of ensuring the maintenance of contact with young people in the future. But, just as there is a price to be paid by young people for participating in the talking relationship, so mothers also pay a price. For mothers, knowledge means power without authority; they continue to be the responsible parent, but cannot act on information, even when they disapprove of their sons' or daughters' activities. Through creating channels of communication, mothers endeavour to exert influ-ence though without appearing to constrain, something which young people are highly attuned to and seek to avoid. Mothers' predicament is manifest in maternal worry – based on a combination of responsibility and impotence.

In contrast, fathers' historical surrender of authority appears not to be matched to the same extent by a new form of tie with sons and daughters at this phase of the life course. While some mothers re-create their rela-tionships, taking on the role of communicator, fathers depend upon mothers to act as mediators of information and relationships between themselves and their children. Their main means of reconnection with young people is through the joking relationship which attempts to smooth away status differences and substitute egalitarian familiarity. However, just as young people resist talking relationships with their mothers, so they are often ambivalent in their response to joking relationships with fathers and perceive the underlying inequality.

Notes

1 The following table shows the reported quality of relationship with non-resident biological parent, by sex of young person:

| | Non-resident mother | | Non-resident father | |
| | Females | Males | Females % | Males % |
Quality of relationship				
Excellent /good	[10]	[10]	50	60
Fair	[3]	[3]	21	21
Poor/very poor	[8]	[7]	29	19
Base	21	20	52	80

2 The following table shows the reported quality of relationship with resident 'step-parent', by sex of young person:

| | Resident stepmother | | Resident stepfather | |
| | Females | Males | Females % | Males % |
Quality of relationship				
Excellent/good	[4]	[3]	[10]	[20]
Fair	–	[2]	[8]	[5]
Poor/very poor	[4]	[2]	[8]	[3]
Base	8	7	26	28

This analysis includes one young man who did not answer the question about his relationship with his resident stepmother, and six who did not answer the question about their relationships with their resident stepfathers. In this latter case, all six reported 'good' or 'excellent' relationships with fathers. We cannot tell if this is an accurate description of the situation, or if, because relations with stepfathers were good, stepfathers were seen as fathers.

3 Seven of these young people (two young women and five young men) are not included in the pair analyses because neither parent was interviewed.

4 Seventeen out of 25 daughters and 24 out of 29 sons said that they thought their mothers' views of the relationship were favourable. Eleven out of 23 daughters and 16 out of 25 sons said that their fathers' views were favourable.

5 Proportions of parents and young people saying the young person would turn to them are: mothers and daughters, 16 and 17 out of 23, respectively; mothers and sons, 11 and 10 out of 22, respectively; fathers and daughters, 4 and 5 out of 12, respectively; and fathers and sons, 1 and 4 out of 5, respectively.

6 On the issue of agreement, 11 daughters' and four sons' accounts agree with the statements of their respective mothers. Neither of the fathers' statements agree with those of their sons.

11 Conclusion

The study described in this book amassed a very large amount of data as a result of the two approaches used: 843 questionnaires completed by young people, and 142 in-depth interviews with young people and their parents. As is usual in research projects of this scale, we have been able in this book to draw on only a proportion of the information collected. Despite this limitation, a formidable set of themes and findings has emerged. We are not attempting any formal summary of these in this brief final chapter. Instead, we pick out several key themes we see our study as highlighting, and consider some of the ways in which these interface with contemporary debates about health, the role of young people, and family life.

The main conceptual focus of the study has been young people in the context of the household. In addition, we have located the household focus within broad structural divisions as seen through the prisms of cultural/ethnic origins, gender – of young people and their parents – and social class. The main substantive concern of the study is broad, covering the health, illness and health-related behaviour of young people.

Young people and their health

Teenagers are commonly thought to be a 'social problem' group in a variety of ways. Indeed, our study found parents much more liable to generalize about teenagers and their behaviour than were teenagers about adults and *their* behaviour. Parental responses indicate an underlying fear of teenagers as out of control, particularly in public places, and therefore a threat to the adult social order. Strikingly, this view is usually held about teenagers in general rather than one's own or other particular teenagers. While the teenage years are often characterized, especially in psychological paradigms of development, as necessarily emotionally turbulent, our study found that in the main young people attribute their emotional difficulties to 'real' problems: those of renegotiating parental relationships, coping with the demands of school and a labour market unreceptive to their needs and talents, finding an acceptable pathway through the maze of commercial and risk-taking pressures that confront young people today. In this situation, health itself is often not a priority for young people. Illnesses such as cancer and heart disease are in fact less likely to be perceived by young people as significant threats to health than unemployment, the destruction and pollution of the environment, and the threat of nuclear war.

Another commonly held view of teenagers is that they are, by and large, a healthy group (with the exception of risk-taking behaviours such as sex, smoking, drinking and drug-taking). We found more illness and use of health services in our study population than this view would suggest. Thirty-nine per cent of our sample of young people reported long-term or recurrent illness; 9 per cent had been in hospital in the year up to the study, 35 per cent had attended a hospital casualty department, and 84 per cent had seen their GPs.

Responsibility for young people's health

Taking the interview accounts of mothers, fathers and young people within the same households, we examined what goes on in families with respect to young people's health. Since health is a multi-faceted phenomenon, it is unsurprising that the notion of taking responsibility for health did not grab the attention of our study participants. In so far as the notion has meaning, parents and young people take it to refer to bodily health, especially young people's diet and personal cleanliness. While more parents and young people say they think 16-year-olds should be responsible for themselves than identified this as a parental responsibility, in practice this happens less often, and parents assume more than a watching brief over young people's health by taking steps actively to intervene (which are often resisted by young people in a variety of ways).

Drawing upon the accounts of different household members, we identified a number of different ways in which health issues are negotiated in practice between parents and young people. Our study suggests that when young people reach 16, for a significant proportion of households there is little change in the status quo. With respect to household meal practices, nearly half of young people continue to eat *en famille* at least for the evening meal; in around half of the households mothers see themselves, and are seen by young people, to be largely responsible for their diet. The delegation of responsibility to young people for meal preparation and food decisions is common. However, this pattern appears to have less to do with the transfer of health responsibility to young people and more to do with mothers' entry into full-time employment. We found only two cases where young people take total responsibility for their own diet.

Similarly, with respect to 'risk' activities, notably smoking, alcohol and drugs, nearly half of the young people engage in none of these activities. With respect to drug-taking, an activity on which parental fears are often focused, the majority of young people are not involved in the 'drug scene'. For most who are, this involvement is limited to the occasional use of cannabis. Only 13 of the 843 young people in our study report using cocaine or heroin. Young people are actually *less* likely than their parents to approve of people in their age group participating in risk activities, including drug-taking, smoking, drinking and sex.

Where young people are not involved in any of these, they are not in conflict with their parents. With respect to health service use, as young people get older they begin to visit the GP unaccompanied. However, mothers are still active in identifying signs of illness in their young people, helping them to decide what to do about symptoms, making GP appointments and accompanying young people to the doctor, especially daughters, and especially in respect of the onset of significant illness. Fathers play a negligible role in these respects. Young people tend to go alone to the GP for routine or follow-up visits.

Contrary to popular supposition, levels of conflict between parents and young people were low in our study, and much less was reported than we had expected. With respect to diet, a small group of young women actively resist taking part in family meals; this is often connected with their tendency to slim or become vegetarian. An even smaller group are locked in a struggle with respect to risk activities. There is evidence suggesting that sometimes conflict had taken place in the past, when young people were younger. The evidence concerning the changes in young people's behaviour over time (up to 15 months elapsed between the questionnaire survey and the household study) indicates their initiation into new activities, as well as their rejection of former habits. These changes are difficult to interpret, however, since responses are likely to be affected by the research context; in particular, young people may be unwilling to admit to activities such as drug use in a face-to-face interview with an adult.

In some households, young people engage in new behaviours without their parents' consent. This group consists disproportionately of young men of Asian origin, who are especially concerned to keep relationships with young women secret from their strongly disapproving parents. In a further group of households, parents condone young people's unhealthy or risk behaviours. With the notable exceptions of parents of Asian and Middle Eastern origin, most parents accept (moderate) alcohol consumption by young people, since they themselves drink. A small group of mothers indulge the food preferences of their sons who stick to the 'faddy' eating habits of childhood. Several mothers took pre-emptive action concerning their daughters' emergent sexuality by accompanying them to the GP for prescriptions for the contraceptive pill. Young people themselves negotiate this outcome, which is found almost exclusively among those of UK-born parents.

Rules and regulations

As a way of examining the issue of health responsibility in practice, our study explored the rules which operate within households concerning the regulation of young people and the ways in which young people negotiate rules with their parents with respect to a wide range of issues relating to health and illness. Contrary to expectation, parental rules are rarely articulated with respect to risk behaviours. The main concern of parents and young people revolves around the issue of going out or staying in. Some parents are concerned about the moral aspects rather than the health consequences of young people's social encounters outside the home; they heavily discourage mixing with peer groups. By contrast, other parents regard a certain degree of freedom from parental control as young people's right, though parents also fear the dangers of the external world.

In accordance with their particular normative views of adolescence, parents differ in their modes of regulation of their young people. Those who see adolescence as a personal quest for individual autonomy seek to renegotiate relationships; they seek to be 'like friends' with their young people, and to be on an equitable footing with them. At the same time, they continue to feel responsible for them, and are thus forced to control them through covert or invisible means. In return for a measure of autonomy, parents require their young people to supply them with information concerning their whereabouts. In this context, as in many others, the creation of a 'talking relationship' is a gendered role, performed by mothers rather than fathers. Moreover, mothers act as mediators between young people and fathers. Maternal communicative strategies prove generally more successful with daughters than with sons.

By contrast, parents who regard adolescence as an ascribed status expect young people, as they grow older, to take on greater responsibility for others in their families and kin groups. They do not emphasize the rights of the individual, but expect young people to remain connected to their families. These parents are less concerned to conceal the fact and mode of regulation in their dealings with their sons and daughters. Expectations concerning what young people do or do not do are self-evident and are not expected to be negotiable.

Culture

One of the central themes which emerges from the study is the cultural specificity of the idea of adolescence. As noted above, not all parents view the teenage years as normally and necessarily a progressive quest for independence, leading to inevitable separation from the family group. Instead parents, especially those who were born and brought up in Asian and Middle Eastern countries, regard the transition to adulthood as entailing greater responsibility towards others – notably those in the household or kin group. In this view, enlarged responsibility towards others substitutes for enhanced rights of the individual to autonomy. These cultural views carry over into the ways parents control and regulate the behaviour of their young people. While parents generally tend to restrict their daughters more than their sons, this is especially so within households where both parents were born outside the UK; in these households going out without a chaperon is heavily discouraged for young women. Parents fear the effects of exposure to 'immoral' practices, especially the risk of sexual activity. It is interesting that many young women describe restrictiveness in terms of choice rather than constraint.

In accordance with greater parental restrictiveness, these young people emerge as less likely to smoke, drink alcohol, and take drugs than their white peers. Though only a very small percentage of young people are likely to engage in all three 'risk' activities – that is, to be current smokers, to have drunk any alcohol in the past week and to have ever taken drugs – white young people are five times as likely to have done so (15 per cent) as Asian young people (3 per cent). Moreover, Asian young men, but not Asian young women, are also more likely to eat healthy diets than other groups. Since ethnic origin is statistically independent of social class in our study, this latter finding is unlikely to result from greater household income of these families. Moreover, healthy diets are generally more likely to be found among young women. Possibly important are the facts that many Asian young people are vegetarian and that Asian young men express a concern about (slight) physical build.

The fit between parental restrictiveness and not engaging in risky activities is far from perfect, however, among the sons or daughters of parents born outside the UK. Those young people who do flout household rules are careful to keep their activities secret from their parents. This means that parents and their young people do not enter into communication or negotiation with respect to activities which may adversely affect the latter's health. Thus parents do not discuss these matters in terms of the agenda of health education, since risky behaviours are heavily sanctioned as immoral, and because parents do not subscribe to the model of individual autonomy and responsibility.

Gender and young people

According to our data, gender is a strong differentiator of young people's health beliefs, health status and health behaviour. Young men and fathers are more likely than young women and mothers to view health as being within their individual control. Mothers place greater importance upon health than fathers and the young. These beliefs have some resonance with health status. In so far as feeling in control is associated with not admitting to illness, young men are more likely than young women to report, and to be reported by their parents, as having good health. They are also likely to suffer less illness. On the other hand, young men's health problems disproportionately involve accidents, a tendency which paradoxically suggests a loss of control.

Young women also seek treatment more frequently than young men from both primary and secondary health care services. However, young men are granted more autonomy by their parents than young women, especially in respect of going to the GP. But when it comes to self-medication, young women are more likely to treat their own illnesses.

The study also shows that patterns of risk behaviour are gendered. Young women are more likely to engage in smoking. Young men are more likely than young women to drink larger quantities of alcohol, though not to drink more often. There are no differences with respect to drug-taking. Young women eat more healthily than young men, a pattern which reflects their greater preference for vegetarianism, and a tendency to be unhappy with their body size and hence to engage in slimming. While patterns vary across the different activities, these also tend to cluster. Young women with parents born in the UK are more likely than all other groups to be involved in smoking, alcohol consumption and drug-taking.

Gender and parenting

Our study highlights gender differences in the parenting of young people and the respective influence of mothers and fathers upon the health and health-related behaviour of their young people.

Although the great majority of mothers of the study 16-year-olds are in employment, mothers feel, in contrast to fathers, that, over the course of parenthood, they have fitted their employment around their family lives rather than vice versa. They see themselves as having more responsibility for their young people, and in practice, they do the lion's share of the household chores. They are more available in the home because their employment hours are on average shorter, and they are more likely than fathers to attempt to control the activities of their young people.

Most young people report good relationships with their parents, though this is less likely to be the case with respect to step-parents and non-resident fathers. Young people report being emotionally closest to mothers, and are most likely to turn to them with respect to personal matters. Mothers are the persons with whom young people get on best and with whom they are most likely to discuss personal, developmental, sexual and health matters. Interestingly, discussion with parents is likely to be associated with turning to health professionals; it would appear that a habit of confiding learnt in the home facilitates other types of communication about health. Mothers keep an eye on their young people for signs of illness and accompany them to the doctor. At the same time, however, mothers are less likely than fathers to feel they can influence their sons and daughters and more likely to worry a great deal about them.

Social class

In many developed countries in the 1990s, social class remains a considerable discriminator of life chances. Death and illness rates, and measures of quality of life, show that the poorest are also the most disadvantaged in health terms. In our study, working-class parents and their young people are less likely to say that health is important (compared with those from middle-class backgrounds), and the health of teenagers of working-class origin is more likely to be rated less than good both by themselves and by their parents. In addition, those expecting to enter the labour market at 16 are more likely to report poor health than those planning to stay in education; most of these young people are likely to enter manual or low-status manual employment. However, few differences emerge with respect to reported illness or use of services.

The relationship between class position and risk activities is complex. To some extent smoking functions, as it does for adults, as a marker of both low social class and high life stress, especially for young women. However, like alcohol consumption and drug use, which are associated with having one or both parents in high-status occupational groups and private education, smoking rates among young people reflect their higher levels of disposable income from after-school jobs.

Class also affects parental views of adolescence. Those whose young people join the labour market see their transition to adulthood as ascribed rather than achieved, that is, they see young people's autonomy as contingent upon a scheduled change in status, rather than as part of the developmental process of adolescence.

Some research and policy implications

As a recent report on *The Health of Youth* puts it: 'Adolescence and youth form an old topic of conversation, but a rather new one for scientific inquiry and for sound action based on knowledge' (WHO, 1989: 60). Most adult attempts to control and alter young people's behaviour have not been based on information from young people themselves about their health beliefs and behaviours. This exercise of acquiring knowledge depends on access to young people's views. To this end the kinds of qualitative in-depth interviews we carried out in our study are coming to be regarded as increasingly important. A review by the International Planned Parenthood Federation (1992) of work in the area of adolescent sexual and reproductive health drew attention to the failures of many education programmes for young people because of lack of such knowledge.

Programmes for educating the young in healthy behaviour tend to be derived from an 'adultist' framework which may take little account of young people's real everyday orientations to health. Health education interventions are not the only culprits here, however; the health services in most countries are geared to adult needs and perceptions. The lack of co-ordination of the different sectors that have an impact on young people's health – education, employment, social services, health – is a further problem.

The current emphasis upon parental responsibility in controlling young people's anti-social behaviour occurs in an economic climate in which young people's future, in terms of job opportunities, is bleak. It is also a moral climate in which the rights and responsibilities of community and citizenship have been ousted in favour of the values of the marketplace. Parents are being required to fill an economic and a moral vacuum. Yet they appear to have little or no role within a model of health education which emphasizes the individual responsibility of young people for their own actions. Health education interventions targeted at young people have tended to be based in schools, rather than embracing both home and school contexts. In the UK, the Health Education Authority, as the main agency responsible for health education, is currently undergoing a process of 'rediscovering' the importance of the family as a context for health education (see Mauthner and Sharpe, 1992). Systematic reviews now in progress of health education initiatives show that effectiveness is often inadequately measured, and that where the design of such initiatives does allow reliable conclusions about effectiveness to be drawn, such programmes are often considerably less effective than they are claimed to be (see, for example, Loevinsohn, 1990). The need for more rigorous evaluation of different inter-sectoral approaches to health promotion for young people is important.

Our own study indicates that the extent to which parents confer responsibility on their young and how much autonomy they give them is tied to their ideas of what it means to be an adolescent – assumptions concerning the relationship between biological and psychological development, and how these translate into the social and economic rights and responsibilities they expect young people to acquire at 16. This diversity of ideas is differentiated by culture, gender and class. It, too, needs to be reflected in a diversity of models of health education.

This study suggests that health educators need to rethink their assumptions concerning young people as well as the role of parents. What young people (and their parents) do, or do not do, with respect to health is part and parcel of everyday life and may not be perceived as having anything to do with health issues in the narrow sense at all. Our study shows that information from young people themselves, and from young people and their parents in a household context, presents a considerable challenge to conventional adult views of teenagers. The state of the nation's health in the future depends upon the fitness of today's teenagers. If young people are to lead healthier lives, strategies are required which match the complexity of their lives. Key actors in the process of change, young people are not a 'race apart'. They connect with society in diverse ways. Culture, gender and social class all influence young people's health status, behaviour and beliefs, especially by shaping the ways in which parents interpret the tasks of parenting, and the ways in which parents and their young people relate to each other.

Bibliography

Acheson, Sir Donald (1991) 'The Health Divide', *The Guardian*, 13 September.

Aggleton, P. (1987) *Rebels without a Cause?: Middle Class Youth and the Transition to Work*. London: Falmer Press.

Allatt, P. and Yeandle, S. (1992) *Youth Unemployment and the Family: Voices of Disordered Times*. London: Routledge.

Apter, T.E. (1990) *Altered Loves: Mothers and Daughters during Adolescence*. Hemel Hempstead: Harvester Wheatsheaf.

Ariès, P. (1973) *Centuries of Childhood* (translated from the French by Robert Baldick). Harmondsworth: Penguin.

Balding, J. (1989) *Young People in 1988*. Exeter: HEA Schools Health Education Unit.

Baric, L. (1979) 'Acquisition of the smoking habit', *Health Education Journal*, 38, 71–6.

Barker, D. (1972) 'Young people and their homes; spoiling and keeping close in a South Wales town', *Sociological Review*, 20, 4, 569–90.

Beail, N. and McGuire, J. (eds) (1982) *Fathers: Psychological Perspectives*. London: Junction Books.

Beardsworth, A. and Keil, T. (1992) 'The vegetarian option: varieties, conversions, motives and careers', *Sociological Review*, 40, 253–93.

Becker, M.H. (1973) 'The health belief model and personal health behaviour', *Health Education Monograph*, 2, 324–508.

Bernstein, B. (1971) *Class, Codes and Control, Vol 1. Theoretical Studies towards a Sociology of Language*. London: Routledge and Kegan Paul.

Bernstein, B. (1975) *Class Codes and Control, Vol 3. Towards a Theory of Educational Transmissions*. London: Routledge and Kegan Paul.

Blaxter, M. (1990) *Health and Lifestyles*. London: Tavistock/Routledge.

Blaxter, M. and Patterson, E. (1982) *Mothers and Daughters: A Three Generational Study of Health Attitudes and Behaviour*. London: Heinemann Educational Books.

Bowie, C. and Ford, N. (1989) 'Sexual behaviour of young people and the risk of HIV infection', *Journal of Epidemiology and Community Health*, 43, 1, 61–5.

Brannen, J. and Collard, J. (1982) *Marriages in Trouble: The Process of Seeking Help*. London: Tavistock.

Brannen, J. and Moss, P. (1991) *Managing Mothers: Dual Earner Households after Maternity Leave*. London: Unwin Hyman.

British Medical Council (1990) *The BMA Guide to Living with Risk.* London: Penguin.

Bush, P.J. and Iannotti, R.J. (1988) 'Pathways to health behaviours' in D.S. Gochman (ed.), *Health Behaviour and Emerging Research Perspectives.* New York: Plenum.

Central Statistical Office (1991) *Social Trends 21.* London: HMSO.

Central Statistical Office (1993) *Social Trends 23.* London: HMSO.

Charles, N. and Kerr, M. (1988) *Women, Food and Families.* Manchester: Manchester University Press.

Chisholm, L. (1990) 'A sharper lens or a new camera? Youth research, young people and social change in Britain' in L. Chisholm, P. Buchner, H. Kruger and P. Brown (eds), *Childhood, Youth and Social Change: A Comparable Perspective.* Basingstoke: Falmer Press.

Chisholm, L., Buchner, P., Kruger, H. and Brown, P. (eds) (1990) *Childhood, Youth and Social Change: A Comparable Perspective.* Basingstoke: Falmer Press.

Cohen, P. (1984) 'Against the new vocationalism' in I. Bates, J. Clarke, P. Cohen, D. Finn, R. Moore and P. Willis (eds), *Schooling for the Dole? The New Vocationalism.* London: Macmillan.

Coleman, J. (1990) *The Nature of Adolescence* (2nd edn). London: Routledge.

Collins, L. (1984) 'Concepts of health education: a study of four professional groups', *Journal of Institute of Health Education,* 22, 3, 81–8.

Cornwell, J. (1984) *Hard-earned Lives: Accounts of Health and Illness from East London.* London: Tavistock.

Crompton, R. and Mann, M. (1986) *Gender and Stratification.* Cambridge: Polity Press.

Cunningham-Burley, S. (1985) 'Constructing grandparenthood: anticipating appropriate action', *Sociology,* 19, 3, 421–36.

Davies, R. (1987) 'Hopes and fears: children's attitudes to nuclear war'. Lancaster: Centre for Peace Studies Occasional Paper No. 11.

Davis, A. (1979) 'An unequivocal change of policy: prevention, health and medical sociology', *Social Science and Medicine,* 13a, 129.

Davis, F. (1963) *Passage through Crisis: Polio Victims and their Families.* Indianapolis: Bobbs-Merrill.

Davis, J. (1990) *Youth and the Condition of Britain: Images of Adolescent Conflict.* London: Athlone Press.

Dean, A. (1990) 'Culture and community', *Sociological Review,* 38, 3, 517–63.

Delphy, C. (1979) 'Sharing the same table: consumption and the family' in C.C. Harris (ed.), *The Sociology of the Family: New Directions for Britain.* Sociological Review Monograph 28, University of Keele.

d'Houtaud, A. and Field, M.G. (1984) 'The image of health: variations in perception by social class in a French population', *Sociology of Health and Illness,* 6, 30–9.

DHSS (1980) *Inequalities in Health: Report of a Research Working Group.* London: HMSO.

DHSS (1984) *Report of the Committee on Medical Aspects of Food Policy* (COMA Report). London: HMSO.

DHSS (1989) *Prevention of Health, Everybody's Business.* London: HMSO.

Douglas, M. (1966) *Purity and Danger: An Analysis of the Concepts of Pollution and Taboo.* London: Routledge & Kegan Paul.

Douglas, M. (1984) 'Standard social uses of food' in M. Douglas (ed.), *Food in the Social Order.* New York: Russell Sage Foundation.

Downie, R.S., Fife, C. and Tannahill, A. (1992) *Health Promotion Models and Values.* Oxford: Oxford University Press.

Erikson, E. (1968) *Identity: Youth and Crisis*. New York: Norton.

European Community (1989) *Young Europeans in 1987*. Luxembourg: Office for the Official Publications of the European Communities.

Finch, J. (1989) *Family Obligations and Social Change*. Cambridge: Polity Press.

Fox, B.A. and Cameron, A.G. (1989) *Food Science, Nutrition and Health* (5th edn). London: Edward Arnold.

Frankenberg, R. (1993) 'Trust, culture, language and time', Consent Conference No. 2, Young People's Psychiatric Treatment and Consent. London: Social Science Research Unit.

Frazer, E. (1988) 'Teenage girls talking about class', *Sociology*, 22, 3, 343–58.

Freidson, E. (1970) *Profession of Medicine: A Study in the Sociology of Applied Knowledge*. New York: Dodd Mead.

Furnham, A. and Gunter, B. (1989) *The Anatomy of Adolescence: Young People's Social Attitudes in Britain*. London: Routledge.

Gardner Merchant (1991) *School Meals Survey*. London: Burson-Marsteller.

Giddens, A. (1991) *Modernity and Self-identity: Self and Society in the Late Modern Age*. Cambridge: Polity.

Gilligan, C. (1982) *In a Different Voice: Psychological Theory and Women's Development*. Cambridge, Mass.: Harvard University Press.

Graham, H. (1979) 'Prevention and health; every mother's business. A comment on child health policies in the 1970s' in C.C. Harris (ed.), *The Sociology of the Family: New Directions for Britain*. Sociological Review Monograph 28, University of Keele.

Graham, H. (1984) *Women, Health and the Family*. Brighton: Wheatsheaf.

Graham, H. (1987) 'Women's smoking and family health', *Social Science and Medicine*, 25, 47–56.

Green, G., Macintyre, S. and West, P. (1989) 'West of Scotland 20–07: Health in the Community: Distributions of basic information from the first sweep of data collection on the 15 year old cohort'. Glasgow: MRC Medical Sociology Unit Working Paper No. 14.

Green, G., Macintyre, S., West, P. and Russell, E. (1991) 'Like parent like child? Associations between drinking and smoking behaviour of parents and their children', *British Journal of Addiction*, 86, 745–58.

Griffin, C. (1985) *Typical Girls?* London: Routledge and Kegan Paul.

Guardian (1993) 'The head of the family', *The Guardian*, 23 February.

Health Education Authority (1992) *Today's Young Adults*. London: The Bath Press.

Health Education Council (1983) *A Discussion Paper on Proposals for Nutritional Guidelines for Health Education in Britain*. National Advisory Committee on Nutrition Education. London: Health Education Council.

Hein, K. (1988) 'Issues in adolescent health: an overview', *Carnegie Council on Adolescent Development Working Papers*. New York: Carnegie Corporation.

Hewitt, R. (1988) *White Talk, Black Talk: Inter-racial Friendships and Communication among Adolescents*. Cambridge: Cambridge University Press.

Holland, J., Ramazonoglu, C., Sharpe, S. and Thomson, R. (1992) 'Pressured pleasure: young women and the negation of sexual boundaries', *Sociological Review*, 40, 2, 645–74.

Hopkins, N. (1989) 'Adolescent health careers: a self-categorization approach'. Unpublished paper, University of Bristol.

Iannotti, R.J. and Bush, P.J. (1988) 'Origins and stability of children's health beliefs relative to medicine use', *Social Science and Medicine*, 27, 345–52.

International Planned Parenthood Federation (1992) *Adolescent Sexual and Repro-ductive Health.* Paris: Centre International de l'Enfance.

Jamieson, L. (1987) 'Theories of family development and the experience of being brought up', *Sociology*, 21, 4, 591–607.

Jensen, B.B. (1991) 'Health education in holistic perspectives and children's con-cepts of health' in D. Nutbeam, B. Hagland, P. Farley and P. Tillgren, *Youth Health Promotion.* London: Forbes Publications.

Jones, G. and Wallace, C. (1992) *Youth, Family and Citizenship.* Buckingham: Open University Press.

Klein Walker, D. (1982) 'Comparisons between inner city and private school adoles-cents' perceptions of health problems', *Journal of Adolescent Health Care*, 3, 82–90.

Knight, R.A. and Hay, D.A. (1989) 'The relevance of the health belief model to Australian smokers', *Social Science and Medicine*, 28, 12, 1311–14.

Lader, D. and Matheson, J. (1990) *Smoking among Secondary School Children in 1990* (OPCS). London: HMSO.

Leonard, D. (1980) *Sex and Generation: A Study of Courtship and Weddings.* London: Tavistock.

Levenson, P.M., Morrow, J.R. and Pfefferbaum, B.J. (1984) 'Attitudes towards health and illness – a comparison of adolescent, physician, teacher and school nurse views', *Journal of Adolescent Health Care*, 5, 254–60.

Lewis, C. and O'Brien, M. (eds) (1987) *Reassessing Fatherhood: New Observations on Fathers and the Modern Family.* London: Sage.

Locker, D. (1981) *Symptoms and Illness: The Cognitive Organisation of Disorder.* Lon-don: Tavistock.

Loevinsohn, B.P. (1990) 'Health education interventions in developing countries: a methodological review of published articles', *International Journal of Epidemi-ology*, 19, 788–99.

Marmot, M.G. and McDowell, M.E. (1986) 'Mortality decline and widening social inequalities', *Lancet*, 2 August, 274–6.

Marmot, M.G., Shipley, M.J. and Rose, G. (1984) 'Inequalities in death – specific explanations of a general pattern', *Lancet*, 5 May, 1003–6.

Marmot, M.G., Kogevinas, M. and Elston, M.A. (1987) 'Social/economic status and disease', *Annual Review of Public Health*, 8, 111–35.

Marshall, T.H. (1950) *Citizenship and Social Class and Other Essays.* Cambridge: Cambridge University Press.

Martin, C. and McQueen, D. (eds) (1988) *Readings for a New Public Health.* Edinburgh: Edinburgh University Press.

Martin, J. and Roberts, C. (1984) *Women and Employment: A Lifetime Perspective.* London: Department of Employment and OPCS.

Mauthner, M. and Sharpe, S. (1992) *Families, Communications and Health: A Litera-ture Review.* London: Social Science Research Unit.

Mayall, B. (1986) *Keeping Children Healthy: The Role of Mothers and Professionals.* London: Allen & Unwin.

Mayall, B. (1989) 'Trumpets over the range or never a may but one or what you will: a brief history of adolescence'. Unpublished paper.

McKee, L. and O'Brien, M. (eds) (1982) *The Father Figure.* London: Tavistock.

McRobbie, A. (1991) 'The politics of feminist research: between talk, test and action' in A. McRobbie, *Feminism and Youth Culture: From Jackie to Just Seventeen.* London: Macmillan.

Mennell, S., Murcott, A. and Otherloo, A.H. van (1992) *The Sociology of Food: Eating, Diet and Culture.* London: Sage Publications.

Miller, J.B. (1976) *Toward a New Psychology of Women.* Boston, Mass.: Beacon Press.

Millstein, S. (1981) 'Conceptions of illness in young adolescents', *Paediatrics*, 68, 6, 834–9.

Moggach, D. (1993) 'Calling all wicked stepmothers', *She*, April.

Murcott, A. (1983) *The Sociology of Food and Eating.* Aldershot: Gower.

Murray, M., Swan, A., Johnson, M. and Bewley, B. (1983) 'Some factors associated with increased risk of smoking by children', *Journal of Child Psychology and Psychiatry*, 24, 223–32.

Naidoo, J. (1986) 'Limits to individualism' in S. Rodmell and A. Watt (eds), *Politics of Health Education, Raising the Issues.* London: Routledge & Kegan Paul.

Natapoff, J.N. (1978) 'Children's views of health: a developmental study', *American Journal of Public Health*, 68, 995–1000.

Nutbeam, D., Hagland, B., Farley, P. and Tillgren, P. (1991) *Youth Health Promotion.* London: Forbes Publications.

Oakley, A. (1992) *Social Support and Motherhood: The Natural History of a Research Project.* Oxford: Blackwell.

Oakley, A. and Rajan, L. (1991) 'Social class and social support – the same or different?' *Sociology*, 25, 1, 31–59.

Oakley, A. and Rajan, L. (forthcoming) 'What did your baby eat yesterday?', *European Journal of Public Health.*

Oakley, A., Rajan, L. and Robertson P. (1990) 'A comparison of different sources of information on pregnancy and childbirth', *Journal of Biosocial Science*, 22, 477–87.

Oakley, A., Brannen, J. and Dodd, K. (1992) 'Young people, gender and smoking in the United Kingdom', *Health Promotion International*, 7, 2, 75–88.

Observer (1992) 'Cigarette advertising hooks the 11 yr olds', *Observer*, 1 November.

Oechsle, M. and Zoll, R. (1992) 'Young people and their ideas on parenthood' in U. Bjornberg, *European Parents in the 1990s: Contradictions and Change.* New Brunswick, NJ: Transaction.

Offer, D. and Sabshin, M. (eds) (1984) *Normality and the Life Cycle.* New York: Basic Books.

OPCS (1989) *General Household Survey 1987.* London: HMSO.

OPCS (1990) *General Household Survey 1988.* London: HMSO.

OPCS (1991) *General Household Survey 1989.* London: HMSO.

Pahl, J. (1989) *Money and Marriage.* London: Macmillan.

Parsons, T. (1951) *The Social System.* Glencoe, Il.: Free Press.

Parsons, T. (1956) *Family: Socialisation and Interaction Processes.* London: Routledge & Kegan Paul.

Parsons, T. (1958) 'Definitions of health and illness in the light of the American social structure' in E. Jaco (ed.), *Patients, Physicians and Illness.* Glencoe, Il.: Free Press.

Perry, C.L. (1991) 'Conceptualizing community-wide youth health programs' in D. Nutbeam, B. Hagland, P. Farley and P. Tillgren, *Youth Health Promotion.* London: Forbes Publications.

Pill, R. and Stott, N.C.H. (1985) 'Preventive procedures and practices among working class women – new data and fresh insights', *Social Science and Medicine*, 21, 975–83.

Pill, R. and Stott, N.C.H. (1986) 'Looking after themselves: health protective behaviour among British working class women', *Health Education Research*, 1, 111–19.

Radcliffe-Brown, A.R. (1962) 'Introduction' in A.R. Radcliffe-Brown and D. Forde (eds), *African Systems of Kinship and Marriage*. London: Oxford University Press.

Research Unit in Health and Behavioural Change (1989) *Changing the Public Health*. Chichester: Wiley.

Richards, M.P.M. (1982a) 'Introduction' in N. Beail and J. McGuire (eds), *Fathers: Psychological Perspectives*. London: Junction Books.

Richards, M.P.M. (1982b) 'How should we approach the study of fathers?' in L. McKee and M. O'Brien (eds), *The Father Figure*. London: Tavistock.

Rutter, M., Tizard, J. and Whitmore, K. (1976) *Educational Health and Behaviour*. London: Longman.

Sharpe, S. and Oakley, A. (1991) 'Parental influences on young people's smoking'. Unpublished report. London: Social Science Research Unit.

Smith, A. and Jacobsen, B. (1988) *The Nation's Health: A Strategy for the 1990s*. London: King Edward's Hospital Fund.

Smith, G.D., Bartley, M. and Blane, D. (1990) 'The Black Report on socio-economic inequalities in health 10 years on', *British Medical Journal*, 301, 373–7.

Solantaus, T. (1987) 'Hopes and worries of young people in three European countries', *Health Promotion*, 2, 1, 19–27.

Solantaus, T. (1991) 'Young people and the threat of nuclear war: "Out there is a world I belong to". A literature review', *Medicine and War*, 7 (supplement 1), 1–95.

Stacey, M. (1991) *The Sociology of Health and Healing*. London: Routledge.

Stone, L.J. and Church, J. (1968) *Childhood and Adolescence: A Psychology of the Growing Person* (2nd edn). New York: Random House.

Swadi, H. (1988) 'Drug and substance use among 3,333 London adolescents', *British Journal of Addiction*, 83, 935–42.

Tones, B.K. (1983) 'Education and health promotion: new directions', *Journal of the Institute of Health Education*, 21, 121–31.

Twigg, J. (1983) 'Vegetarianism and the meaning of meat' in A. Murcott, *The Sociology of Food and Eating*. Aldershot: Gower.

Vegetarian Society (1991) *The 1991 Food Survey. Trends in Vegetarianism amongst Adults and Young People*. Altrincham: Vegetarian Society.

Verbrugge, L.M. (1985) 'Gender and health: an update on hypotheses and evidence', *Journal of Health and Social Behaviour*, 26, 156–82.

Voysey, M. (1975) *A Constant Burden: Reconstruction of Family Life*. London: Routledge & Kegan Paul.

Walkerdine, V. and Lucey, H. (1989) *Democracy in the Kitchen: Regulating Mothers and Socialising Daughters*. London: Virago.

Whitehead, M. (1987) *The Health Divide: Inequalities in Health in the 1980s*. London: Health Education Council.

Williams, D.R. (1990) 'Socioeconomic differentials in health: a review and re-direction', *Social Psychology Quarterly*, 53, 81–99.

Willis, P. (1977) *Learning to Labour: How Working Class Kids Get Working Class Jobs*. Farnborough: Saxon House.

Windsor, R.A., Baranowki, T., Clark, N., Cutter, G. (1984) *Evaluation of Health Promotion and Education Programs*. Palo Alto, Calif.: Mayfield Publishing.

WHO (1946) *Constitution*. New York: WHO.

WHO (1989) *The Health of Youth*. Geneva: WHO.

Index

relationships with stepchildren,
  59–61, 185, 206, 212
responsibilities, 59
Stott, N.C.H., 68, 69
street games, 34
stress, 70, 74, 83, 117, 188
structural patterns, 8
studying, 135
subversion, 7
suicide, 69, 76
surveillance of young people, 4
Swadi, H., 119, 120

Tones, B.K., 70
trainers (footwear), 26, 34, 41
truancy, 141, 170
Twigg, J., 153

unemployment, 3, 6, 35, 36, 73, 181
United States, 36, 70

vegans, 120
vegetarianism, 104, 110, 120, 146,
  153–4, 209, 212
  ethnic differences, 107, 123, 211
  gender differences, 107, 123
Vegetarian Society, 120
Verbrugge, L.M., 85
videos, 127
violence, 2, 34, 37, 69, 131

virginity, 133, 169, 202
voting, 29
Voysey, M., 90
vulnerability of young people, 4

Walkerdine, V., 4, 6, 136
Wallace, C., 2–4, 6, 8, 71
weight problems, 105–6, 119, 151–2,
  154, 156
Whitehead, M., 68
Williams, D.R., 83
Willis, P., 3
Windsor, R.A., 5
Women and Employment survey, 21
World Health Organization (WHO),
  68, 103, 213
worrying, 205
  about children's whereabouts, 49,
    66, 138–9
  about health, 73
  gender differences, 90, 142, 187,
    197
  by young people, 73, 80

Yeandle, S., 14, 136, 137
Young Europeans Survey, 20
youth training schemes, 13, 36

Zoll, R., 4

CHILD HEALTH MATTERS
CARING FOR CHILDREN IN THE COMMUNITY

Sally Wyke and Jenny Hewison (eds)

The 1990s will be a time of considerable change in the organization and delivery of child health care services. On-going reforms of the National Health Service and the welfare state coupled with significant ethnic and social changes in British society mean that health care professionals are being forced to rapidly adjust their working practices. Such change cannot be achieved without information about the needs, characteristics and perceptions of service users or without up-to-date information about new developments and problems in community health care.

This book provides some of this information and presents it in a form accessible to those people in the front line of organizing and delivering child health care. It will therefore be an invaluable resource for health service managers, general practitioners, community paediatricians, community nurses and health visitors and will also be of interest to students of sociology and community medicine.

Contents
Introduction – Section 1: Resources for care – Women, child care and money – Section 2: Perspectives on health – Dealing with children's illness: mothers' dilemmas – Understanding the mother's viewpoint: the case of Pathan women in Britain – Ideologies of child care: mothers and health visitors – Section 3: Using health services – Children with a cough: who consults the doctor? – Whether or not to consult a general practitioner: decision making by parents in a multi-ethnic inner-city area – 'Appropriate' use of child health services in East London: ethnic similarities and differences – Section 4: Available knowledge – The promotion of breastfeeding – Childhood asthma: strategies for primary and community health – Child sexual abuse and the trials of motherhood – Children with HIV infection: their care in the community – Index.

Contributors
Andy Clarke, Sarah Cunningham-Burley, Caroline Currer, Robert Drewett, Heather Fletcher, Jenny Hewison, Jenny Kitzinger, Una Maclean, Berry Mayall, Jacqueline Mok, Jennie Popay, Ian Russell, Elizabeth Watson, Sally Wyke.

176 pp   0 335 09393 0 (Paperback)   0 335 09394 9 (Hardback)

CHILDREN'S CONSENT TO SURGERY

Priscilla Alderson

> If I didn't want the operation, my parents wouldn't make me have it. If I was going to die they'd make me. It would be the only sensible thing to do, but I'd agree.
>
> (Gemma, aged 11)

When are children old enough to understand medical information? When are they mature enough to make wise decisions in their best interests? This challenging new book explores these difficult questions through detailed qualitative research. It is based on in-depth interviews with 120 children undergoing surgery, their parents, and many of the staff caring for them in four city hospitals. In their own words, the child patients challenge many accepted ideas about their rights, interests and abilities. *Children's Consent to Surgery* is essential reading for a wide range of health professionals as well as social scientists with an interest in childhood, children's services and ethics.

Contents

Surgery at school age – Limb lengthening – Children's human rights – Children's legal rights – Reviewing research about children – Hoping for benefit: children's reasons for having surgery – Giving information: adults' views – Understanding information: children's responses – Making a wise choice: competence to consent – The many stages of surgery – Respecting children's consent – Children named in interviews – Glossary of medical terms – Index.

224 pp   0 335 15732 7 (Paperback)   0 335 15733 5 (Hardback)

CHILDREN, TEENAGERS AND HEALTH: THE KEY DATA

Caroline Woodroffe, Myer Glickman, Maggie Barker and Chris Power

> An invaluable source of information for anyone concerned with policies on child health.
>
> Dr Sheila Adam, Director of Public Health,
> North West Thames Regional Health Authority

What are the current patterns of health and illness among children and teenagers? What changes have taken place in recent years? What factors influence health? What are the health differences between parts of the UK, between sexes, ethnic groups, and social classes? This book uses a wide range of statistics from official and academic sources to answer these questions. Clear graphical presentation allows trends and comparisons to be seen at a glance.

This book is an essential reference for anyone concerned with child health, whether in the health and social services or the many areas of public policy which have an impact on health. The presentation makes the data easily accessible to non-specialists, enabling wider informed public debate on how best to improve the health of children and teenagers in the UK.

Contents
Introduction – Population and family – Mortality and morbidity – Socioeconomic environment – Physical environment – Cultural environment – Endpiece – Note on official data sources – Glossary – Index.

208pp   0 335 19125 8 (Paperback)

330